The Seabiscuit STORY

From the Pages of the Nation's Most Prominent Racing Magazine

Edited by John McEvoy

EP
ECLIPSE PRESS

Essex, Connecticut

An imprint of Globe Pequot, the trade division of
The Rowman & Littlefield Publishing Group, Inc.
4501 Forbes Blvd., Ste. 200
Lanham, MD 20706
www.rowman.com

Distributed by NATIONAL BOOK NETWORK

British Library Cataloguing in Publication Information available

Library of Congress Cataloging-in-Publication Data Available

ISBN 978-1-4930-7337-5 (paperback)

♾™ The paper used in this publication meets the minimum requirements of American
National Standard for Information Sciences—Permanence of Paper for Printed Library
Materials, ANSI/NISO Z39.48-1992.

The Seabiscuit STORY

Contents

Introduction

It can only be described as amazing. Today — ninety years after his birth, eighty-three years following his final race, and seventy-six years after his death — the legend of Seabiscuit continues to grow. His presence in the public consciousness dwarfs that of every other American racehorse, including such legends as Secretariat and Man o' War. Few horses qualify as being larger than life, but surely Seabiscuit does. "Amazing" is the only word for it.

The popular Seabiscuit with Red Pollard up poses for the cameras at Belmont Park.

During his racing career in the late 1930s, Seabiscuit became an idol for a nation caught in the throes of the Great Depression and in dire need of a hero. He was the subject of a biography, two movies, and countless photos and articles in print publications (he was a most willing subject, having perfected his camera "pose" much like John Henry would years later). There were Seabiscuit parlor games, Seabiscuit hats, and in 1938 he was the most extensively covered public figure in the nation's newspapers. (President Franklin D. Roosevelt, who once delayed a staff meeting to listen to a radio broadcast of a Seabiscuit race, was runner-up.)

More than six decades later, Seabiscuit charged back into prominence with the publication in 2001 of Laura Hillenbrand's wonderful account of his life and the major people in it. Hillenbrand's critically acclaimed *Seabiscuit: An American Legend* was relished not only by racing people but hundreds of thousands of others intrigued by the saga of the so-called "ultimate underdog." The book dashed onto the hardcover bestseller lists and, thereon, mirrored the tenacity of its hero. The paperback version showed similar strength.

Hillenbrand's book was the third devoted to Seabiscuit, one of which — Ralph Moody's *Come on Seabiscuit* — was reissued after being out of print for years. Hillenbrand's illuminating effort, with its deft delving into the crannies of history surrounding her subject, serves as the source of the

new movie *Seabiscuit,* released in July 2003. (It was the second cinematic recounting of Seabiscuit's story, the first — starring Shirley Temple — having been produced in 1949. Also, in 1940, a newsreel documentary was devoted to his life.) Another major medium settled on Seabiscuit as a subject in April 2003, when PBS aired a sixty-minute documentary on him.

Now comes this Eclipse Press effort in honor of the horse. Utilizing the extensive files of its parent entity, *The Blood-Horse,* Eclipse Press presents the epic of Seabiscuit as it unfolded in the pages of that weekly magazine. This provides the reader with an "at the time, on the spot" feeling, from Seabiscuit's nondescript early years to his days of fame and glory. He was

SEABISCUIT
Retirement of the World's Leading Money Winner Has Been Announced. Jockey J. Pollard Up.

being written about by a variety of people, some who dismissed his talents and others who recognized his worth.

The Blood-Horse has been chronicling horse racing since 1916. Its coverage of Seabiscuit started with three short articles in 1935 (the first one in the issue dated July 6) and eventually totaled 101 entries. Some are short; others run to thousands of words. The vast majority are fascinating from an historical standpoint, providing as they do details of how Seabiscuit's career unfolded on a week-to-week basis. Then, following his retirement, *The Blood-Horse* published several retrospective pieces on his life and times. Also included here are the obituaries that appeared in the magazine of Seabiscuit's owner Charles S. Howard (1950); his trainer, Tom "Silent Tom" Smith (1957); and jockey John "Red" Pollard (1981).

Most of *The Blood-Horse* stories were unsigned, having been contributed by correspondents in the field or written by staffers in the Lexington headquarters of the publication. Some bylines do appear, including those of three of American racing's most notable writer-observers: Joe Palmer, John Hervey ("Salvator"), and David Alexander. Palmer's contributions reflect his gift for humorous understatement, including this observation on the reported discrepancy in the measured distance from muzzle to buttock of match race rivals Seabiscuit and War Admiral: "As nearly as can be estimated with-

out getting the two of them up in the office," Palmer wrote, "they are much the same length." Hervey, a renowned racing historian, ponders the history of the Santa Anita Handicap and Seabiscuit's efforts in that race. Alexander, a close friend of Pollard, Seabiscuit's primary jockey, contributes a memorable tribute to that colorful character.

Seabiscuit had, in essence, two racing "careers," distinguished by his accomplishments, or lack thereof, for his two owners. In his first career, under his breeder Wheatley Stable's banner, Seabiscuit learned on the job and improved his skills before moving on to his second, much more successful, career with Charles S. Howard.

Wheatley Stable was owned by Mrs. Henry Carnegie Phipps and her brother, Ogden Mills, and was one of the Eastern establishment's most prestigious operations. Seabiscuit's sire was the notoriously ill-tempered Hard Tack (a son of Man o' War), his dam the unraced mare Swing On (by Whisk Broom II). On paper this was a promising confluence of genes, and so it turned out. But Seabiscuit represented a startling anomaly for his sire, as Hard Tack sired only eleven other stakes winners and was eventually relegated to the U.S. Army's Remount Service.

During the first sixteen months or so of his racing career, the light-bodied Seabiscuit proved he had an iron constitution. Under the training of legendary Hall of Fame horseman James F. "Sunny Jim" Fitzsimmons, Seabiscuit made his first start on January 19, 1935, finishing fourth and earning $50. His next start, in which he finished second, came three days later. A pattern was established. Fitzsimmons entered Seabiscuit as if the trainer were on speed-dial to the racing secretaries' offices. The little bay colt made a mind-boggling thirty-five starts at two, finally breaking his

Mrs. H. C. Phipps bred Seabiscuit and raced him in her Wheatley Stable name early in his career.

maiden in his eighteenth attempt. He was entered to be claimed five times that season — three of those occasions for as little as $2,500. There were never any takers.

When Seabiscuit finally did win, he equaled the track record in a five-furlong allowance event for a purse of $1,000 at old Narragansett Park on June 22, 1935. Next time out, also at Narragansett, he won again, setting a new track mark for the same distance. This was in a "claiming stakes," a race that seems by definition to embody contradiction but was not uncommon in those days. Then ensued a thirty-seven-race, seventeen-month gap before, having developed into a high-class performer, Seabiscuit produced the second of what was to be his twelve track record performances (a fact that, looking back, might cast some doubt on the accuracy of the 'Gansett timer). Seabiscuit finished his first season of competition with five wins and a desultory but deserved ranking of No. 28 on the Experimental Free Handicap.

One of Seabiscuit's neighbors under Fitzsimmons' shedrow was William Woodward's 1935 Triple Crown winner Omaha. Another was Woodward's 1936 Horse of the Year Granville. A *Blood-Horse* story included here describes Seabiscuit's role as a workmate for Omaha.

Seabiscuit's "first career," for Wheatley Stable, encompassed forty-seven races, of which he won nine while earning $18,395. When Howard acquired him for $7,500 in August of

Introduction

1936, he had thickened physically into a robust specimen (at his physical peak at five, he was muscular enough to merit the description of being "a big horse on short legs"). Seabiscuit was considered both well bought and well sold. Howard was looking for a decent allowance horse; Fitzsimmons was willing to cull this much-used racing machine. That Seabiscuit would go on to become the world's leading money winner, a Horse of the Year, and a national icon would have been considered an absolutely preposterous proposition.

〜

Charles Stewart Howard, the Georgia-born one-time bicycle racer and repairman who became the largest auto dealer in the world through his Buick agency in California, was no stranger to good fortune in the horse business. He paid $500 for the yearling Coramine at Saratoga in 1935 and she developed into a stakes winner. So did the $1,300 purchase Porter's Cap a few years later. Howard and his son, Lin, acquired Seabiscuit's extremely able stablemate Kayak II for some $7,500 in Argentina. Howard later imported Noor, who defeated the great Citation four straight times. But those rewarding transactions paled before Howard's acquisition of Seabiscuit. Indeed, the sum of Howard's accomplishments suggests it was not so much serendipity as vision and enthusiasm that led to his myriad successes.

Turned over to trainer Tom Smith,

a man who raised the art of reticence to a new level, Seabiscuit began his remarkable transformation. He ran fourth behind the grand mare Myrtlewood in his first start for Howard, then two races later recorded the first of his stakes wins under the crimson and white colors. Seabiscuit was ridden in these races, as he would be ridden a total of thirty times, by the iconoclastic Canadian-born Red Pollard. Seabiscuit's other most frequent race partner was Hall of Famer George (The Iceman) Woolf, who was employed during the two periods when Pollard was sidelined as the result of serious riding injuries.

Racing for Howard, Seabiscuit made forty-two starts and won twenty-four. Seabiscuit also finished second seven times and third seven times, going unplaced but four times. He earned $419,265. That sum, combined with his earlier gleanings for Wheatley, enabled him to surpass Sun Beau as the world's leading money winner in 1940. Howard, an enthusiastic bettor, cashed numerous huge wagers on his pride and joy.

Seabiscuit set twelve track records and equaled two others at distances from five furlongs to a mile and one-quarter. He carried 130 or more pounds thirteen times, winning eight of those races, and writers at the time compared him favorably to such vaunted weight carriers as Exterminator, Discovery, and Equipoise. He deserved the compliment, although it should be kept in mind that this group pales by compari-

11

son with a later cadre of such marvels as Round Table, Forego, and Kelso. The latter two each carried 130 pounds or more twenty-four times, with Forego winning thirteen and Kelso twelve. Round Table won seventeen of twenty-five such burdensome tests.

Seabiscuit made his biggest splashes at ages five and seven. In 1938 he won his oft-postponed, thunderously bally-hooed Pimlico match race with 1937 Triple Crown winner War Admiral. That event ranks as one of this country's all-time best-known sporting events. After being away from competition for nearly a year due to injury, Seabiscuit returned in 1940 to finally win the major West Coast prize that had twice narrowly eluded him, the $100,000 Santa Anita Handicap. Then this "miracle horse" was retired.

Despite being voted champion handicap horse at four and five and Horse of the Year at five and retiring as the world's leading money winner, Seabiscuit in 1999 was rated only twenty-fifth on *The Blood-Horse*'s list of the top 100 American Thoroughbreds. His relatively low ranking — compared to

the level of his fame — may have resulted from the fact that he was ineffective on wet tracks, lost half of his ten photo finishes, never won beyond a mile and one-quarter, was beaten by fillies nine times during his career, and had a moderate lifetime winning percentage of only 37.

At stud Seabiscuit sired just four stakes winners. His chances were compromised by the fact that he was bred almost exclusively to Howard's own moderately pedigreed mares. Seabiscuit's years as a stallion were spent on Howard's Ridgeway Ranch, where he was often ridden by his admiring and grateful owner, sometimes being used to herd cattle. Seabiscuit was good at it, too.

It seems unlikely that, decades from now, there will be a horse so interesting and so well-known, one whose exploits are based in racing but both embody and transcend it, one whose legend has become woven so brightly into the national fabric. Seabiscuit was special, and the stories in this book help to tell why that is so.

Out of Obscurity

S eabiscuit's name first appeared in *The Blood-Horse* in the issue of July 6, 1935. The story reported the first of what would be Seabiscuit's twenty-seven career stakes wins — the Watch Hill Claiming Stakes at Narragansett Park on June 26. This came in Seabiscuit's nineteenth race of the season; he had finally broken his maiden in his previous start.

Two other Seabiscuit-related items were published in *The Blood-Horse* that year, both also recounting minor stakes wins by the super-active Wheatley Stable youngster.

While Seabiscuit was toiling away in relative obscurity as a two-year-old, American racing was celebrating a glittering addition: Santa Anita Park. The Arcadia, California, showplace first opened its doors on Christmas Day, 1934, its inaugural meeting highlighted by the running of the Santa Anita Handicap — the race that Seabiscuit would become indelibly associated with when he won it in 1940. The gross purse of $108,400 for the inaugural Santa Anita Handicap was a world record. The event, run in February 1935, attracted the best field ever assembled to that time for a winter race in the United States, including stars such as Equipoise, Twenty Grand, and Mate.

That first running of the Big 'Cap, as it became known, was taken by the converted steeplechaser Azucar. Favored in the huge field of twenty was the great Equipoise. Unfortunately, the "Chocolate Soldier" broke down in what was the final race of his career.

Other racing headlines in 1935 included Omaha's Triple Crown victory. A stablemate of Seabiscuit, Omaha won the Kentucky Derby, Preakness, and Belmont Stakes just as his sire, Gallant Fox, had five years earlier.

In 1936 Seabiscuit was the subject of a half-dozen *Blood-Horse* items as he captured stakes in Michigan, Ohio, New York, and

California. His first stakes victory with jockey Red Pollard aboard came on September 7 in the Governor's Handicap at Detroit. Seabiscuit displayed the competitive spirit that was to become his trademark when making up several lengths and posting a nose victory in the Scarsdale Handicap at old Empire City on October 24. On December 12 he scored his easiest and richest triumph up to that point in his career when he took the World's Fair Handicap at Bay Meadows.

Although he had improved tremendously, Seabiscuit was not yet being mentioned as a member of the top echelon. That group included fellow three-year-olds Bold Venture, winner of the Kentucky Derby and Preakness, and Belmont Stakes hero Granville, as well as reigning handicap leader Discovery.

July 6, 1935
SEABISCUIT WINS

The Watch Hill Claiming Stakes ($2,500 added, 2-year-olds, five furlongs), on June 26, was the first stakes at Narragansett Park in which Alfred Vanderbilt did not have an entry. With the Maryland sportsman out of the field, the crowd made Wheatley Stable's Seabiscuit (108) a strong favorite, and the Hard Tack colt performed in accord with expectation. Jockey F. Horn had him close to Sandy Mack's pace for the first quarter, then wore the Prince of Wales colt down. At the quarter-pole Seabiscuit was safely in front, and he increased his margin to two lengths at the end, with Mrs. G.W. Ogle's Infidox (108) in second place. Third, a length father back, was Labonte and Seguin's Zowie (102), with the Branncastle Farm entry of Challephen (108) and The Hare (105) fourth and fifth. Herondas (108), Sandy Mack (105), and Royal Ballad (105) made up the rest of the field. The winner was entered to be claimed for

$5,500, and carried three pounds extra for the odd $500. Time, :22⅘, :45⅗, :59⅗ (new track record), track fast. Stakes division, $2,795, $500, $250, $125.

Seabiscuit was making his nineteenth start. He has won two races, finished second five times, third four times, has earned $4,970. He is the second winner for his sire's first crop, of four foals, and is his first stakes winner. Hard Tack stood at Horace N. Davis' Blue Grass Heights Stock Farm, near Lexington, but was moved this year to Claiborne Stud, Paris, Ky. Swing On, dam of Seabiscuit,

Hard Tack, sire of Seabiscuit.

did not race. Her first foal, Query, won at two in 1934. Balance produced Flippant (Broadway Stakes, Bayview Handicap), Hornpipe (Amsterdam Stakes), the winners Scales, Even Up, Abby and High Wire, and the producer Flutter. She is half-sister to Distraction (Wood Memorial, Colorado, Flash Stakes, Yonkers, Champlain, Bay Shore, Edgemere, Pierrepont Handicap), Blondin (Empire City Derby, Long Beach Handicap, and sire), Swinging (good race mare and dam of Equipoise), etc. *Balancoire II won in France, and produced six winners and the producers Wiggle Waggle, *Escarpolette (dam of Alyssum, Depression, etc.) and *See Saw II. She is sister to Night Rider (Triennial, Hurstbourne Stakes) Melody (Acorn Stakes, in England, grandam of King Nadi), and Mediant (Foam Stakes, Great Eastern Handicap in the United States, and the Stewards' Cup, Champion Sprint Handicap, etc. in England).[Editor's Note: Seabiscuit's pedigree appears in Ch. 5, "The Legend Lives," p. 112.]

October 26, 1935
SEABISCUIT SURPRISES

The mid-week attraction at Agawam Park was the Springfield Handicap ($2,500 added, 2-year-olds, six furlongs), run October 17. It brought out a field of eight juveniles, of which Mr. G.W. Ogle's Infidox (117) was the favorite. From break to finish, however, the winner was Wheatley Stable's Seabiscuit (109),

Wheatley Stable's trainer, Sunny Jim Fitzsimmons.

which Jockey J. Stout got away in motion. The Hard Tack colt led at every post, shaking off a belated challenge from Infidox in the stretch. C.V. Whitney's Bright Plumage (117), beginning slowly, came well despite being forced to race on the outside most of the way, and closed with a good burst of speed to take second place from Infidox by a head, though a length behind the winner. W. Hartman's Aboveboard (107) was fourth, another length and a half behind. The others were Professor Paul (102), Bereit (95), Black Mistress (96), and Sandy Beach (118). Time, :23⅘, :46, 1:11⅘, track fast. Stakes division, $2,030, $500, $250, $100.

November 2, 1935
SEABISCUIT'S ARDSLEY HANDICAP

The second consecutive stakes success for Wheatley Stable's Seabiscuit (112) was the Ardsley Handicap ($2,500 added, 2-year-olds, 5¾ furlongs), run at Empire City on October 23. The Hard Tack colt, winner of the Springfield Handicap at Agawam Park on October 17, was indifferently supported for the race, went to post as third choice. The first half-mile was a closely fought duel between Seabiscuit and Knowing (110), a Dunboyne gelding which broke in front and led the Hard Tack colt for four furlongs, though never able to draw out. Entering the stretch Knowing fell away, and Seabiscuit, disposing quickly of William Ziegler, Jr.'s Wha Hae

(115), drew out to win by three lengths. Wha Hae weakened rapidly, finished in third place, two lengths behind Brookmeade Stable's Neap (107), which passed tired horses to finish second. C.V. Whitney's Tatterdemalion (114) was fourth, closing some ground after being outrun in the early furlongs. The others were Knowing and Holdum Brown (108). Jockey F. Kopel rode the winner. Time, :23, :47, 1:08⅘, track fast. Stakes division, $2,835, $500, $250, $125.

Seabiscuit has now started 33 times, has won five races, finished second six times, third five times, and has earned $11,510.

August 8, 1936
SEABISCUIT'S MOHAWK STAKES

Over from Suffolk Downs came Wheatley Stable's Seabiscuit (3-y-o,

109), to run in the Mohawk Claiming Stakes ($2,000 added, 3-year-olds and up, one mile) at Saratoga August 3. The Hard Tack colt entered for $6,000 proved much the best, winning by six lengths with speed to spare. Ridden by Jockey J. Stout, Seabiscuit was off in front, was rated steadily, came away in the stretch when ready. Second was Mrs. A.A. Baroni's Ann O' Ruley (112), which finished fast after being outrun for six furlongs. Two lengths behind her was Alfred Vanderbilt's Balkan Land (3-y-o, 109), which had been well up throughout. Mrs. F. Ambrose Clark's Goldeneye (3-y-o, 109) was fourth, two lengths farther back, and was followed by the favorite, Kate (112), Jair (3-y-o, 100), and Captain Jinks (3-y-o, 102). Time, :24⅖, 48⅕, 1:12⅖, 1:38⅖, track fast. Stakes division, $2,960, $400, $200, $100.

Seabiscuit has started 46 times, won

The three-year-old Seabiscuit easily winning the Mohawk Claiming Stakes at Saratoga.

eight races, finished second eight times, third six times, earned $17,595. In 1935 he won the Watch Hill Claiming Stakes and Ardsley Handicap. The first crop of foals by Hard Tack, which stood at Horace N. Davis' Blue Grass Heights Stock Farm, near Lexington, until his removal in 1935 to A.B. Hancock's Claiborne Stud, Paris, came in 1933. It included four foals, all of which won at two, all of which have also won at three this year. One other stakes winner, Grog, was included. Swing On, dam of Seabiscuit, did not race. Her first foal, Query, won at two, 1934. Seabiscuit is her second. Her foal of 1934, Beaten Biscuit, has not yet started. Balance produced Flippant (Broadway Stakes, Bayview Handicap), Hornpipe (Amsterdam Stakes), the winners Scales, Even Up, Abby, and High Wire, and the producer Flutter. She is half-sister to Distraction, Blondin, Swinging (good race mare and dam of Equipoise, etc.).

September 12, 1936
SEABISCUIT GOES WELL

Although Myrtlewood (126) was scratched from the Governor's Handicap ($5,000 added, 3-year-olds and up, 1⅛ miles) at Detroit September 7, a field of 12 starters, including a number of horses of some class, went to the post in the event. Favorite and leader for the first quarter-mile was Finance (120), but the *Bull Dog colt dropped rapidly back thereafter. B. Hernandez's Biography (104) went next into the lead, but was carried too fast by Mrs. C.S. Howard's Seabiscuit (3-y-o, 109), which had always been close to the lead. In the

Mr. and Mrs. Charles S. Howard.

stretch Biography tired, and Seabiscuit went on to win. Rushing on him were two early trailers. One was F.M. Alger, Jr.'s *Azucar (112) which moved up from tenth place to come very fast in the stretch. Driving even faster was Mrs. J. Chesney's Professor Paul (3-y-o, 99), which moved later than *Azucar, passed him in the drive. Professor Paul took second place, a neck behind the winner, a length and a half in front of *Azucar. Biography was fourth, followed by Paradisical (108), Safe and Sound (103), Cristate (106), Marynell (104), Woodlander (100), Finance, Heart Break (101), and Alsang (3-y-o, 95). Jockey J. Pollard rode the winner. Time, :23⅖, :47, 1:12, 1:38, 1:50⅖, track fast. Stakes division, $4,290, $800, $400, $200.

In 50 starts, Seabiscuit has won 10 races, finished second eight times, third seven times, and has earned $23,055, including Watch Hill Claiming, Mohawk Claiming Stakes, and Ardsley Handicap.

October 3, 1936
SEABISCUIT'S HENDRIE HANDICAP

Mrs. C.S. Howard's Seabiscuit (3-y-o, 115) won his second stakes at Detroit September 26, when he took the lead in the Hendrie Handicap ($2,500 added, 3-year-olds and up, 1¹⁄₁₆ miles) near the three-eighths pole, and drew out to win by four lengths. Mrs. J. Chesney's Cristate (114) was second, two and one-half lengths in front of H. W. and W.J. Young's Safe and Sound (108), with I.J. Collins' Paradisical (114), the favorite, in fourth place. Marynell (106) and Professor Paul (3-y-o, 113) were the other members of the field. Jockey J. Pollard rode the winner. Time, :24⅘, :48⅗, 1:13, 1:38⅕, 1:44⅖, track fast. Stakes division, $2,010, $450, $200, $150.

In 52 starts, Seabiscuit has won 11

races, finished second eight times, third seven times, and has earned $25, 065.

October 31, 1936
SEABISCUIT JUST GETS UP

Mrs. Charles S. Howard's Coramine disappointed her owner in the Ardsley Handicap, but the California sportswoman did not have long to wait for consolation. The next race, at Empire City on October 24, was the Scarsdale Handicap ($5,000 added, 3-year-olds and up, one mile and 70 yards), and the winner, after a desperate drive, was Mrs. Howard's Seabiscuit (3-y-o, 116), a 12-to-1 outsider.

Favorites in the race fared very poorly. Mrs. Ethel D. Jacobs' Jesting (112), which got to the front after a half-mile, bore over going into the second turn, caused a jam in which Snow Fox (3-y-o, 116), the 3-to-1 favorite, was knocked back, cut down so badly that he was later destroyed. Another sufferer was Sgt. Byrne (119), split second-choice, which was running third when the

The Howards' Seabiscuit (outside) beating Jesting in the Scarsdale Handicap at Empire City.

crowding occurred. Emileo (3-y-o, 116), which shared second regard, was forced back sharply when moving up near the turn. Jesting seemed a certain winner, reaching the eighth-pole two lengths in front of the hard-running Piccolo (3-y-o, 105½), which carried the C.V. Whitney silks, with the third-place Wha Hae (3-y-o, 109) falling back. From sixth place came Seabiscuit, making up four lengths in the closing furlong, under a hard drive by Jockey J. Pollard. In the last strides the Hard Tack colt caught Jesting, won by a nose. Piccolo, gaining rapidly on Jesting, failed by a head to catch him, took third place three lengths in front of T.B. Townsend's Steel Cutter (106). In order followed Wha Hae, Prince Abbot (112½), Emileo, Esposa (115), Sgt. Byrne, Exhibit (113), with Snow Fox, pulled up, completing the field. Time, :23⅗, :47⅗, 1:12⅕, 1:39⅕, 1:44, track fast. Stakes division, $5,570, $1,000, $500, $250.

Seabiscuit in 55 starts at two and three has won 12 races, finished second eight times, third nine times, has earned $31,035.

December 5, 1936
SEABISCUIT TAKES THE RECORD

The Bay Bridge Handicap ($2,500 added, all ages, one mile) at Bay Meadows November 28 resulted in a victory for a California owner, but was won with a horse which must be considered an invader. Mrs. C.S. Howard, whose husband is a San Francisco automobile dealer, has had several horses racing this fall in California, but Seabiscuit (3-y-o, 116), Coramine, and others have been racing only in the East. Seabiscuit made his first western start in the Bay Bridge Handicap, had been freshened for a month, was made favorite.

Seabiscuit was shuffled back at the start, trailed the field for a quarter-mile. Then Jockey J. Pollard started sending him up, tried to get through on the last turn. He got in close quarters, was forced to take up. He then sent his mount around the field, was carried wide on the stretch turn. But Seabiscuit was so much the best that these repeated misfortunes made little difference. He headed H.C. Hatch's Uppermost (114) in the stretch, drew out to win by five lengths, though eased up through the last 50 yards. Third, a half-length behind Uppermost, was Hynes and Beezley's Velociter (107), a neck in front of Mrs. M.C. Rush's Noble Count (3-y-o, 108). In order followed Wildland (3-y-o, 105), Watersplash (104), Coldwater (106), and Arson (108). Time, :23⅗, :46⅘, 1:11⅗, 1:36 (new track record), track fast. Stakes division, $1,970, $500, $200, $10.

An unusual angle of the race was that all of the placed horses have held Bay Meadows' track record for a mile. Velociter set a new mark of 1:36⅗ this season. A few days later Uppermost cut it to 1:36⅕. And now Seabiscuit has lowered it to 1:36, and the three record-makers finished one-two-three, in the order of their best performances.

Seabiscuit has now started 57 times, of which 35 times were at two. He has won 13 races, finished second eight times, third 10 times and has earned $33,505. He has won four previous stakes this year.

December 19, 1936
CANTER FOR SEABISCUIT

The World's Fair Handicap ($10,000 added, all ages, 1³⁄₁₆ miles) at Bay Meadows on December 12 was both the richest and the easiest triumph in the record of Mrs. Charles S. Howard's Seabiscuit (3-y-o, 113). Jockey J. Pollard broke the Hard Tack colt alertly, sent him to the front when the field had got well under way. After a half-mile Seabiscuit was five lengths in front, going easily. Mrs. M.C. Rush's Noble Count (3-y-o, 106) was nearest at this point, with Tick On (115) and Watersplash (101) pressing him closely. However, none could throw down a challenge to the leader, and though Seabiscuit's lead was cut to three lengths after six furlongs, it was only because Pollard had him well in hand. The other three fell back after a mile, leaving a six-length margin to the leader, and F.M. Carr's Wildland (3-y-o,

101) and Millsdale Stable's Giant Killer (3-y-o, 107) began their runs. At the eighth-pole Seabiscuit's lead was back to three lengths, but he drew away again to win by five. Wildland was two and a half lengths in front of Giant Killer, with Noble Count a length and a half farther back. Seabiscuit, already holder of the one-mile record at Bay Meadows (1:36) added the 1³⁄₁₆-mile record to his trophies. Time, :23, :47, 1:11⅗, 1:36⅖, 1:55⅗ (new track record), track fast. Stakes division, $8,000, $2,000, $1,000, $500.

Seabiscuit has earned $41,505, winning 14 races from his 58 starts at two and three, finishing second eight times, third 10 times. The World's Fair Handicap was his sixth stakes victory this year, most important of his others being the Governor's Handicap at Detroit and the Scarsdale Handicap at Empire City. He won three smaller stakes at two.

Stardom

Seabiscuit truly came to the fore as a major American racehorse as a four-year-old in 1937. He won his seasonal debut on February 9, then was defeated in two straight races by Rosemont. Seabiscuit's road to that year's title as champion handicap horse was probably smoothed by Rosemont's early departure from the scene. Rosemont went unplaced in his only two subsequent starts and was retired. A son of The Porter, Rosemont had won stakes every year he raced. As a three-year-old he won the important Withers Stakes and finished third in the Belmont Stakes.

After suffering the first of what would be his two heartbreaking defeats in the rich Santa Anita Handicap (his initial $20,000 runner-up purse was the largest he had ever earned in one race), Seabiscuit went on a roll. Previously, he had never managed to put together back-to-back wins. This year, Seabiscuit sizzled through a five-month stretch during which he reeled off seven handicap victories in a row from California to Massachusetts.

Transcontinental travel by racehorses had been a rarity in the past, but Seabiscuit's era was replete with equine tourists, including such champions as Equipoise, Discovery, Challedon, Kayak II, Stagehand, Pompoon, and Marica who raced at tracks from coast to coast.

Seabiscuit broke a twenty-year-old Empire City track record in one of those victories. In another, the Marchbank Handicap, he eclipsed Tanforan track marks for the half-mile, six furlongs, and mile while en route to an easy victory in the mile and one-eighth event. He showed great determination in taking the Brooklyn Handicap, drawing praise from *The Blood-Horse*'s Eastern-based correspondent who noted that Seabiscuit's "three (earlier) rich victories in California were scored against inferior competition." Seabiscuit's win in the Butler Handicap gave him "leadership of the handicap division," and it was following that race that his photograph first appeared in the magazine. An impressive tally in the Massachusetts Handicap, his foremost achievement up to that point, capped the win streak.

The 1937 season also saw Seabiscuit involved in the only dead heat of his career, saw him set a single-season earnings record, and produced the first reports of a possible match race against War Admiral, whose Triple Crown triumph had made him a close runner-up in the monetary standings for the season.

War Admiral, generally regarded as the great Man o' War's best son, enjoyed an unbeaten season at age three in 1937. In addition to his Kentucky Derby-Preakness-Belmont sweep, War Admiral captured five other events and earned $166,500. Seabiscuit, arguably Man o' War's best grandson, narrowly topped that total with his $168,590.

March 6, 1937
ROSEMONT'S CLIMAX

The 1935 Santa Anita Handicap went to a cast-off steeplechaser. The 1936 event was won by a vastly improved plater which had been claimed for $3,500. The 1937 running ($100,000 added, 3-year-olds and up, 1¼ miles), made more orthodox Turf history by going to a horse which was bred and raised by his owner and had been a recognized stakes contender in each of his four seasons on the track.

When Foxcatcher Farms' Rosemont won the San Antonio Stakes on February 20, he insured himself a position as favorite for the $100,000 event. On February 24 he came out in the morning to go a handy mile and an eighth in 1:54⅖, and Trainer Richard E. Handlen apparently judged his charge fit enough without working over the full distance of the big race. On February 27 Rosemont took up top weight of 124

pounds, and was made the betting favorite at nearly 4 to 1.

Rains during the latter part of the week had made a slow track probable, but Santa Anita officials worked hard to make a fast strip. Machines such as those used to melt asphalt on city streets were sent over the track, flames drying out the mud. Though the track was not quite fast, it was classified as good. Time of the handicap, as well as of other races during the day, indicated that it was not more than a second off its usual speed. Mindful of the difficulty with the start of the Santa Anita Derby a Saturday earlier, track authorities had wooden stalls built to place at the end of the gate, so that every starter came out of an individual compartment.

A.C.T. Stock Farm's Special Agent, obviously trying to clear the way for his stablemate, Indian Broom, shot away at high speed, with E. and W. Janss' Boxthorn behind him. The California-bred Don Roberto, an animal almost as large as Whopper, was third by the time the back stretch had been reached, and Mrs. Charles S. Howard's Seabiscuit, in close quarters at the start, had moved up to fourth. The favorite was eleventh after a half-mile, nine lengths behind the flying Special Agent, which had covered the distance in :45⅘. For another quarter-mile Special Agent held his speed, covering six furlongs in 1:10⅗. The order of the horses immediately behind him did not change, and Harry Richards had not moved on Rosemont. At the mile there were still no changes among the leaders, but both Time Supply and Rosemont were beginning their runs, and the leaders were dropping back. Rosemont had stepped up to sixth place, six lengths behind the pace. Turning into the stretch, with three-sixteenths of a mile straightaway, Special Agent had enough, and Jockey J. Pollard drove Seabiscuit into the lead. Boxthorn and Don Roberto retired, and Indian Broom moved forward to take up where his stablemate had left off. At the eighth-pole Special Agent was clinging to Seabiscuit, which was leading him a head. Indian Broom was two lengths behind and charging hard. But Rosemont, clear and on the outside was running fastest. He had three and a half lengths to make up in the last furlong, and he made them up. Special Agent and Indian Broom he swept aside, but Seabiscuit fought it out to the last stride. Locked together the leaders went under the wire, and the photo-finish sign went up. Clem McCarthy, broadcasting the race from well above

the finish line, said, "Rosemont got up by a short nose, I think." Some two minutes later, after scrutiny of the photograph, officials ordered up Rosemont's number.

Rosemont's success story, which rose to its climax with victory in "the world's richest race," differs somewhat from those of recent Turf heroes, in that there has not been a time when he was not recognized as a good horse. The story, however, has just enough of the element of luck in it, to make it a good one. On February 28, it was announced that Rosemont would not race again, but would be retired to stud. However, on the next day Trainer Handlen denied this, said Rosemont would be pointed for the Narragansett Special next summer.

Garden Rose [dam of Rosemont], herself a winner, was bred by Edward Beale McLean, and was put up for sale in the dispersal of that sportsman's Belmont Plantation stock in June, 1931. She went for $4,300 to Preston M. Burch, who was either bidding for William du Pont or shortly sold Garden Rose privately to him. She had been bred four times to Messenger, a Fair Play stallion now owned by Mr. du Pont, and her first foal, Sweet Tidings, was a winner at two and three. Her second, Parties, was to win a total of 30 races in five seasons, but had not won at the time of the dispersal. Her third, a yearling which went to Mrs. Thomas H. Somerville (sister to Mr. du Pont) for $1,500 was named Garden Message, won 16 races, including the Pimlico Nursery Stakes, Sprightful Claiming Stakes (by disqualification), Oakdale

Claiming Handicap, and Marlboro Stakes. Her fourth, Rose Bearer, which was sold with her as a weanling, and raced in Foxcatcher Farms' colors, won one race at two. Mr. du Pont sent Garden Rose to *The Satrap, a stallion which Mr. du Pont had imported, and which was sent back to England last year. Her foal to *The Satrap's cover was Roseanna, which won two races at two last year. She has a 1937 2-year-old by *Teddy.

Rosemont himself came up once for auction, when Foxcatcher Farms held a dispersal sale in December, 1932. He went for $1,900, and Garden Rose for $3,600, but both went to J. W. McComb, who bid them in for Mr. du Pont.

Apparently but an incidental fact in the purchase of Garden Message was the fact that she was in foal to The Porter, already a proven stallion for which John Hay Whitney paid $27,000 at the same sale. But this foal, born April 18, 1932, was Rosemont, which has now started 21 times, won seven races, finished second six times, third three times, and has earned $168,750, becoming the one hundred and fourth horse to earn $100,000 or more.

Garden of Allah, Rosemont's second dam, also was a winner, and produced Dream of Allah (also by Colin and winner of Providence Handicap, and dam of the stakes winner Islam, Time Supply's sire, Time Maker, and three other winners). Garden of Allah also produced the winners Loughland and Devil's Garden (also producer), and the producer Girl of Allah. She was a sister to the good winner Sky Pilot.

Frances Hindoo, Rosemont's third dam, produced also the steeplechase winner Zellwood. She was a sister to Pepper (Ohio, Seabreeze, Carnarsie, McLaughlin, Crocker Stakes), Nihil, Kinski, Benroe, and Greetings and to the producers Dingle Farfalla, Da Rimini, Dordica, Frantic, and Halloo, from which descend the stakes winners General J. M. Gomez, Everett, Belzoni, Earlocker, Ginger Clark, Mission Bell, etc.

Francesca, Rosemont's fourth dam, was a stakes winner (Clarendon Hotel Stakes) and also produced the winners Missive and Billo O., and the producer Franconia. She was a sister to Iroquois (Epsom Derby, St. Leger), and Jaconet, dam of the stakes winners and sires Sir Dixon and Belvidere, the winners Hindoonet, Blacklock, and Lady Pepper (also producer) and the producers The Niece (dam of Uncle), Mattie T. Cambric, Intrepid, Magna Charta, and Little Mary. The next dam was Maggie B. B.

March 13, 1937
CONSOLATION FOR SEABISCUIT

The San Juan Capistrano Handicap ($10,000 added, 3-year-olds and up, 1⅛ miles) is primarily a consolation event for horses which have failed in their major objective, the Santa Anita Handicap. Head Play won it in its first year; Whopper won it in 1936. This winter it was regarded as almost a foregone conclusion that Mrs. C.S. Howard's Seabiscuit (120), just beaten in the rich handicap, would take the consolation event.

Principal contention was expected to

come from A.C.T. Stock Farm's entry of Special Agent (116) and Indian Broom (118), and the same strategy that was used unsuccessfully in the $100,000 event, of sending Special Agent out to make the pace, was used again. For six furlongs Special Agent set a hot pace, but could never shake off Seabiscuit. When the pacemaker weakened, Seabiscuit shot into the lead and Jockey J. Pollard, perhaps mindful of criticism of his ride in the Santa Anita Handicap, took no chances. He kept the son of Hard Tack going until his lead was overwhelming, then took him in hand to win by seven lengths. Indian Broom, lacking his usual dash in the stretch, could not catch his stablemate, but Raoul Walsh's *Grand Manitou (108), showing considerable improvement, charged up to take second place, three-quarters of a length in front of Special Agent, which led Indian Broom by a neck. Red Rain (114) was fifth, had never been dangerous. Apparently outclassed were Goldeneye (107), Silk Mask (105), Star Shadow (110), Gold Seeker (110), and Chanceview (112), which finished in the order named. Seabiscuit cut three-fifths of a second from the track record which Time Supply had set, under 116 pounds, last winter. Time, :22⅘, :46⅗, 1:11, 1:36⅕, 1:48⅘ (new track record), track fast. Stakes division, $9,200, $2,000, $1,000, $500.

Seabiscuit has started 62 times, won 16 races, finished second nine times, third 10 times, and has earned $71,750. His dam, Swing On, did not race, and Seabiscuit is her second foal. Her third foal, also by Hard Tack, has not raced. Her first foal, Query, won at two. Balance produced Flippant (Broadway Stakes, Bayview Handicap), Hornpipe (Amsterdam Stakes), and the winners Scales, Even Up, Abby, and High Wire, and the producer Flutter. She was a half-sister to Distraction, Blondin, Swinging (good race mare and dam of Equipoise), etc.

April 24, 1937
SEABISCUIT RACES WELL

Perhaps the most improved horse in the handicap division is Mrs. C.S. Howard's Seabiscuit. He raced in the upper claiming division at two. At three he was a stakes horse in what might be called second flight handicap events. At four he is a real danger in any field. After a bitter stretch fight he surrendered to Rosemont in the Santa Anita Handicap, virtually mowed down his field in the San Juan Capistrano Handicap a week later. He was rested until the running of the Marchbank Handicap ($10,000 added, 3-year-olds and up, 1⅛ miles), at Tanforan on April 17.

Though Seabiscuit (124), despite a heavier impost than he had previously carried, was bet down to 2 to 5, he had worthy opposition in the A.C.T. Stock Farm entry of Special Agent (113) and Indian Broom (116), the latter a winner of the event in 1936, in world record time. But Seabiscuit, best on performance, was also favored by racing luck. Jockey J. Pollard shot him at once to the front, took him in hand on the first turn, and waited for challenges. None came, and Seabiscuit galloped to the finish three lengths in front of Raoul Walsh's *Grand Manitou (110), which ran a very good race to beat Hunt, Beezley, and Boeing's Sobriety (109) a head for third place. Special Agent had good early speed, though no match for the winner's pace, but he tired to finish fourth. Don Roberto (108), Sir Oracle (3-y-o, 103), and Indian Broom completed the field. Jockey Pollard, who may have wondered why Indian Broom did not come up to contest the issue with Seabiscuit, found after the race that the Taylor color-bearer had been eliminated on the first turn. He stumbled leaving the gate, then got in close quarters on the turn. He stumbled again, went to his knees, almost unseated Ralph Neves. When he recovered he had lost all chance, and he was galloped behind the field, pulled up in the stretch. It is very doubtful that he could have threatened the Hard Tack colt, but he might have made a race of it. Time, :22%, :45%, 1:10%, 1:36, 1:48%, track

fast. It is worthy of note that Seabiscuit cracked Tanforan's track records for half-mile, six furlongs, and one mile in passing, might have reached Indian Broom's world record of 1:47% for the 1% miles had he ever been fully extended. (Indian Broom's fractional time was :24%, :48, 1:11%, 1:35%, 1:47%.) Stakes division, $8,200, $2,000, $1,000, $500.

Seabiscuit has started 63 times in three seasons, won 17 races, finished second nine times, third 10 times, and has earned $79,950. He has won 11 stakes, finished second in two, third in four others.

June 5, 1937
SEABISCUIT GETS ANOTHER

Weight concessions of 16 to 26 pounds failed to stop Mrs. C.S. Howard's Seabiscuit (127) at Bay Meadows May 22, in the Bay Meadows Handicap

Seabiscuit (inside) defeating Aneroid by a nose in the Brooklyn Handicap at Aqueduct.

($10,000 added, 3-year-olds and up, 1¹⁄₁₆ miles). The Hard Tack colt, galloping along close to the pace which Ed Janss' Boxthorn (111) set for the first seven furlongs, went to the front when Jockey Pollard called on him in the stretch, won easily by a little more than a length. The real surprise of the race was the winner's stablemate, Exhibit (105), which came very fast through the stretch to take second place, a nose in front of M.C. Walker's Watersplash (103). Boxthorn was fourth, a length farther back, having tired after he was headed. Sallys Booter (110), Mickeys Man (101), Don Roberto (107), and Valiant Fox (103) completed the field. With the exception of the winner, the race failed to draw any horses which have much business racing for $10,000, and Seabiscuit's victory was almost conceded before the race. He was backed at 1 to 10, and raced like it. Time, :24, :47⅘, 1:11, 1:37⅗, 1:44⅘, track fast. Stakes division, $7,530, $2,000, $1,000, $500.

Seabiscuit's score is now 64 starts, 18 wins, nine times second, 10 times third. He has earned $87,530. He also won the Marchbank Handicap at Tanforan, on April 17.

July 3, 1937
BROOKLYN HANDICAP

The Brooklyn Handicap, which came up for its forty-ninth running at Aqueduct June 26, has had a history which reflects the fortunes of racing in New York. Originally run at Gravesend (the first running was in 1887), it began as a $5,000 added event, gradually increased in value until the early '90's, when it was worth around $18,000 to the winner. Then it dropped again, became a $7,500 added affair. With the turn of the new century, the Brooklyn again became increasingly richer, reached its peak in 1908, when Celt defeated Fair Play for a purse worth $19,750 to the winner. The next years were troubled ones for New York racing, and the Brooklyn fell below $5,000 for the first time. In 1911 and 1912 it was not run at all, began again in 1913 with a purse worth $3,125 to Whisk Broom II. It grew slowly but steadily in value, while such fine horses as Grey Lag, Mad Play, Exterminator, and Peanuts were adding their names to the winners' list. In 1931 it had reached a second peak, being worth $13,900 to the winner, Questionnaire. Then the depression struck, and when Discovery won the event in 1934 it was worth but $2,925. Discovery also won the 1935 and 1936 runnings, when the Brooklyn had been made a $10,000 added race. This year New York racing is having a banner season, and the Brooklyn, still a dependable barometer, was endowed with $20,000 in added money, reached a third peak, was worth more to the winner than any running except that of 1908. During the Brooklyn's long history, the distance was decreased once, in 1915, from 1¼ miles to 1⅛ miles.

The 1937 running found J.A. Manfuso's Aneroid (122) sharing public favor with Mrs. C.S. Howard's Seabiscuit (122). The Hard Tack colt had rolled up an impressive record during the winter, but his three rich victories in California were scored against

Seabiscuit winning the Butler Handicap, his fifth straight stakes victory.

inferior opposition. Aneroid, on the other hand, had been running against the best the East had to offer, had won four stakes, had turned in an exceptionally brilliant effort in the Suburban Handicap. When the field got to the post, Aneroid was even-money favorite; Seabiscuit was at 6 to 5.

When the start came, Seabiscuit was the quickest. Jockey J. Pollard rushed him to the front, then took a good hold on him. Bulwark (101), one of the lightweights, came up to the challenge and Seabiscuit raced him into defeat. Then, on the turn, Aneroid moved forward. He had been well rated in third place through the first six furlongs, and he came down on the outside in the stretch. With three furlongs to go Seabiscuit led by a half-length. At the eighth-pole this had been cut to a head. Through the final, hard-fought furlong the two raced almost together, but Seabiscuit stuck it out, won by a nose. Five lengths farther back Greentree Stable's Memory Book (114) had raced up to take third place, three

lengths in front of Maemere Farm's Maeriel (105). In order finished Gold Seeker (107), Bulwark, Rosemont (127), Rust (106), and Scotch Bun (102). Rosemont had come forward with a rush nearing the last turn, got to fourth place, then tired steadily. He pulled up sore. Time, :23⅗, :47, 1:11⅖, 1:37, 1:50⅕, track fast. Stakes division, $18,025, $4,000, $2,000, $1,000.

By his game stretch effort, Seabiscuit became the one hundred and sixth horse to earn more than $100,000 in America. He has started 65 times, won 19 races, finished second nine times, third 10 times, and has earned $105,505. This places him in ninety-fourth position among American money-winners of all time. His previous stakes victories this season were the San Juan Capistrano, Marchbank, Bay Meadows Handicaps.

July 17, 1937
SEABISCUIT'S BUTLER HANDICAP

The third Butler Handicap ($20,000 added, 3-year-olds and up, 1³⁄₁₆ miles) was run at Empire City July 10, with six horses making up the field. The favorite, with four consecutive stakes victories behind him, was Mrs. C.S. Howard's Seabiscuit (126), for which may be claimed leadership of the handicap division. The start was good enough, but James Butler's Caught (102), which had been fractious at the gate, came over to the inside from the outside post position. Corinto (109) and Finance (119), which formed the entry of Mrs. Emil Denemark, were annoyed, as was William Ziegler's Esposa (108). Seabiscuit, in number one post position, and B.M. Byers' Thorson (107), next to him, escaped the crowding. Seabiscuit went out to dispute with Caught for the leadership, and Thorson, outrun, was taken under restraint. Seabiscuit went to the front, disposed of Caught in a half-mile. Esposa came up after six furlongs, but was bothered again and tired. Then Corinto made his bid, and at the end of a mile he was racing side by side with Seabiscuit. He faltered in the stretch, and the son of Hard Tack drew away. Thorson, which had moved up gradually, raced hard through the stretch to take second place, a length and a half behind Seabiscuit, three lengths in front of Corinto. Esposa was fourth, another length away. Caught and Finance, the latter of which pulled up lame, finished in order. Time, :23, :48, 1:12, 1:38⅖, 1:58⅗, track fast. Stakes division, $18,025, $4,000, $2,000, $1,000.

Seabiscuit has now started 66 times, won 20 races, finished second nine times, third 10 times. The Butler Handicap raised his earnings to $123,530, of which $82,025 was won this year.

July 31, 1937
YONKERS HANDICAP

The Empire City record for 1$\frac{1}{16}$ miles stood for almost exactly 20 years after the 4-year-old Spur, on July 28, 1917, went the distance in 1:44⅗ under 122 pounds. On July 24, in the Yonkers Handicap ($7,500 added, 3-year-olds and up, 1$\frac{1}{16}$ miles), Racing Secretary John B. Campbell assigned 129 pounds to Mrs. C.S. Howard's Seabiscuit, and the 4-year-old cut two-fifths of a second from Spur's record. Weight was Seabiscuit's principal opponent, for the field he met was not a high-class one. Mrs. Ethel D. Jacobs' Jesting (108) went out to make the pace under sufferance, while Jockey J. Pollard was in second place with Seabiscuit. After about five furlongs he let the favorite run, and Seabiscuit moved at once into the lead. Though Jesting held on well through the stretch, he was overmatched, and Seabiscuit drew steadily away to win by four lengths. Mrs. Emil Denemark's Corinto (109) was third, three lengths behind Jesting, a like distance in front of B.M. Byer's Thorson (110). Dark Hope (114) and Roustabout (109), the latter of which ran far below his best form, were the others. Time, :23⅗, :47⅖, 1:11⅗, 1:38, 1:44⅕ (new track record), track fast. Stakes division, $8,225, $1,500, $750, $275.

Seabiscuit, running his string of victories to six in succession, was making his

Seabiscuit with trainer Tom Smith and jockey Red Pollard after winning the Yonkers Handicap.

sixty-seventh start. He has won 21 races, finished second nine times, third 10 times, and has earned $131,755, of which $90,250 has been gained this year. The Yonkers moved him from ninety-fourth to eighty-ninth place among American money winners.

August 14, 1937
SEABISCUIT'S RICHEST VICTORY

The brilliant series of victories scored by Mrs. C.S. Howard's Seabiscuit, comparable to no other handicap performance since Discovery's sweep of eight successive stakes in 1935, was stretched to seven at Suffolk Downs August 7, when the Hard Tack colt justified pre-race predictions to win the Massachusetts Handicap ($50,000 added, 3-year-olds and up, 1⅛ miles). It was the richest race in the career of the one-time plater, possibly the best field he has turned back.

There was some criticism of the 130-pound impost Secretary H.D. Monroe assigned to the C.S. Howard colt, but it

was the heaviest package Seabiscuit has ever carried. Jockey J. Pollard, who has ridden the colt in all of his races this year, was in the saddle, and he broke his mount alertly, after a six-minute delay to post. Hobson C. McGehee's Fair Knightess (108) also came away flying, and when she offered battle for the lead Pollard let her go. Trouper (100) also had early speed, and in the first quarter-mile he moved into second place. He began falling back immediately, and Seabiscuit was soon in second place, some two lengths behind the *Bright Knight filly. Pollard had a light hold on his mount down the backstretch, but Seabiscuit gradually gained. Mid-way around the last turn Pollard called on him, and Seabiscuit responded gamely. At the eighth-post he had caught the filly, and at the end he had drawn clear. Mrs. E. D. Jacobs' *Caballero II (108), a Chilean-bred horse which was established as a dangerous threat, came fast in the stretch to wear down Fair Knightess in the last 70 yards and take second place by a length. Raoul Walsh's *Grand Manitou (104) was fourth, two and a half lengths farther back. In order followed Calumet Dick (116), Esposa (113), Aneroid (128), New Deal (107), Trouper, *Sahri II (110), War Glory (108), Black Gift (107), and White Cockade (110). Time, :23⅕, :48, 1:11, 1:36, 1:49 (new track record), track fast. Stakes division, $51,780, $10,000, $5,000, $2,500, $1,250.

Seabiscuit won the Mohawk Claiming Stakes last year, running to be claimed for $6,000. No one wanted him at that figure, and he was later sold to Charles S. Howard, San Francisco automobile dealer, for a price variously reported at $6,000 and $8,000. Either way he has proved very much of a bargain, winning $142,030 this year, enough to make him second money-winner of the season to date, some $2,500 behind War Admiral. For his three seasons, his record is 68 starts, 22 wins, nine times second, 10 times third. He has earned $183,535, taking him from eighty-ninth to twenty-third place among American money winners.

August 28, 1937
TWO MORE FOR SEABISCUIT

Two more starts are scheduled for Seabiscuit before the son of Hard Tack and Swing On returns to California for the opening of the Bay Meadows meeting. Owner Charles S. Howard's present plans are to pass up the $25,000 added Narragansett Special to race his 4-year-old in the $10,000 added Hawthorne Gold Cup September 11, and then send the handicap champion to Maryland for the $10,000 added Havre de Grace Handicap September 29.

October 23, 1937
SEABISCUIT'S CONTINENTAL HANDICAP

On October 12 at Jamaica, Mrs. C.S. Howard's Seabiscuit (130) went out in quest of the title of leading money winner of the year. He came back with it by a margin of five lengths, running easily, leading all the way after the first few strides. Mrs. Ethel D. Jacobs' *Caballero II (117), considered his most formidable rival, got to the front at the break, but

Jockey J. Pollard hustled the Hard Tack colt down on the inside, was in front going to the first turn. For six furlongs *Caballero II stayed at his head. Then, rounding the last turn, Seabiscuit began coming away, shook off his opposition, and won well within himself. *Caballero II went gamely to keep second place by two lengths from Cleaveland Putnam's Moon Side (112), which was a length in front of B.M. Byers' Thorson (112). In order followed Chanceview (109), Preeminent (117), Pasha (3-y-o, 105), Danger Point (3-y-o, 106), Rust (105), Two Bob (103), Strabo (3-y-o, 108½), and He Did (112). Time, :24, :48, 1:12⅘, 1:44⅘, track fast. Stakes division, $9,250, $2,000, $1,000, $500.

On the following Saturday, Seabiscuit ran a dead heat with Heelfly in the Laurel Stakes.

October 23, 1937
DEAD HEAT AT LAUREL PARK

When Coldstream and Red Rain ran a dead heat in the 1935 Saratoga Special, it was the first dead heat in a stakes event for many years. Last year the only dead heat in an important race was in a steeplechase stakes, between *Rioter and Rock Lad. This year there have been two such instances. The Arlington Futurity was a dead heat between Teddy's Comet and Tiger, and on October 16 the finish of the Laurel Stakes ($7,500 added, 3-year-olds and up, one mile) found Mrs. C.S. Howard's Seabiscuit (126) and T.P. Morgan's Heelfly (3-y-o, 114) finishing together. For the 3-year-old, it was the best race

Seabiscuit winning the Continental Handicap by five lengths at Jamaica in New York.

he had run against worthy opponents; for Seabiscuit it was his second race of the week (the other being the Continental Handicap at Jamaica). If Seabiscuit had won the Laurel Stakes outright he would have become the winner of $200,000.

Seabiscuit was off well from an outside post position, was held in third place while Everglade Stable's Deliberator (116) fought with E.D. Shaffer's Floradora (108) for the lead. When the filly shook off Deliberator, Seabiscuit moved up to second place. Then A.C. Compton's Clingendaal (3-y-o, 110) made his bid, went up to wrest the lead from the *Bull Dog filly, which immediately dropped out of the race. In the stretch Jockey J. Pollard sent Seabiscuit forward, seemed an almost certain winner. But here Heelfly entered the picture. He had broken with a blindfold, this being the result of his usual unruly behavior, at post. He was away

slowly, dropped to last place, as the blindfold was snatched away. For six furlongs he was last, then came forward with a rush. When Seabiscuit took the lead at the eighth-pole, Heelfly was at his head. A few strides farther and the two were head and head. Thereafter neither yielded an inch. Laurel Park's patrons waited some 10 minutes while placing judges studied the photograph, then saw the dead heat sign go up. A length and a half behind the leaders, Deliberator was third, with Clingendaal fourth, a length farther back. Then came Fair Knightess (113), Tabitha (108), and Floradora. Time, :24, :47⅕, 1:12⅖, 1:37⅗, track fast. Stakes division, $4,337.50 each, $750, $350. The time was one-fifth second slower than Jack High's track record, set in 1932 under 118 pounds.

The race brought Seabiscuit's record to 71 starts, 24 wins, nine seconds, 11 thirds. He has earned $198,622.50, of which $157,117.50 has been earned this year, making him the leading money winner of 1937. If he succeeds in holding this position, it will be the first time a horse older than three years had been leading money winner since 1915, when the 7-year-old Borrow led the list. He is now seventeenth on the list of American money winners, just behind Crusader, just in front of Discovery.

The 3-year-old Heelfly had no such record to show, but has proved himself among the better performers of his age during the latter part of the season. He has started 22 times, won 12 races, finished second four times, third three times, and has earned $30,592.50. Previously this year he had won the Warren and Potomac Handicaps.

November 13, 1937
SEABISCUIT LEADS THE FIELD

At the beginning of the current year, Charles S. Howard's Seabiscuit was not included on the list of American money winners published by the *American Racing Manual*, since that list now includes only horses which have won $50,000 or more. But his second in the Santa Anita Handicap placed him in that favored group. By mid-season he had reached that picked band which has won as much as $100,000. Steadily he moved forward on the list. When he won the Continental Handicap at Jamaica October 12 he became the leading money winner of the year. A dead heat in the Laurel Stakes four days later lacked a little of putting him into the group of winners of $200,000. Then a fall flurry of three victories took War

Admiral again to the top among 1937 money winners. But at Pimlico November 5, in the Riggs Handicap ($10,000 added, 3-year-olds and up, 1 3/16 miles), Seabiscuit went again into the leading position for the year. He will not be threatened again, as War Admiral is through for the season and no other horse is in a challenging position.

Seabiscuit (130) turned in one of his best performances in the Riggs, though the 3-year-old Burning Star (114), getting 10 pounds by scale was getting to him at the finish. But the Hard Tack colt raced to a new track record, under 17 pounds more than the previous record holder, Dark Hope, had carried. Seabiscuit, ridden by J. Pollard, was

Trainer Tom Smith (left) and owner C. S. Howard (right) accepting the Riggs Handicap trophy.

away well, but not in the first flight. War Minstrel (3-y-o, 110) made the early pace, with Infantry (110) just behind him. Chanceview (107) was third for a quarter-mile, then yielded that place to J.A. Manfuso's Aneroid (119). That son of The Porter, moving fast down the back stretch, went to the front after a mile. The early pacemakers had faded by that time, and it was Seabiscuit which challenged. Racing clear on the outside, he wore Aneroid down, and was leading him by a half-length at the eighth-pole. Here came a more desperate challenge by Burning Star, Shandon Farm's winner of the Travers and other stakes. He had begun more slowly than Seabiscuit, had moved later. He was wearing the handicap champion down during the closing yards, but the furlongs ran out, and Seabiscuit beat him by a neck. Mrs. Ethel D. Jacobs' *Caballero II (116), which had been in good position throughout, had been passed by both of the leaders, finished third, three-fourths of a length behind Burning Star. Aneroid, faltering in the last furlong, was fourth, a half-length farther back. In order followed the Lawrence Realization winner Unfailing (3-y-o, 109), Firethorn (120), War Minstrel, Thorson (115), Chanceview, Count Stone (105), and Infantry. Time, :23⅘, :47, 1:11⅗, 1:37, 1:57⅗ (new track record), track fast. Stakes division, $10,025, $1,500, $1,000, $350.

Money winning, like mountain climbing, gets harder at high altitudes. The $10,025 which Seabiscuit won took him past but one more horse on the list of American money winners. This was Crusader, which had formerly occupied sixteenth place. In all Seabiscuit has started 72 times, won 25 races (including a dead heat), finished second nine times, third 11 times, and has earned $208,585. His record for this year is 14 starts, 11 wins, one second, one third, earnings of $167,080. (War Admiral earned $166,500 this year.)

Seabiscuit was named champion older male for 1937 despite losing the Bowie Handicap to Esposa (inside) in his final start of the year.

November 13, 1937
RECORDS AND PROSPECTS
By Joe H. Palmer

In 1912, when there was virtually no racing in New York, and when a sweep of the Kentucky Derby and the Preakness would have netted $6,300, the 4-year-old Star Charter led the list of money-winning horses with a total of $14,655, the lowest amount that has placed a horse at the top during the present century. In 1915, when none of the present classic races were worth as much as $17,000 to the winner (Derby, $11,450; Travers, $2,150; Preakness, $1,275; Belmont Stakes, $1,825; Futurity, $16,590; Hopeful Stakes, $9,150), the 7-year-old Borrow led the list of money winners with $20,195. In both years racing was more or less on the rocks, this period being the lowest ebb of many years.

With the exception of these two years, the 1937 season is the first since 1900 (and I have no available figures for earlier years) that the leading money-winning horse has not been a 2- or 3-year-old. Seabiscuit, then, is the first horse of the century in the handicap division to lead the winning list in a year when racing was normal. Furthermore, the $167,080 he has earned this year is the greatest amount any handicap horse has won in a single season. Again my figures go back only to 1900, but since purses were generally lower in earlier years, I should guess that Seabiscuit's record was never surpassed in America. Not even such great racers as Equipoise, Sun Beau, Discovery, or Exterminator got as much in any one season. Indeed, only five horses since 1900, of any age, have earned as much in a year's racing. These are Gallant Fox ($308,275), Zev ($272,008), Top Flight ($219,000), Twenty Grand ($218,545), and Mate ($214,775).

So when Seabiscuit came down, in new track record time, at Pimlico last Friday, he was setting what is probably a new American record for one-season earnings by a horse four years old or up. It is true that a horse is not to be measured wholly in terms of money won. Many persons deny Seabiscuit a ranking as a really great horse, basing this largely on the fact that his opposition has not been of really high caliber. But as the *American Racing Manual* remarks in its introduction to the list of money winning horses, "greatness, in whatever way achieved, evokes admiration."

Seabiscuit's owner and trainer are reported to be studying the weights for the Bowie Handicap ($10,000 added) on November 11. Should the Hard Tack colt win that race, he would move two places forward on the all-time list of American winners, to fourteenth place, just behind Sarazen. Should his great objective, the Santa Anita Handicap, be attained, he would move into fourth place, just behind Zev. Should he stay sound, he might have the ghost of a chance to get at Sun Beau's world record of $376,744. Should he have as many pounds on him as there are "ifs" in this program, he couldn't win for $200 at Shreveport.

November 20, 1937
ESPOSA BEATS SEABISCUIT

William Ziegler, Jr.'s, Esposa has won eight stakes events this season, has been a capable performer in earlier years, is now nearing the $100,000 mark in earnings. But what was perhaps her crowning achievement came at Pimlico November 11 when she defeated Seabiscuit by a nose, cut one and two-fifths seconds from a 26-year-old track record. The durability of the track record was no great matter for surprise, since there has been no assault on it for at least 12 years, but her chances against Seabiscuit had been estimated by Pimlico's bettors at 15 to 1.

The occasion was the Bowie Handicap ($10,000 added, 3-year-olds and up, 1⅝ miles) on November 11, the race having been lengthened from a previous distance of 1½ miles. Seabiscuit (130), already leading money winner of the year, was out to make his owner the leading money winner also, since the C.S. Howard stable was only a few thousand dollars behind Milky Way Farm. Shandon Farm's Burning Star (3-y-o, 114), which had been wearing Seabiscuit down at the same weights in the Riggs Handicap, was the only one of the field of eight given much of a chance against the Hard Tack colt.

Regal Lily (3-y-o, 109), coupled with Firethorn (116) to form the W.M. Jeffords entry, was the early pacemaker, the Chilean *Caballero II (113) close behind her. Pollard took Seabiscuit to the inside on the first turn, holding him well under restraint. Half-way down the backstretch he moved out and began closing on the leaders. A quarter-mile from the finish he was third, gaining rapidly. But as the leaders reached the stretch, they swung out from the rail. Through the gap Nick Wall drove Esposa, and the Espino mare responded willingly. Seabiscuit, on the outside, drove on into the lead, but Esposa was running harder. Some 20 yards from the finish she got her nose in front, kept it there to the end. Seabiscuit, beaten for the fourth time in 15 starts this year, easily took second place from Burning Star, which finished a length and a quarter behind him, going strongly at the end. Firethorn rushed up on the stretch turn, got into second place, but lost ground when forced to circle his field, finished fourth, a length behind Burning Star. Regal Lily, *Caballero II, Red Rain (106½), and Challephen (107) completed the field. Time, :25, :50⅕, 1:15⅕, 1:41, 2:06⅗, 2:32, 2:45⅕ (new track record), track fast. Stakes division, $9,375, $1,500, $1,000, $350.

Esposa has now started 72 times, won 16 races (eight stakes in 1937), finished second 17 times, third 10 times and has earned $90,200. She is as well up in her own division as Seabiscuit in his. Seabiscuit, whose second money increased his total earnings to $210,085, is sixteenth on the list of money winning horses in America. Esposa is in fourteenth place among American money-winning fillies and mares.

A Match for the Ages

Nineteen-thirty eight was by far Seabiscuit's biggest news-making year. It began with a relatively verbose statement from trainer Smith about his star runner's physical condition, followed with Smith's dismissing as false a rumor that an attempt had been made to "sponge" Seabiscuit (insert a sponge in the horse's nasal cavity to hamper his breathing), and went on to include twenty-four additional *Blood-Horse* stories about the Howard runner.

This was the year that the famed "Jones Boys" — the father and son training team of Ben and Jimmy — won the first of their eight Kentucky Derbys. They sent out the Kansas-bred Lawrin to win the sixty-fourth Run for the Roses for Herbert J. Woolf's Woolford Farm. Aboard Lawrin was jockey Eddie Arcaro, posting the first of five Kentucky Derby victories in what would be his legendary career.

Seabiscuit's campaign began with two gut-wrenching losses, the first in the San Antonio Handicap on February 26. Conceding twelve pounds, he was beaten a nose by Aneroid, a leading member of the handicap division whom Seabiscuit had defeated in the previous year's Brooklyn 'Cap. Two weeks later Seabiscuit lost the Santa Anita Handicap by the same slim margin to Stagehand, a three-year-old, to whom he was giving a whopping thirty pounds. Although he did not contest any of the Triple Crown races, Stagehand, at the end of the year, was voted the championship of his division.

Two match races served as focal points of 1938 for Seabiscuit. The first was held at Del Mar on August 12. Interestingly, Seabiscuit took on Ligaroti, a horse owned by Charles Howard's son Lin in partnership with Bing Crosby. Any notion that this event was a familial exercise in courtesy went by the wayside when the race began. Jockey Noel "Spec" Richardson, who had ridden

Seabiscuit to victory in the Agua Caliente Handicap in March, did everything he could to beat him while piloting Ligaroti in the match. Nevertheless, Seabiscuit — under George Woolf — prevailed. Both jockeys were subsequently suspended for "foul riding" after a battle that recalled the Don Meade-Herb Fisher contretemps in the 1933 Kentucky Derby. Meade, on eventual first-place finisher Brokers Tip, and Fisher, astride runner-up Head Play, repeatedly flailed at each other in a bitterly fought stretch duel. A classic photo of this infamous "Fighting Finish" showed Meade tugging on Fisher's jacket with his right hand as they neared the wire, Fisher's left hand gripping Meade's right boot. Neither horse was disqualified. Both jockeys drew thirty-day suspensions for their on-track actions. Fisher was handed an additional five days for assaulting Meade in the jockeys' room after the race.

Long before the Del Mar event, the racing press had been reporting plans for a match race between Seabiscuit and War Admiral. That pot of expectation simmered all summer, but the flame beneath it was several times lowered as proposals fell through. Finally, track president Alfred G. Vanderbilt lured Seabiscuit and War Admiral to Pimlico for a face-off in the Special on November 1. For a relatively modest purse of just $15,000, the country's two premier runners shipped down to Baltimore. What occurred there went down in racing history.

January 29, 1938
SEABISCUIT TAKES IT EASY

Comparative idleness of Charles S. Howard's Seabiscuit, now at Santa Anita Park, has given rise to reports that the Hard Tack horse was not doing well. On January 17 Trainer Tom Smith denied such reports, said that Seabiscuit was not in hard training, was being given only slow gallops, would not be raced until the Santa Anita Handicap. He said:

I have despaired of getting Seabiscuit into any race prior to the Santa Anita Handicap with less than 132 pounds. I will not run him with 132 pounds. So what is the use of training him?…We had him all ready for a race on New Year's Day; then they weighted him out of it. Not that he couldn't have won. We simply do not want him to carry 132 pounds until after the Santa Anita Handicap. Then we will try him at any weight and against any kind of a field.

February 12, 1938
SEABISCUIT WORKS

A standard source of news is the workouts of candidates for important races. When candidates do not work out, stories on the reason for idleness immediately become rife. So idleness of

Seabiscuit at Santa Anita Park has given rise to innumerable rumors of unsoundness, illness, and the like. On February 1 Seabiscuit came out with Jockey Pollard in the saddle, went a quarter in :23⅗, a half in :46⅕, finished out six furlongs in 1:12. Trainer Tom Smith said he was satisfied, said a rumor that an attempt had been made to sponge Seabiscuit was "silly."

February 26, 1938
SEABISCUIT'S STUD PLANS

After his racing career is over, Seabiscuit will enter stud in southern California, Owner C.S. Howard announced February 17, saying that he hoped to establish a nursery in that section. But, hoped Owner Howard,

Seabiscuit will be kept in training in an attempt to surpass Sun Beau's money-winning record.

March 5, 1938
SANTA ANITA PARK

Climax of the 56 days of racing at Arcadia comes March 5, with the fourth running of the $100,000 Santa Anita Handicap. Seabiscuit and Pompoon will vie for favoritism in the race. Sceneshifter will have a good many backers. Many bettors will go along with Aneroid. If the winner does not come from these four, it will be the major upset of the California season.

Pompoon has been idle since his smart victory in the San Carlos Handicap. Sceneshifter, recent overnight winner,

The Seabiscuit team in morning training.

has also been withheld. Those who insisted Seabiscuit should have at least one race before starting in the big handicap found him in action February 26, getting beat a nose by Aneroid. He was giving the son of The Porter 12 pounds, will have to concede him 10 in the big race, will have a furlong farther to go. And 10 pounds at 1¼ miles is perhaps as great a concession as 12 pounds at 1⅛ miles. Pompoon carried 124 pounds in his winning race, will drop off four of them in the Santa Anita Handicap, will have to carry his burden three-sixteenths farther. On February 23 Oscar Otis, in the *San Francisco Chronicle*, reported that Pompoon pulled up lame from a work, but this has not been confirmed from other sources. Johnny Gilbert will probably ride Pompoon, the veteran Raymond Workman will be on Seabiscuit, Jack Westrope on Sceneshifter, Charley Rosengarten on Aneroid.

The remainder of the field is uncertain. *Amor Brujo, beaten under 116 pounds at 1⅛ miles by Sweepalot and Warfellow, may not pick up his allotted 120 in the big race. Whichcee, second to Bill Farnsworth last week in a six-furlong race run in 1:10⅗, will probably go along with Indian Broom to form the A.C.T. Stock Farm entry, though Indian Broom, with 108 pounds, was decisively beaten by Aneroid and Seabiscuit February 26, will have to carry 116 pounds on March 5. Time Supply turned in a good effort in the San Antonio Handicap, will probably start. Calumet Dick pulled up lame after that race, is doubtful. Today may be a starter, though his performance in the San Antonio does not indicate much chance for him. Dark horse is A.A. Baroni's Star Shadow. Under 107 pounds, he was second to Pompoon (124) in the San Carlos, closed well after being outrun, to finish a length behind the Pompey colt. He is in with 108 pounds in the big race and on his best performance could be dangerous at the weights.

Last week the track had two million-dollar days. On February 22 the turnover reached a new record for the meeting, when $1,370,807 was wagered. Through 46 days of racing, the turnover is approximately $29,500,000, or about $640,000 daily. This is likely to increase rather than diminish through the two remaining weeks, and it seems probable that the betting at Santa Anita Park this season will be the highest ever registered on a pari-mutuel track.

March 5, 1938
BRADLEY AND SEABISCUIT

On February 24 it was reported that E.R. Bradley had offered $50,000 for Seabiscuit, *after* the Santa Anita Handicap, win or lose. It was also reported that the offer was $100,000. Owner Charles S. Howard was not interested, at either figure, said: "Seabiscuit is not for sale at any price."

March 5, 1938
REVENGE FOR ANEROID

Last June 26, after J.A. Manfuso's Aneroid had swept through four spring stakes, and was well on his way toward the top of the handicap division, he met Charles S. Howard's Seabiscuit in the Brooklyn Handicap, at Aqueduct.

Seabiscuit, making his first Eastern start of the season, had most of his present reputation still to make, and Aneroid was a slight favorite to beat him. But Seabiscuit broke in front and was never headed, and though Aneroid was gaining slowly at the end Seabiscuit lasted to win by a nose. Thereafter Aneroid dropped out of the picture, placed in only one later stakes in 1937, while Seabiscuit went on to the leadership of the division.

At Santa Anita Park February 26, exactly eight months later, Seabiscuit went to post a 2-to-5 favorite in the San Antonio Handicap ($7,500 added, 3-year-olds and up, 1⅛ miles). Aneroid broke in front and was never headed, and though Seabiscuit was gaining at the end Aneroid lasted to win by a nose. But though revenge may have been sweet enough to Aneroid's owner, and to Aneroid's jockey, Charley Rosengarten, it was not complete. In the Brooklyn Handicap Aneroid and Seabiscuit were level at 122 pounds; in the San Antonio Seabiscuit carried 130 pounds, Aneroid 118.

During the early stages of the race, Lucas B. Combs' Woodberry (108) was second, with A.C.T. Stock Farm's Indian Broom (108) third. After a half-mile Woodberry dropped back, and the Brooms horse went up to challenge. Seabiscuit, in slightly tight quarters at first, ran under restraint in fourth place to the stretch, then moved up strongly. He disposed of Indian Broom easily, might have caught Aneroid in a few strides more. Indian Broom was third, a length and a half behind him, with Mrs.

F.A. Carreaud's old Time Supply (114) getting fourth place, a head farther back, after being fairly close to the pace throughout. Woodberry was fifth, tiring a trifle toward the end. In order followed *Frexo (110), Gosum (109), Calumet Dick (116), Today (115), Over the Top (112), *Sahri II (109), Grey Count (109), and *Limpio (110), the latter coupled with Seabiscuit. Calumet Dick pulled up so lame that Jockey Shelhamer dismounted before bringing him back to the judges' stand; *Sahri II might have been closer had she not been hampered in the stretch by a loosened bandage, but could hardly have been a dangerous contender in any case. Time, :23⅖, :47, 1:11⅘, 1:37⅖, 1:50, track fast. Stakes division, $7,125, $1,200, $600, $300.

In 49 starts, Aneroid has won 15 races (including six stakes), finished second seven times, third seven times, and has earned $55,110. He was foaled at Greentree Farm, Lexington, on April 12, 1933. At the Walnut Hall sale at Boyce, Va., in 1934, he was sold for $300 to Dion K. Kerr, his present trainer, who sent him out at two under the silks of E. Bruner. Last year Mr. Bruner sold him to the present owner. Through his whole racing career, however, Aneroid has been in charge of the same trainer, and in most of his important victories has been ridden by Charley Rosengarten. Outburst [dam of Aneroid], a winner, was half-sister to the stakes winners Toro ($142,530 and successful sire), Brocado, and Good Goods, and the winner Light Brigade. Aneroid was her first foal. Her only other foal through 1935 was No Dice, also a winner and placed in three stakes. *Brocatelle [Aneroid's second dam] was a good producer, as above. *Pietra [third dam] also produced Irish Lassie (dam of the stakes winner Easter Stockings) and June Rose (dam of Brown Bud). She was half-sister to Pomegranate, stakes winner and dam of Prunus, stakes winner and leading sire in Germany four successive seasons.

March 12, 1938
STAGEHAND'S GREAT DOUBLE

Had any one predicted, when the Santa Anita Park meeting opened, December 25, that a colt which was then a maiden 2-year-old would take both of the richest stakes of the meeting, there might have been reasonable doubt of his sanity. But Maxwell Howard's Stagehand, which was noticed, if at all, only because he was a brother to Sceneshifter and trained by famous Earl Sande, came back to the winner's circle after the Santa Anita Handicap with two startling records. He had earned more money than any other horse had ever garnered in the same space of time ($133,800 in 12 days) and he had set a new track record for 1¼ miles. Meeting one of the most powerful fields the rich handicap had ever mustered, the 3-year-old had given weight by scale to 15 of his 17 opponents, had received a concession only from the recognized champion handicap horse Seabiscuit, which gave him seven pounds by scale.

Indian Broom was the only withdraw-

al of the 19 overnight entries, Whichcee being left to carry the A.C.T. Stock Farm hopes. Seabiscuit was favorite at 19 to 10, the Maxwell Howard entry of Stagehand and Sceneshifter second, J.H. Louchheim's Pompoon third. The selection proved sound, but not in the right order.

The start, which came in three minutes, was a good one. Count Atlas bore over, seriously interfering with Seabiscuit, but George Woolf quickly righted the Hard Tack horse. Pompoon got away swerving, but was quickly straightened. There were no other sufferers, and the remainder of the race was free of interference. Sprinting to the front went Whichcee, with Aneroid hard after him. Primulus was fourth, Count Atlas fifth. Of the strongly backed horses, Pompoon was first, racing in seventh place around the first turn, some five lengths behind the leader. Stagehand was ninth, two heads behind Pompoon, and Sceneshifter was twelfth, two lengths farther behind. Rounding the turn Aneroid wrested the lead from Whichcee, and Woodberry moved up into second place. Whichcee was third and falling back at the six-furlong-post, with Pompoon leading the second flight, two lengths farther back. Finding racing room on the back stretch, Woolf suddenly moved with Seabiscuit. The Hard Tack horse went sweeping forward, took the lead on the turn, and observers later questioned the wisdom of rushing him so hard. At all events Seabiscuit turned into the stretch in front and on the rail, with Aneroid, a head behind, still holding on

Turning for home in the Santa Anita Handicap, Seabiscuit (left), Aneroid (right), and eventual winner Stagehand (no blinkers).

gamely. Woodberry was in third place, falling back, and now Stagehand came rushing forward. With a quarter-mile to go he was fourth, two and a half lengths behind Seabiscuit. At the eighth-pole Seabiscuit still had a head lead over Aneroid, but Stagehand had closed the gap, was lapped on the leaders. The final furlong was a bitter struggle between Seabiscuit and Stagehand, both horses running straight and hard at a pace which carried them six lengths out from the field. But the 3-year-old never ceased to gain. With a remarkable display of stamina he cut Seabiscuit's lead away inch by inch, had his nose in front at the finish. Stewards ordered a photograph as a matter of precaution, but those on the finish line had had little doubt of the result. In third place, six lengths behind the driving leaders, came Pompoon, game but not good enough. Nelson A. Howard's Gosum, next to last for six furlongs and fourteenth at the quarter-pole, closed fast to pass tired horses and take fourth place, two lengths behind Pompoon, four lengths in front of the exhausted Aneroid, which finished almost together with Star Shadow and Sceneshifter, both of which had raced evenly but without much chance.

The pace of American racing usually results in a series of successively slower quarters. But both Seabiscuit and Stagehand, after comparatively slow fourth quarters, quickened the pace through the stretch. Seabiscuit covered the final quarter-mile in 24⅘ seconds, four-fifths of a second faster than his previous quarter. But Stagehand made up slightly more than two lengths, ran his final quarter in about 24⅗ seconds to complete one of the most brilliant performances a 3-year-old has ever shown so early in the year.

Stagehand, second winner in four Santa Anita Handicaps which was purchased from J.E. Widener (*Azucar, previous holder of the track record which Stagehand broke, was the other), raced eight times at two without winning, got one second, one third, and $260. In his first start at three, at Santa Anita on January 2, he was second. Since that time he has won five successive races, including the Santa Anita Derby and Handicap. In all he has started 14 times, won five races, finished twice second, twice third, and has earned $137,060. The Santa Anita Handicap victory thrust him well up in the ranks of the winners of $100,000 or more (there are now 108 of them), placing him fifty-first among American money winners, just behind My Dandy.

March 12, 1938
NOTES OF THE HANDICAP

In last year's Santa Anita Handicap Seabiscuit was bothered at the start, got to the front in the stretch, led by several lengths at the eighth pole, lost by a nose to Rosemont. The 1938 running was almost a repetition of that experience.

Jockey Jack Pollard prevented from riding Seabiscuit by an injury several weeks ago, was permitted to leave a Pasadena hospital to watch the Santa Anita Handicap from a parked car.

March 19, 1938
SEABISCUIT'S WEIGHT
By Joe H. Palmer

Sympathizing to some extent with C.S. Howard's disinclination to run Seabiscuit at heavy weights, I should like to hear him state his position differently. For the San Juan Capistrano Handicap Seabiscuit was assigned 135 pounds, was held out because of the weights. Now, in the Santa Anita Handicap, under 130 pounds, Seabiscuit finished six lengths in front of all but Stagehand. Since he could have met, in the San Juan Capistrano, the horses he had beaten six lengths or more a week earlier, 135 pounds is no immoderate assignment. Refusal to run him at that weight is tantamount to refusing to run him in fair handicaps. I have insisted for some time that when an owner is fortunate enough to possess a high-class horse 4 years old or more, he should have a chance at as liberal rewards as the owner of a high-class 2- or 3-year-old. But I wish Mr. Howard would frame his refusal in some such way as this: "I will not run him in handicaps. I will put him in weight-for-age races, or weight-for-age races with moderate allowances, or I will put him in the stud."

Seabiscuit, and others of his caliber, ought to have opportunities in weight-for-age races. But he ought not to be allowed in handicaps at weights which are unfair to the chances of other horses. The present set-up can hardly be a permanent one, and already some of the richer handicaps have become farces. The owner of a tremendous gate attraction can say to a race track that he will not start his gate attraction unless he gets all the best of the weights. The results we have seen. The solution seems obviously to be more weight-for-age races and handicaps that are handicaps.

April 2, 1938
AGUA CALIENTE HANDICAP

Only stakes event of the meeting which is in progress at Agua Caliente this year was the Agua Caliente Handicap ($12,500 added, 3-year-olds and up, 1⅛ miles), run March 27. If it was not made for C.S. Howard's Seabiscuit, the Hard Tack horse was certainly made for it. Under 130 pounds, a burden less trying than the same weight at 1¼ miles, Seabiscuit had no opposition of any class to face, and though weights on the other horses ranged from 108 pounds down to 98, this was largely a handicapping gesture, and Seabiscuit could have won had the remainder of the field been permitted to ride with only the lightest jockeys they could pick up. In fact three of the lightweights had to carry overweight from one to three pounds because no riders could be found to make their weights.

Seabiscuit went to the front at once, with Jockey N. Richardson in the saddle. He kept a moderate pace for a half-mile, with no very serious challenges to repulse. Then he drew leisurely away, was in hand at the finish, won by two lengths from E.E. Fogelson's Gray Jack (103), a Class D contender at Santa Anita Park. Mrs. R.J. Murphy's Little Nymph (98), also a Class D performer, was third, a head farther back, with Kozinsky Brothers' *Amor Brujo (108) fourth. Warfellow (103), San Luis Rey (99), Sir Ridgway (100), and Top Radio (98) completed the field. Time, :23⅘, :47, 1:11⅘, 1:37, 1:50⅗, track fast. Stakes division, $8,600, $2,500, $1,250, $500.

Though the two horses have not met, War Admiral and Seabiscuit have been running a race since last summer for money winning honors. After War Admiral's victory in the Widener Cup Handicap, and Seabiscuit's second, on the same day, in the Santa Anita Handicap, both stood almost together, with earnings of $231,625 for War Admiral, $231,285 for Seabiscuit. Seabiscuit's Agua Caliente victory gave him undisputed possession of thirteenth place among American money winners, with a total of $239,885. He has started 76 times, won 26 races, finished 12 times second, 11 times third. Seabiscuit is the second foal of his dam, Swing On, which did not race. Her first foal, Query, won at two. Her third, a brother to Seabiscuit, has not raced. Balance produced Flippant (Broadway Stakes, Bayview Handicap), Hornpipe (Amsterdam Stakes), and the winners Scales, Even Up, Abby, and High Wire, and the producer Flutter. She was half-sister to Distraction, Blondin, Swinging (good race mare and dam of Equipoise), etc.

45

April 16, 1938
WAR ADMIRAL VS. SEABISCUIT

With the beginning of the northern and eastern racing season it was inevitable that a special race between Samuel D. Riddle's War Admiral and Charles S. Howard's Seabiscuit would become an engrossing subject for everyone concerned with racing. For race tracks and newspapers such an event was a "natural." Both the principals were unquestioned leaders, both had an exceptional amount of color and drawing power, and they had never met. Last week the air was full of it.

Herbert Bayard Swope, chairman of the New York Racing Commission, began with a suggestion that the Suburban Handicap be stepped up from $20,000 to $50,000 on the condition that Man o' War's most famous son and most famous grandson would start. On April 6 Mr. Swope talked by telephone to Mr. Howard, who suggested that Belmont Park offer a $100,000 purse for a special race at its fall meeting. Mr. Swope took that idea to Mr. Riddle and to Joseph E. Widener, head of the Belmont Park organization, got their approval.

The same day John D. Hertz, speaking for Chicago's Arlington Park, made an offer of a $100,000 race to be run at the Arlington Park meeting, which begins June 27, closes July 30, but stipulated that a third horse be invited, as, for instance, Stagehand, if he wins the Kentucky Derby. Mr. Hertz's suggestion was for a race at a mile and a quarter, under weight-for-age conditions, essentially the same as the conditions which had been thought of in connection with the Belmont Park proposal. The Arlington Park race would presumably have been set for closing day, as Mr. Howard has stated his intention to leave Seabiscuit in California to compete in the $50,000 added Hollywood Handicap, to be run at the new Hollywood Park on July 16.

Toward the end of last week it began to look as if Belmont Park might win out in the bidding for what promised to be the greatest "match race," as newspapers insist on calling it, since Man o' War was pitted against Sir Barton in 1920. Messrs. Swope, Riddle, Howard, and Widener were getting down to details of weight, post position, etc. Then it

Triple Crown hero War Admiral.

began to be intimated that C.V. Whitney, a powerful member of the directorate of the Westchester Racing Association (Belmont Park), might oppose such an enormous outlay for a special race when New York's regular weight-for-age races had been left begging. Mr. Whitney was off deep sea fishing, out of reach of newspaper men.

During the week-end, Suffolk Downs, speaking through Board Chairman Charles F. Adams, entered the bidding. Mr. Adams suggested a $100,000 race to be held at the Boston track July 9 (closing day), with six to 12 starters, and $70,000 to the winner.

Tuesday of this week, April 12, Belmont Park's directors met, with C.V. Whitney among those present. After the meeting there was another proposal before Messrs. Riddle and Howard. Belmont Park was willing to put up $100,000 for a special race to be held at the great Long Island course not in September, but on Decoration Day, May 30. The Belmont Park directors had excellent arguments to make along with their revised offer. They felt that five or six months was too long a time between arranging and running; that too many things might happen; that the horses ought to be left free to engage in competition during the summer, especially in New York's weight-for-age races for which both are eligible, including the Whitney Stakes, Saratoga Cup, and Jockey Club Gold Cup; that since both horses are now sound and ready and public interest at a high point, the Decoration Day date would be best.

After the decision of the Belmont

Park directors was made known, Mr. swope agreed to the wisdom of their reasoning. The next move was up to Messrs. Howard and Riddle.

April 23, 1938
TRACK RECORD UNDER 133 POUNDS

Though he has repeatedly refused to start Seabiscuit under weights above 130 pounds, Charles S. Howard left his horse in the Bay Meadows Handicap ($15,000 added, 3-year-olds and up, 1⅛ miles) under 133 pounds. Thirteen overnight entries had been made, as there seemed some doubt that Seabiscuit would start. But when it became apparent that he would, the field was reduced to seven, six of which received weight concessions of 20 to 29 pounds from the Hard Tack horse.

Seabiscuit, with Jockey George Woolf up, stood quietly in his compartment until the field was lined up, got away well. Primulus (105) went out to make the pace, and Seabiscuit swung along behind her under restraint. For six furlongs the Sweep On mare set a rather brisk pace, but for the last quarter-mile had Seabiscuit at her head. As the leaders went into the turn, Woolf gave his mount rein, and Seabiscuit moved easily to the front. Primulus fell away, and Nelson A. Howard's Gosum (113) moved up to challenge. At the eighth-pole Seabiscuit was only a length ahead of the Hotweed colt, and Woolf shook him up. Seabiscuit came away to win by three lengths, was well in hand at the finish. Third, a length and three-quarters behind Gosum, was Neil S.

McCarthy's Today (112), running a good race but overmatched. Advocator (109), a *Sickle gelding which is a stablemate of Seabiscuit, came up well in the stretch to finish fourth, a nose behind Today. Sweepalot (109), Primulus, and Don Roberto (104) completed the field. Time, :23⅗, :47⅘, 1:11⅗, 1:37, 1:49, track fast. This was a track record for Bay Meadows, was no record for Seabiscuit, which had run 1⅛ miles in the same time at Suffolk Downs last August. Stakes division, $11,270, $3,000, $1,500, $750.

The race was Seabiscuit's seventy-seventh start. He has won 27 races, finished second 12 times, third 11 times. He has earned $251,155. The Bay Meadows Handicap purse lifted him above his famous grandsire, Man o' War ($249,465), leaves him in twelfth place among American money winners, some $2,000 behind Exterminator. Seabiscuit may start in the Dixie Handicap at Pimlico, for which he has been assigned 130 pounds, but would have stiffer opposition than the Bay Meadows race afforded. Victory in that $20,000 added event would put him above Exterminator, Victorian, Display, Twenty Grand. Victory in the $100,000 special with War Admiral would carry him into second place, with only Sun Beau ($376,744) between him and the title of leading money winner of the world.

April 30, 1938
SEABISCUIT ARRIVES

On April 25 Charles S. Howard's Seabiscuit was unloaded at Belmont Park, after a 3,000-mile journey from the Pacific Coast. He shipped well, unloaded quietly amid the popping of flash bulbs, was scheduled to have an unlimbering gallop on April 26. Jockey Pollard, now recovering from a broken collar bone, will reach Belmont Park soon, and no hard workout is planned before his arrival. Said Trainer Tom Smith: "War Admiral will know he's been in a horse race, win or lose." There is some possibility that Seabiscuit will be sent after the Dixie Handicap, on May 11, at Pimlico.

On the same day Belmont Park officials confounded expectation with the announcement that there would be no advance in prices on the day of the big race. Unlike the Papyrus-Zev race, when admission ranged from $5 to $22, the War Admiral-Seabiscuit event will be available at prices ranging from $1.50 to $10. C.V. Whitney, vice president of the Westchester Racing Association, said in making the announcement: "This is the public's race."

May 28, 1938
THE BIG RACE IS OFF

Five years ago Belmont Park scheduled a special race between the two outstanding fillies then in training, Top Flight and Tred Avon, set the date for Decoration Day, May 30, 1933. A few days before the race Top Flight went lame, and the race was never run.

For Decoration Day in 1938 Belmont Park had scheduled a far greater special race, between Samuel D. Riddle's War Admiral and Mrs. Charles S. Howard's Seabiscuit. On this page and the next of this issue we were going to tell our readers about that race, because it was going to be one of the great events in American Turf history.

But just as the press was about to start rolling came the news that the War Admiral-Seabiscuit race had been declared off. Reason: Seabiscuit was not in condition.

Presumably the bidding will now be reopened for the greatest gate attraction now available to American race tracks.

We ask the indulgence of our readers if a few references to the special race remain in this week's issue.

July 23, 1938
SEABISCUIT'S GOLD CUP

The Hollywood Gold Cup ($50,000 added, 3-year-olds and up, 1¼ miles) at Hollywood Park July 16 drew a field of 10, including Charles S. Howard's Seabiscuit (133) and nine horses which have been racing steadily on the Coast this year. At the weights several other starters seemed to have a chance, and though Seabiscuit came through with a good victory, it was by no means a runaway.

A.C.T. Stock Farm sent out Whichcee (114) and Indian Broom (120) against the Hard Tack horse, while A.A. Baroni's Silver State Stable started three, Specify (3-y-o, 109), Star Shadow (114), and No Dice (105). Specify, which won the Hollywood Derby a week earlier, was quickest at the beginning, and at the end of a half-mile was six lengths in front of the field. Whichcee and Indian Broom were nearest, while Seabiscuit, away between horses, was outrun for that distance, trailed in ninth place. For the next quarter-mile the position of the leaders did not alter much, except that Specify drew farther out and Indian Broom came up and took a head lead over his stablemate. But Seabiscuit's position altered radically. Brought up fast approaching the turn, he was in fifth place with a half-mile to go.

Whichcee went back into second place on the turn, began cutting steadily into Specify's margin. An eight-length lead was cut to six, then to four. But before Whichcee could get near enough to challenge, Seabiscuit had passed him with a strong charge. In the last eighth Specify was done. Just before Seabiscuit reached him he began bearing out, and George Woolf, not to be caught outside a tiring horse, cut to the inside. He went past Specify easily, and Seabiscuit drew out to win by a length and a half. Specify just lasted to take second place by a nose from Whichcee, with Binglin Stable's *Ligaroti (118) five lengths away fourth. In order followed Indian Broom, Warfellow (105), Star Shadow (114), *Sahri II (109), No Dice, and Grey Count (105). Time, :23⅘, :47⅕, 1:11⅖, 1:37⅗, 2:03⅘ (new track record), track fast. Stakes division, $37,150, $10,000, $5,000, $2,500, $1,000.

The race was Seabiscuit's seventy-ninth start. He has won 28 races, finished second 13 times, third 11 times, and has earned $290,305. The victory moved him five places forward among leading American money winners, and he is now in sixth place. Immediately ahead of him is Mate, with $301,810.

When Equipoise moved up on the turn in the Santa Anita Handicap of

1935, Sun Beau's great record of $376,744 in earnings was in danger. But a tendon bowed and Equipoise finished seven and a half lengths away from leading money winning honors. Since that time Sun Beau has had no serious challenge, but it is Mr. Howard's hope that Seabiscuit will offer one. The Hard Tack horse has $86,439 to go to reach Sun Beau's total, has twice been withdrawn from races this year against War Admiral because of leg trouble.

July 30, 1938
DEL MAR'S SPECIAL

Undeterred by the fate of other specially arranged races this year, the Del Mar Turf Club last week announced a $25,000 race in which the invited starters are Seabiscuit, *Ligaroti, and Whichcee. Seabiscuit, owned by Charles S. Howard, and *Ligaroti, owned in partnership by H.L. (Bing) Crosby and Lindsay C. Howard, son of Seabiscuit's owner, are regarded as certain starters. The Hard Tack horse will carry 126 pounds. *Ligaroti will have 110, and Whichcee, if he starts, 106.

July 30, 1938
SEABISCUIT STAYS

July 19 Charles S. Howard was quoted by the San Francisco *Chronicle* as saying that he had virtually abandoned plans for a campaign at Saratoga and other Eastern tracks with Seabiscuit. The special race at Del Mar, engaging *Ligaroti and possibly Whichcee, will be his next objective, and there may be a special at Longacres. According to the *Chronicle*, Mr. Howard said:

"Cancellation of the gold cup at Chicago, plus the unfavorable weather conditions in the East, make it inadvisable to ship to the Atlantic Coast at this time. Apparently there will be races available for Seabiscuit on the Coast, perhaps one or two events in San Francisco this fall which will round out a schedule.

"If the proposed Del Mar and Longacres events materialize we will stay West. Only in the event that everything falls flat, and that appears highly unlikely, will we ship East."

August 13, 1938
SEABISCUIT'S "EARNINGS"

On his way to attempt to surpass Sun Beau's record earnings of $376,744, Charles S. Howard's Seabiscuit now faces two special races. At Del Mar, on August 12, he meets *Ligaroti, South American racer, owned jointly by Bing Crosby and Mr. Howard's son, Lindsay C. Howard, the latter also being *Ligaroti's trainer. Seabiscuit will carry 130 pounds, *Ligaroti 114.

The Longacres track offered a special race to Seabiscuit with $10,000 added, at one mile. Mr. Howard refused to accept unless the purse was raised to $25,000, the distance to 1⅛ miles. These conditions were met, the date set for August 27 (to be postponed one week in case of rain), with Seabiscuit to carry 132 pounds, *Ligaroti 115, A.A. Baroni's Specify 105.

Should Seabiscuit win both races, his earnings will approximate $340,000, placing him second on the list of money winners.

Meanwhile New York's Bill Corum suggested, if Seabiscuit passed Sun Beau by means of special races against such competition, that Mr. Kilmer send his stallion into the lead again by racing him, for $50,000, against Exterminator's Shetland pony, Peanuts.

August 20, 1938
SEABISCUIT GETS HIS SPECIAL

At Del Mar on August 12, as scheduled, Charles S. Howard's Seabiscuit (130) met *Ligaroti (114), owned by Mr. Howard's son Lindsay C., in partnership with Bing Crosby, in a race rather obviously designed to help Seabiscuit along the road to the position of leading money winner. This object was achieved, but in other respects the race was hardly a success. *Ligaroti held on to the Hard Tack horse all the way, was beaten by a head, in track record time of 1:49 for 1⅛ miles. But after the race both George Woolf, on Seabiscuit, and Noel Richardson, who rode *Ligaroti, were suspended for foul riding. Richardson claimed that Woolf grabbed *Ligaroti's bridle in the stretch. Woolf asserted that Richardson had grabbed his whip hand, and then had claimed a foul "to save his own skin."

Stewards apparently believed both, suspended them for the rest of the meeting, requested that the California Horse Racing Board continue the suspension for the rest of the year.

Woolf attributed the narrowness of Seabiscuit's victory partly to Richardson's tactics, partly to the fact that his riding orders included instruc-tions to restrain Seabiscuit and "make a race out of it."

Before the race, Seabiscuit had earned $290,305. If the $25,000 received for the exhibition race is counted, he has earned $315,305, is fourth among American money winners, behind Sun Beau, Equipoise, Gallant Fox, fifth among money winners of the world.

August 27, 1938
SEABISCUIT'S ENGAGEMENT

With the proposed $25,000 special at Longacres apparently abandoned, Charles S. Howard was quoted in the San Francisco *Chronicle* as saying that Seabiscuit would be shipped to Chicago for the Hawthorne Gold Cup, the shipment to be made at the last possible moment, with preliminary training at Del Mar.

August 27, 1938
DENIAL AND EXPLANATION

The Del Mar track has had more trouble getting rid of the Seabiscuit-*Ligaroti match than it had getting it. Prodded by varied and conflicting stories of the events leading up to the suspension of Jockeys Woolf and Richardson, stewards decided on August 17 that a public statement, though five days late, could help the situation. So the official view of the happenings in the special was released:

Coming to the one-sixteenth pole, Seabiscuit started to move on, but Jockey Richardson reached out and grabbed Seabiscuit's saddle cloth and held on to it until he got practically to the 70-yard pole, where *Ligaroti had moved up considerably, and at

A desperate finish in the match race at Del Mar with Seabiscuit (inside) nosing out Ligaroti.

this point he let go of the saddle cloth and tried to grab Jockey Woolf's wrist. Woolf fought to get his arm loose, and about 20 yards from the finish reached out and grabbed *Ligaroti's bridle rein and held on to it from there across the finish.

This apparently settled the matter of foul riding, but unsatisfied newspapermen still referred pointedly to the unusual fact that the official photograph of the finish had not been publicly displayed.

On another tack, Seabiscuit's owner, Charles S. Howard, issued an indignant denial to the published story that Woolf had instructions to restrain Seabiscuit and "make a race out of it." Said Mr. Howard, with some heat:

Any fool writing racing ought to know that a race run in 1:49, with the first mile in 1:36⅘...couldn't be fixed in that manner. The whole thing, to anyone versed in how races are run, is obviously a false alarm...Just to keep the records straight, I will make public the riding orders given Seabiscuit. Jockey Woolf was told to go to the front around the first turn, to get clear of *Ligaroti, because the latter has a habit of lugging in to the rail... Once on the back stretch Woolf was told to take back slightly and get on the outside, letting *Ligaroti go up on the rail. Seabiscuit always runs well from behind...Woolf was told to make his move on the outside at the far turn, and win as far off as he could...As the race turned out, Seabiscuit was not able to ever get more than a neck in front of *Ligaroti, had to stay in on the rail.

Meanwhile one thing appeared plain: All tracks which have gone to trouble and expense to get a special race involving Seabiscuit or War Admiral have had cause to regret it.

October 1, 1938
SEABISCUIT THIRD IN MUD

Charles S. Howard's Seabiscuit was scratched out of the Hawthorne Gold Cup Saturday, September 17, because the track was muddy, was shipped on to Belmont Park, where he started in the Manhattan Handicap ($5,000 added, 3-year-olds and up, 1½ miles) on Tuesday, September 20, despite the fact that the track was slushy from rain which fell that morning. It was generally supposed that the son of Hard Tack would be withdrawn from the Manhattan because of the rain, but he went to the post, perhaps because his owner and trainer wanted to know what he could do on such a track and at such a distance. The Howard star, assigned 128 pounds, was opened at 9 to 10 in the betting, but got only moderate support, his price going as high as 8 to 5, and closing at 6 to 5. Of the four which opposed him the most support was given Brookmeade Stable's Handcuff (3-y-o, 109½, including 1½ pounds overweight).

Seabiscuit, ridden by George Woolf, broke well, but was soon taken under restraint, as Belair Stud's *Isolater (108) and Walter M. Jeffords' Regal Lily (108) began a stubborn battle which lasted all the way around Belmont Park's 12-furlong track. R.A. Moore's Piccolo (100) dropped into third place, followed by Handcuff. Woolf, possibly because he wanted to watch Handcuff, as she seemed the one to beat, took Seabiscuit in behind the entire field and followed the others down the back stretch. *Isolater, ridden by Jimmy Stout, drew away to a lead of a length or slightly more. Before the half-mile pole was reached Jack Westrope asked Handcuff for her speed and guided her to the outside. Woolf took Seabiscuit to the inside. Both Seabiscuit and the filly passed Piccolo without difficulty, and there were three lengths to go to catch up with Regal Lily, which was now running well lapped on *Isolater. Handcuff failed to show anything in the home stretch, and Woolf set out to catch the leaders. He drew his bat and Seabiscuit finished well, but made only a negligible reduction of the distance between him and the leaders. Regal Lily pressed *Isolater hard through the last furlong, but the Belair horse was the winner by a head from the daughter of Man o' War. Seabiscuit was three lengths back of the leaders, having acquitted himself well under high weight and over an unfavorable track. Handcuff failed utterly in the stretch, finished 10 lengths behind the favorite, two lengths ahead of Piccolo. Time, :24⅗, :49, 1:14, 1:39⅕, 2:05⅕, 2:31, track muddy. Stakes division, $4,300, $1,000, $500, $250.

*Isolater has now started 28 times, won seven races, finished second once, third eight times, and has earned $18,625. His first stakes victory was in the Aqueduct Handicap, run September 5.

October 8, 1938
SEABISCUIT WINS A GOOD ONE

Charles S. Howard's Seabiscuit's four victories this year had been scored over inferior opposition, and on the four occasions when he had met capable horses he had been defeated. But in the Havre de Grace Handicap ($10,000 added, 3-year-olds and up, 1⅛ miles) on September 28, Seabiscuit (128) met a good field, got the worst of the racing luck, came on to score a decisive victory in fast time, one-fifth of a second slower than the track record set by Osculator as a 4-year-old under 104 pounds.

With track and distance to suit him, Seabiscuit was made favorite at 1 to 2. He was off well, but on the first turn he was bumped as Marica (124) and Masked General (114) tried to get to contention, and Jockey George Woolf had to take him to the outside. Hal Price Headley's Menow (3-y-o, 120), getting only a pound by scale from the Hard Tack horse, had broken to the front, was steadied along ahead of the field. W.L. Brann's Savage Beauty (103), 116-to-1 outsider, forced a swift pace and Seabiscuit, recovering rapidly from his difficulty, moved into third place on the back stretch. It was fairly obvious, after five furlongs, that the winner was among these three.

Then, as the field swung into the last turn, the fortune that had cost Seabiscuit ground on the first turn swung back in his favor. Menow, which had upset one of the leaders on the handicap division when he beat War Admiral at Suffolk Downs, seemed well on his way to upset another. But on the turn a tendon gave under the strain and Menow began losing ground. He kept going gamely, but both Seabiscuit and Savage Beauty went past him, and in the stretch Seabiscuit had little difficulty shaking off the *Challenger II filly. Ridden out, he won by two and a half lengths, with Savage Beauty a length in front of Menow, which was taken to the outside and pulled up, badly lamed in both fore ankles. Mrs. Louise Viau's Rex Flag (111) was fourth, a length and a half behind Menow. In order followed Esposa (121), which never got into contention, Two Bob (104), Marica, and Masked General. Time, :23⅘, :47⅖, 1:12⅖, 1:37⅖, 1:50, track fast. Stakes division, $8,175, $2,000, $1,000, $500.

The victory, most creditable one for Seabiscuit this year, raised his earnings to $323,980, including $25,000 won in an exhibition race against *Ligaroti last August. This does not change his position among leading American money winners, where he remains fourth. He has started 82 times, won 30 races, finished second 13 times, third 12 times.

October 15, 1938
PIMLICO'S SPECIAL

What Belmont Park offered $100,000 for and failed to get, what Suffolk Downs' $50,000 added Massachusetts Handicap failed to achieve, has been announced for Pimlico's fall program at the comparatively low figure of $10,000. It was announced October 5 that both Charles S. Howard and Samuel D. Riddle had signed an agreement to send Seabiscuit and War Admiral against each other. Each owner will post $5,000 to insure the appearance of his horse,

C.S. Howard (left) and Sam Riddle agreed to a match race between Seabiscuit and War Admiral.

and though the announcement has not been made plain this sum will apparently be forfeited in case of non-appearance. To this the Maryland Jockey Club will add $10,000, making the race worth $15,000 to the winner.

The race is tentatively set for November 1, Pimlico's opening day, with November 3 as substitute date in case the track is not fast. It will be at 1 3/16 miles, with each horse carrying 120 pounds. On November 1 a "neutral person" will inspect the track at 8:30 in the morning. If it is muddy the race will be postponed. If the track is approved the race goes on, according to the agreement, regardless of weather and track conditions later in the day.

War Admiral will probably not start again until the special race comes up. Seabiscuit, it is reported, will go after the $7,500 added Laurel Stakes at Laurel Park October 15. He is also engaged in the Washington Handicap on October 29, but if the race with War Admiral goes through, he will probably pass up that engagement.

October 22, 1938
JACOLA BEATS SEABISCUIT AND RECORD

Charles S. Howard's Seabiscuit apparently is running weight off by winning. Last July he carried 133 pounds and won. In his next start he was given 130, beat *Ligaroti in a special race. When he came east he was given 128 pounds, got beat by *Isolater and Regal Lily. The defeat took no weight from his impost, and he came back under 128 pounds, won at a mile and an eighth. For the shorter Laurel Stakes ($7,500 added, all ages, one mile) on October 15, he dropped weight again, took up 126 pounds. He ran a very good race, got beat two and a half lengths by Edward Friendly's *Jacopo filly (3-y-o, 102), to which he gave 14 pounds by scale.

The race began as a duel between J.A. Manfuso's Aneroid (116) and Mrs. Emil Denemark's Finance (118), and after six furlongs it proved that Finance had cut out more for himself than he could do. He tired badly and fell back, finishing next to last. It was at this stage of the race that Jacola, ridden by Nick Wall, began moving up from a position just behind the leaders. Midway of the last turn she headed Aneroid, tired from his struggle for the lead, and drew clear as she reached the stretch. Wall, who had defeated Seabiscuit on Stagehand in the Santa Anita Handicap, kept her going along nicely, looked back for the odds-on favorite. Seabiscuit was coming; he had left the post well enough, had bettered his position while racing on the outside for nearly the first mile. He saved ground on the last turn, however, and responded to George Woolf's urging. But Jacola was not weakening. She even gained another length through the last furlong, and at the finish Wall had found it safe to ease her up. Seabiscuit, two and a half lengths behind the filly, was an easy second, three lengths in front of The Chief (3-y-o, 116). The latter had started slowly, had been shunted back through the back stretch. When he got clear he came up fast, made a good effort. Four lengths farther back was Aneroid, tiring but nearer to his old

form than in the other two starts of his campaign. In order followed Grey Gold (111), Accolade (114), Mr. Canron (114), Busy K. (118), Nedayr (3-y-o, 116), Mower (111), Finance, and Masked General (114). Time, :23⅕, :47⅘, 1:12⅕, 1:37 (new track record), track fast. Stakes division, $7,825, $1,500, $750, $350.

Jacola has the enviable record of never having run a bad race. She has won eight of her 15 starts, finished second in five, third in one. The only time she was unplaced she was fourth, beaten by the capable fillies Merry Lassie, Handcuff, and Creole Maid. She has earned $42,190, the bulk of her 2-year-old earnings coming from her victory in the Selima Stakes last October. She was foaled May 10, 1935, at A.B. Hancock's Claiborne Stud, Paris, Ky., was sold as a yearling for $1,000. La France [Jacola's dam] did not race. She is also dam of the winners Dick Merrill and Johnstown, the latter winner of the Remsen Handicap at Jamaica at about the time Jacola was being unsaddled. [*Editor's Note: Johnstown went on to win the 1939 Kentucky Derby and Belmont.*]

October 29, 1938
THE PIMLICO SPECIAL
By Joe H. Palmer

About the War Admiral-Seabiscuit special this department is resolutely saying nothing, but about the press brochure recently distributed by Publicity Director Dave Woods no such silence is needed. This offering, some 24 pages in a heavy yellow cover, arrived a few days ago, and is almost large enough to deserve a book review. Included is a complete tabulation of the past performances of the two rivals—not such a big compilation for War Admiral, but a whole lot for Seabiscuit, which has started 83 times, beginning in January of 1935 at Hialeah Park, with a $2,500 claiming tag attracting no one's attention.

Included also is a history of the Maryland Jockey Club and racing in Maryland, from the days when George Washington turned in that extraordinary expense account which states that he lost £1 6s on the races, won £13 at cards, and spent £25 for two "boxes" of claret, which indicates that the presidential nominee of 1789 possessed qualities now played down in political life.

Among other interesting features is a set of measurements of the two horses, made by Dr. Harry C. Crawford, New York veterinarian. They indicate horses of much the same type, with War Admiral, at 15.2½, having a half-inch more height, at 960 pounds, 80 pounds the worst of the weight, the same length from body to ground (35½ inches), same width between eyes (9), same forearm (17½), same stifle (36), same gaskin (17). Seabiscuit girths 72 inches, or two more than War Admiral. At one point Dr. Crawford's efforts seem to have been nullified by a typesetter, for War Admiral's length from nose to tail is given as nine feet, two inches, that of Seabiscuit as seven feet, 10 inches. As nearly as can be estimated without getting the two up in the office, they are much the same length, with Seabiscuit possibly the longer horse. At all events, no horse standing at 15.2¼ has any business being more than nine feet long from nose to tail (any one who stretches the horse's neck and holds his tail out straight is cheating).

This takes little from Mr. Woods' brochure, which will be a considerable aid to those covering the race. It makes one point clear which seems universally misunderstood. Pimlico is putting up $15,000, not $10,000. The owners put up $5,000 each as forfeit, but not as a stakes, and if both horses go the forfeit money is returned to the two owners, does not go to the winner. Anyway, whether the race gets to the track or not, it has resulted in a very good reference book on Pimlico and on two of the best horses of the decade.

October 29, 1938
WAR ADMIRAL AND SEABISCUIT
By Russell F. Oakes

Nobody in Maryland, it seems, is willing to lay odds that Seabiscuit will whip War Admiral or that War Admiral will whip Seabiscuit in the 1³⁄₁₆-mile special race scheduled to take place at Pimlico November 1. There are plenty of betting men around, however, who are willing to lay 2-or-3-to-1 odds that the race won't take place.

Alfred Gwynne Vanderbilt, vice president of the Maryland Jockey Club, who succeeded in getting the owners of War Admiral and Seabiscuit—Samuel D. Riddle and Charles S. Howard—to sign on the dotted line, must be aware of the "Oh, yeah!" attitude so many race-goers have taken toward the scheduled special. However, he shows no sign of concern and goes blithely about his business of talking up and building up Pimlico and its racing.

It is an old story, of course, that attempt after attempt to match War Admiral and Seabiscuit has failed. That is why blasé race-goers and bettors aren't going to believe a War Admiral-Seabiscuit race until they see it.

Some of the edge was taken off the public's interest in the scheduled special by the defeat here October 15 of Seabiscuit. The son of Hard Tack took a thorough plastering in the one-mile Laurel Stakes from Ed Friendly's good filly Jacola. To horsemen and others who really know horses and racing, there was nothing really humiliating about Seabiscuit's defeat. And his owner, the debonair and affable Howard, shows no signs of perturbation over the loss. Sitting in his box the Monday after the race with Kenneth N. Gilpin, Col. John F. Wall, and several other friends, Mr. Howard explained that "it is no disgrace for any horse to lose to as good a filly as Jacola"; that "Seabiscuit did every bit as good in the stakes as he did in last year's version, when he dead-heated with Heelfly"; that "I'm not worried in the least; I know we're going to whip War Admiral."

Horseman after horseman came up to speak to Howard while I sat with him. None of them had anything but words of praise for the manner in which Seabiscuit performed in defeat. Some pointed out that the handicap champion had made Jacola break the track record to whip him; that the winner had carried only 102 pounds to Seabiscuit's

126; that Seabiscuit took the "overland" route, running from five to 10 more lengths than any horse in the field.

I was interested in other things. I wanted to know why Seabiscuit's rider, George Woolf, had worn a spur on his left boot; whether Seabiscuit had begun to get lazy and cunning; whether Howard is genuinely sincere in his desire to pit his horse against the great son of Man o' War. I learned that Seabiscuit is a confirmed "rail-runner," in his owner's opinion, and that Woolf wore the spur to help him keep the horse from "lugging in." I learned that Seabiscuit, as far as his owner knows, has not grown sour, or lazy, or cunning—that he is a willing worker and a good doer. And I learned, to my own satisfaction at least, that Howard is sincerely eager to pit his champion against Sam Riddle's star.

I learned something more: Woolf had instructions in the Laurel Stakes to keep Seabiscuit far out in the track, where there would be little danger of interference from other horses in the big field. The manner in which Woolf rode indicated that such instructions had been given, but as a rule it is next to impossible to gain admission from an owner or trainer when orders of this kind are given to a pilot.

"We told Woolf to stay out in the track, away from all horses," Howard declared. "We wanted to win the race, of course, and we felt that we could win it even if Seabiscuit skimmed the outside rail from start to finish. But victory wasn't nearly as important as protecting the horse from injury."

A box or two removed from Howard sat young Vanderbilt complaining about an "awful sore throat" and denying that Seabiscuit's defeat robbed his scheduled special race of color or anything else. Agreeing with him was young Harry Parr III, his buddy, and treasurer of the Maryland Jockey Club. These gentlemen radiated confidence that the special race will take care of itself.

Barring accident, injury, and sickness, I am confident that on November 1 Seabiscuit and War Admiral will hook up. If the track isn't fast on that day, the horses are to meet two days later.

"I'll be ready with Seabiscuit," Howard said, "no matter how many times the race is postponed because of unfavorable track conditions. But I don't know about Riddle; he might balk beyond November 3. But he probably could be persuaded to stick around with War Admiral if Pimlico decided to up the purse. And Pimlico could do that easily; you know that."

Mr. Howard went on to point out that Mr. Riddle "won't even allow one of his horses to start if Jim Milton is in the starter's stand," then laughed a laugh that seemed to say: "Isn't that ridiculous?"

There Howard struck a point that for some days now has lodged painfully in the sides of Milton's host of Maryland friends. The veteran starter—he is 62—has asked the Maryland Racing Commission to "excuse" him from starting the scheduled special race, and the commission has approved his request. It has been written before that Riddle became irked with Milton for using pincers [used like a twitch on the upper lip] on War Admiral, though Milton says

Champion Seabiscuit working out for the match race.

Triple Crown winner War Admiral working out at Pimlico.

he used the very pincers furnished by Riddle or by his representative for use on Riddle horses. Riddle's criticism of Milton has cut the veteran starter to the core. For many years he and Riddle were good friends. And Riddle, Milton says, is the only owner he has ever sought out in the stands after a race in order to congratulate him; that occurred at Pimlico the day War Admiral won his Preakness. And Riddle congratulated Milton on the start!

It was last year that Mr. Riddle terminated a grievance against Pimlico that had extended since 1926. That year the Philadelphia horseman was irked when Frank J. Bryan, then racing secretary and handicapper at the Maryland Jockey Club track, assigned Crusader 126 pounds for the 2¼-mile Pimlico Cup Handicap, for 3-year-olds and upward. Crusader was regarded, until War Admiral came along, as Man o' War's best son. That he was a first-class horse the records attest. But on that day at Pimlico, a dozen years ago, he should have carried less than 126 pounds in the Cup, Riddle argued. At any rate, the good mare, Edith Cavell, under a feather of 93 pounds, gave Crusader as bad a lacing as Jacola gave Seabiscuit at this course on October 15. Princess Doreen, then a 5-year-old, and carrying 110 pounds, finished third. The time was 3:52⅕, a new record for the race and a mark that still stands.

In view of his long ostracism of Pimlico, it is conceded that Vanderbilt achieved a *coup de maitre* in getting S.D. Riddle's signature for the scheduled War Admiral-Seabiscuit race. Vanderbilt's feat is regarded as all the more remarkable in view of the comparatively small money prize that will go to the winner, and in view of the fact that War Admiral has shown what is interpreted by experts to be a decided dislike for the Pimlico racing strip.

Jim Milton has been starting races in Maryland since the day Havre de Grace was opened back in 1911. Some time later he was employed at Laurel to succeed the late A.B. Dade. It wasn't long afterward that he was taken on at Pimlico. A little later he "took over" at Bowie. He has found that War Admiral, rather than being a "bad post actor," is "docile as a lamb if backed into his stall with the pincers," that he isn't "one-tenth as bad as his daddy was."

But Milton isn't going to be in the starter's stand for what is potentially one of the greatest races in the history of Maryland racing. In his place, probably, will be George Cassidy, starter on the New York tracks and son of the man under whom Milton served part of his apprenticeship. But it is perhaps just as well for Milton. Whatever happens in the race can be no fault of his.

No matter what the outcome of the race, Howard is going to keep Seabiscuit at Pimlico and, "in all probability start him in the other stakes for which he is eligible. Then he'll go, along with the other horses, to California for winter racing."

Asked whether he planned to retire Seabiscuit at the end of 1938 racing, Howard said:

"I have no plans other than to keep the horse in training and at racing as long as he trains soundly and retains his speed."

"When you do retire him," I asked, "where will you stand him—in California or Kentucky?"

"I'll have to stand him in California," laughed the Californian. "Otherwise, I wouldn't dare show my face in my own State."

November 5, 1938
SEABISCUIT'S TRIUMPH

At Pimlico November 1, under good weather conditions and over a track which Jervis Spencer, Jr., had judged to be fast the morning before the race, Glen Riddle Farm's War Admiral and Charles S. Howard's Seabiscuit, each with 120 pounds up, met at long last to decide the question of supremacy which has been disputed since the $100,000 special at Belmont Park last Memorial Day blew up with the withdrawal of Seabiscuit.

For War Admiral it was the twenty-third start; for the year-older Seabiscuit it was the eighty-fourth. For American breeding it was something of a triumph for the Fair Play line, since the two horses are, respectively, son and grandson of Fair Play's great son, Man o' War. With one year more on the Turf than War Admiral, Seabiscuit went into the race with earnings of $325,480 (not $331,405, as published), his owner's eyes on the $376,744 which makes Willis Sharpe Kilmer's Sun Beau the leading money winner of the world. For War Admiral there was no such shining goal, though there have been persistent reports that he will be sent after the $100,000 Santa Anita Handicap next March, and victory in that event would take him very close to Sun Beau's eminence. Seabiscuit, so long as he is sound and unsoured, will race on; War Admiral will enter stud next March.

With Starter George Cassidy substituting for James Milton (who deferred to Owner Riddle's never publicly expressed wish), the two great handicap leaders got off, from a walk-up start, with virtually no delay.

Under a cloudless sky, some 40,000 persons poured into Pimlico, breaking all records for attendance. Two out of three of them, as reflected by the wagering, thought War Admiral would be the winner. So great was the throng that NBC's Clem McCarthy, leaving the paddock before the bugle called the two horses to the track, could not get to the broadcasting booth, roosted on the fence at the finish line to call the race,

mentally blessed Alfred Vanderbilt for removing the "hump" from Pimlico's infield.

Seabiscuit, edging ahead, broke up the first attempt at a start; War Admiral broke up the second. On the third trial they were off, with War Admiral on the inside. Whipped away from the start, Seabiscuit immediately did something few believed he could do; he outran War Admiral down the stretch, came

Seabiscuit alone at the wire but surrounded by admirers in the winner's circle following the match race with War Admiral.

furiously, Pimlico's spectators saw Seabiscuit begin coming away. First a length, then two, then three, and Seabiscuit went over the finish line four lengths in front, took back the title of champion of the handicap division which he had lost, in popular opinion, to War Admiral. When the time was hung out, it was seen that Seabiscuit had cut one-fifth of a second from Pompoon's track records, had run the 1³⁄₁₆ miles in 1:56⅗.

Backers of War Admiral are fairly sure to explain that the colt doesn't like the Pimlico track, will point out that Pompoon took him to a hard drive in the Preakness, that Masked General, but for running out on the stretch turn, might have beaten him in the Pimlico Special last fall. But they will hardly explain it to the satisfaction of Seabiscuit's connections.

After the race, Owner Howard, brought before a microphone, said, "I'm too excited to talk. I'm sorry to beat Mr. Riddle and Mr. Conway, for they're both good sportsmen. But they were running against a little too much horse." Jockey Woolf said, "I wish Red had been on him instead of me." (Jockey Red Pollard, regular rider of Seabiscuit, is still incapacitated as the result of a broken leg suffered last June.) Trainer Tom Smith, notoriously a man of few syllables, muttered into the microphone unwillingly, gave credit to horse and jockey.

For Seabiscuit, the race was the thirty-first victory from 84 starts. He has been 14 times second, 12 times third, and he has earned $340,480. He had been in fourth place among the world's leading

over to the rail on the first turn, two lengths in front of War Admiral. Turning into the back stretch it was a length and a half, then two lengths, then a length and a half again. On the back stretch Charley Kurtsinger sent the Man o' War colt forward, and he ran up to Seabiscuit, for a moment got his head in front. Seabiscuit matched speed with speed, took the lead again, and for nearly six furlongs the two battled head-and-head, around the turn, well into the stretch.

Then with less than a furlong to go, with Kurtsinger and Woolf both driving

Trophy presentation ceremonies with (from left) C.S. Howard, jockey George Woolf, Tom Smith, and Alfred G. Vanderbilt, who organized the match race between Seabiscuit and War Admiral in the Pimlico Special.

money winners. The purse of the special took him to second place, $2,000 past Equipoise, $36,000 behind Sun Beau. It is reported that he will go after the $50,000 added Widener Cup Handicap at Hialeah Park this winter, and victory in that race would take him to the top.

November 19, 1938
SEABISCUIT GOES WEST

Charles S. Howard, considering the 134 pounds which Seabiscuit was assigned for the Bowie Handicap November 15, said, "That means that Seabiscuit will make his next start back home." Seabiscuit, whose owner will

not race him under more than 130 pounds, will be pointed for the Santa Anita Handicap, and there are also reports of a $10,000 race being arranged at Tanforan. Apparently the handicapper at Santa Anita Park is being given his choice between Seabiscuit and a top weight above 130 pounds.

December 10, 1938
HORSES OF THE YEAR, SEABISCUIT

One of those swift reversals of opinion of which the sporting world is so capable made Charles S. Howard's Seabiscuit the "horse of the year." A powerful cam-

YEAR	AGE	STARTS	1ST	2ND	3RD	UNPL.	EARNINGS
1935	2	35	5	7	5	18	$12,510
1936	3	23	9	1	5	8	$28,995
1937	4	15	11	2	1	1	$168,580
1938	5	11	6	4	1	0	$130,395
Totals		**84**	**31**	**14**	**12**	**27**	**$340,480**

paigner at four, Seabiscuit's 5-year-old record was not at all perfect, for up to November 1 he had won five races, in four of which he had indifferent opposition; in the fifth Menow broke down apparently on the way to victory. Aneroid nosed him out in the San Antonio Handicap, Stagehand caught him from behind in the Santa Anita Handicap, War Minstrel beat him badly in the Stars and Stripes Handicap, *Isolater turned him back in the Manhattan, and Jacola held him off in the Laurel Stakes.

Stagehand was conceding weights to all his conquerors, and these defeats did no great damage to his reputation. But to the world of the Turf Seabiscuit had committed a worse sin; in popular opinion he had twice "ducked" a meeting with War Admiral, only horse given much chance at him at level weights. But on November 1 at Pimlico, thanks to Alfred Vanderbilt's enterprise and luck, the two came together at long last.

Four out of five of Pimlico's patrons expected War Admiral to win, most of them expected him to win without great difficulty. Even Seabiscuit's backers were surprised when the Hard Tack colt, laying down a trail of blazing speed, took the track from War Admiral the first time past the stands. On the back stretch War Admiral ran up to him,

and they went head-and-head for six tense furlongs. Then having proved speed and stamina, Seabiscuit revealed in no uncertain terms that characteristic restricted to great horses, a racing heart. In Pimlico's stretch he came away, won by four lengths in new track record time of 1:56⅗ for 1³⁄₁₆ miles, became the "horse of the year."

Seabiscuit was lightly considered as a 2-year-old, and he was raced 35 times that season, beginning during the winter in Florida. He raced in claiming events on several occasions, and was sold by Wheatley Stable to his present owner for a reported price of $7,000.

Seabiscuit's record by years, and the only threat to Sun Beau's eminence as leading money winner since Equipoise bowed a tendon in 1935, is shown above.

December 24, 1938
WAR ADMIRAL AND SEABISCUIT

Last week Marshall Cassidy, official at Hialeah Park, said that the track would consider a special race attracting War Admiral and Seabiscuit. It was possible that this might be a $50,000 special between the two horses; it was also possible that it might be made an invitational affair, with Stagehand, Lawrin, Dauber [1938 Preakness winner], and Pasteurized

[1938 Belmont winner] also included. It was reported from Florida also that both Charles S. Howard and Samuel D. Riddle had agreed to a special race for $40,000, with Seabiscuit giving two pounds to War Admiral, the race to be run sometime in February, at a mile and an eighth.

Neither story was very well confirmed, and Mr. Howard was reported to be considering the 134 pounds assigned Seabiscuit in the Santa Anita Handicap, waiting to see what John B. Campbell would give him in the Widener Handicap, whose weights appear January 4.

Meanwhile Trainer Tom Smith spoke more definitely. Admitting the question of racing in Florida or California had not been decided, he said:

"I'd rather see 'the Biscuit' running for $100,000 and carrying 134 pounds at Santa Anita, than see him carrying 130 pounds for $50,000 in Florida."

Meanwhile Seabiscuit is in light training at Columbia, S.C., and no definite plans for him have been announced. War Admiral, not named for the Santa Anita Handicap, will be sent after the Widener Handicap, with or without Seabiscuit.

December 31, 1938
SEABISCUIT'S BANDAGES

The State, morning newspaper of Columbia, S.C., said December 23 that Seabiscuit had "gone the way of all handicap horses," was so lame that he was finished with racing. The next day, Owner Charles S. Howard, at San Francisco, said he had read the story, had heard nothing from Trainer Tom Smith. It seemed improbable that, reading reports of Seabiscuit's lameness, Owner Howard would have waited for notification by ordinary mail.

At Columbia, Trainer Smith denied the story of unsoundness, said the horse was "sound as a dollar," a comparison not as impressive nowadays as it was a few years ago. Continued Mr. Smith:

"There's nothing to it. Just because 'the Biscuit's' legs were bandaged in the stall does not mean that he is lame. We've used bandages on his legs a long time."

On December 26, with no previous warning, Trainer Smith announced that Seabiscuit would leave Columbia for Santa Anita Park on December 27, with the Santa Anita Handicap as his destination, 134 pounds, Stagehand, and all. Behind him he left stories of special races in Florida, the probability of another meeting with War Admiral.

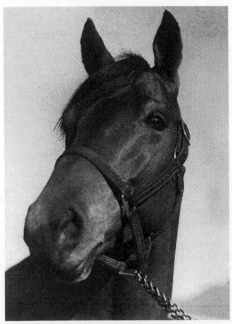

Dual honors in 1938: champion older male and Horse of the Year.

1939-1940

A Glorious Farewell

It was one race and out for Seabiscuit in 1939. On February 14 at Santa Anita, in his first start since the Pimlico match race, Seabiscuit pulled up lame after finishing second in an allowance event. He had ruptured the suspensory ligament of his left fore, necessitating treatment and a long period of recuperation. While sidelined, Seabiscuit was bred to a few mares that spring. He returned to light training late in the autumn. Finally, on December 19 at Santa Anita, Seabiscuit worked a half-mile in a style suggesting he was back in earnest.

In Seabiscuit's absence from competition, Kayak II proved a stalwart substitute for his injured stablemate. Kayak II won eight of his eleven starts. The Argentine-bred banked $170,875 and took down championship honors in the handicap division — a title Seabiscuit had held the two preceding years. Kayak II's six stakes scores included the Santa Anita Handicap, Bowie Handicap, and Hollywood Gold Cup. Few stables in racing history have been blessed by the presence of such a talented "stand-in" for their sidelined star performer. Kayak II concluded his twenty-six race career with fourteen wins, eight seconds, one third, and purses of $213,205.

Seabiscuit's archrival War Admiral, meanwhile, managed only two additional starts following the Pimlico match. War Admiral won a minor stakes at Narragansett just eleven days after the Pimlico Special, then wound up his career with an allowance race win at Hialeah Park in February of 1939 before going to stud.

As the 1940 racing season got underway, doubts about Seabiscuit's ability to return as a full-blown version of his old self were very strong. After all, he was seven years old, had been away from competition for nearly a year, had been at stud, and had already run eighty-five times. Furthermore, his patched up leg was a front one, which would be most severely strained by the heavy weights he would be required to carry. All in all, many observers saw this comeback as attempting the impossible. But owner Howard was determined to return Seabiscuit to competition. Howard wanted his pride and joy to avenge his two photo-finish losses in the Santa Anita Handicap and in so doing surpass Sun Beau as the world's leading money-winning Thoroughbred. Going into the 1940 season, Seabiscuit trailed Sun Beau by just $35,864.

Seabiscuit's first race back did little to dissuade the doubters, nor did his second: he finished third in an allowance race on February 9, 1940, then a well-beaten sixth in the San Carlos Handicap eight days later.

But then the old boy rediscovered his form. As *The Blood-Horse* headline put it, "Seabiscuit's Himself Again." The proof was in his track-record equaling win in the San Antonio Handicap on February 24 in which he defeated Kayak II.

Up next was the race that Seabiscuit had lost twice to nose decisions: the Santa Anita Handicap. His third attempt to win the world's richest race drew extensive *Blood-Horse* coverage, all of it warranted, as Seabiscuit sped to victory and set a career money-winning record of $437,730. That coverage includes the gracious telegram sent to Charles Howard by Mr. and Mrs. Willis Sharpe Kilmer, owners of Sun Beau, whose monetary mark Seabiscuit had at last surpassed in what was his final race.

January 14, 1939
GENERAL ITEMS

Seabiscuit was weighed at Santa Anita Park January 3, scaled 1,080 pounds, or 30 more than his usual racing weight.

January 21, 1939
SEABISCUIT DECLARED IN

When weights for the Santa Anita Handicap were sent out for publication, Secretary Webb Everett included a blank on which sports writers could "pick" the race. Last week the votes were in, with Seabiscuit getting 23 selections for first place, no other horse getting more than four. Stagehand, which will apparently go to Florida, had the four, and three each were received by Dauber and *Ligaroti, the South American including Clem McCarthy [radio's legendary racing announcer] among his backers. Ossabaw, Specify, Xalapa Clown, and Heelfly were each selected by two persons, Norris Royden [a racing official] being one of those who selected the Vanderbilt racer [Heelfly]. Yale O' Nine and Star Shadow each had one backer among the sports writers.

February 4, 1939
SEABISCUIT SCRATCHED

Weight-for-age for 6-year-olds at 1¼ miles in March is 129 pounds in California, and Seabiscuit was assigned four pounds more, or 133, for the Santa Anita Handicap. Weight-for-age for 6-year-olds at six furlongs in January is 132 pounds, and Seabiscuit was assigned four less, or 128, for the San Felipe Handicap at Santa Anita Park January 28. But there were a large number of probables for the race, and none seemed to be "scared" out by Seabiscuit, so Trainer Tom Smith withdrew his charge rather than risk the mishaps which frequently go with a crowded field.

On January 27 Trainer Smith had made a surprising announcement. Ralph Neves, the stable's first-string rider, will be assigned to *Kayak II for the $100,000 race, and the comparatively obscure Gordon Helton, who had 18 winners from 101 mounts last year, is being seriously considered for Seabiscuit. If Helton gallops and rides Seabiscuit until the big handicap, he will be a better pilot for the horse, the trainer thinks, than any jockey not intimately connected with him.

February 18, 1939
SEABISCUIT'S FUTURE

No definite announcement regarding Seabiscuit's rider for the Santa Anita Handicap has been forthcoming from the C.S. Howard stable, but it is reported that Ralph Neves, under contract to the stable, will have the mount. On February 6 Trainer (Silent Tom) Smith was unusually loquacious, said that indications were that *Sorteado and *Kayak II might start also; that the stable would declare to win with Seabiscuit; that if Seabiscuit wins it will be his last race but that otherwise he will continue in training, probably on the West Coast; that Seabiscuit was "as sound as a gold dollar."

February 25, 1939
SEABISCUIT'S STATUS

On February 14 Seabiscuit made his first start since he defeated War Admiral at Pimlico last November 1. He went away from the post stride for stride with Today, dropped back after six furlongs and finished second, with Marica third and last. Seabiscuit pulled up lame, Marica went wrong in her good fore leg. Today has never been entirely sound since he twisted a plate and cut his foot in the Kentucky Derby of 1935. He is owned by Neil S. McCarthy, who purchased him with the contingency that if he raced again a percentage of his earnings would go to C.V. Whitney [who had bred and originally raced the colt].

Trainer Smith said, just after the race, that Seabiscuit definitely had not broken down, that he was expected to recover rapidly. The following day Trainer Smith was afraid there had been a slight rupture of the suspensory ligament on Seabiscuit's left fore leg, but said the horse ate well, walked better than expected. Future book operators put Seabiscuit's odds for the Santa Anita Handicap up from 5-2 to 10-1.

At the end of the week there was only

the smallest chance that Seabiscuit would race in the big handicap, some prospect he might never race again. Photographs indicate there is no bowed tendon, but the left fore leg is still filled. An X-ray had shown that no bone was broken. On February 18 Seabiscuit was walking better, and Trainer Smith hoped to gallop him soon.

However, Seabiscuit's chances for the $100,000 handicap have been greatly lessened because even if he recovers from the injury, he will have to miss badly needed works, will have little time to be tightened for the 1¼-mile struggle. The stable's best horse is now *Kayak II. After the South American was beaten on February 14, Mr. Howard was dissatisfied with Jockey Craigmyle's handling, joked "Next time I'll put Gene Normile up." Last Saturday, he put Jack Adams up, and *Kayak II broke the track record for 1⅟₁₆ miles.

March 18, 1939
SEABISCUIT TO STUD

Sun Beau's rocking crown of leading money winner of the world settled considerably March 8 when Trainer Tom Smith announced that Seabiscuit would be bred to several mares this spring, would be away from the races all year. His first mates will be Fair Knightess, Carvola, and Illeanna, all of which have raced this year, the first two for C.S. Howard. Seabiscuit will be fired, in an attempt to restore the ruptured suspensory ligament of his left fore leg, and will be rested throughout the year. It is the hope of his owner that the firing and the rest will bring him back to

soundness, and that he can be trained for the Santa Anita Handicap of 1940. Prospects that he will ever race again are doubtful, as the year of inactivity will cause him to gain several hundred pounds, and this, with his 1939 stud campaign, may end his racing.

April 1, 1939
SEABISCUIT'S PLANS

Last week an Associated Press story reported that Seabiscuit had "proved unsatisfactory standing at stud" and that he would probably be withdrawn from a breeding farm near Log Angeles. Apparently this was a distortion. Seabiscuit has not been on a breeding farm; he has been with the C.S. Howard stable, which shipped last week to Tanforan. There Trainer Tom Smith said Seabiscuit would be fired, turned out at the Howard ranch near Willits, Calif., in the hope that his injured tendon sheath will mend. Meanwhile he will be bred to two or three mares.

July 8, 1939
DENMARK ENTRY WINS

Mrs. Emil Denmark's Blind Eagle (105) and War Minstrel (108) have been running rather disappointingly of late, particularly the latter, and as a result they got into the Paul Revere Handicap ($10,000 added, 3-year-olds and up, 1⅟₁₆ miles) at Suffolk Downs July 1 with light imposts. They took the race from the start. War Minstrel, which was the only horse to finish in front of both War Admiral and Seabiscuit last year, dashed to the front, but his stablemate, away third, got the lead after about a half-mile. The two ran together, well clear of R.A. Moore's Clodion (116), to the finish, but through the last furlongs War Minstrel had a slight advantage and won by a neck. Clodion was third, a length and a half behind the entry, with Wesley Sears Farm's Xavier (101½) fourth, a length farther back. Mrs. Parker Corning's Thanksgiving (120), made a 7-to-10 favorite, never turned on at all and finished last. F.A. Smith rode the winner. Time, :24⅖, :49, 1:13⅖, 1:40, 1:47, track slow. Stakes division, $9,100, $2,000, $1,000, $500.

War Minstrel, winner of the Stars and Strips Handicap last year [over Seabiscuit], and the Yankee Handicap as a 3-year-old in 1937, raced unplaced in two starts at two. In all he has started 55 times, won 12 races, finished second eight times, third 11 times, and has earned $55,200. He is from the excellent producer War Feathers, dam of War Magic (Diamond State Stakes), War Plumage (C.C.A. Oaks), and others. *Tuscan Red [War Minstrel's granddam] is third dam of Kumohata, winner of this year's Japanese Derby.

Seabiscuit is beginning training again, and if he goes soundly may be back in action this fall.

October 28, 1939
SEABISCUIT TRIES AGAIN

At Tanforan October 24 Charles S. Howard's Seabiscuit was scheduled to arrive to begin training again, in a last attempt to wrest the title of leading money winner of the world from Willis Sharpe Kilmer's Sun Beau. With about $36,000 needed, Seabiscuit went out last winter with an injured suspensory ligament, and it was generally believed that he would never race again. But the

Seabiscuit in the morning.

injury is reported to have healed, with Seabiscuit only 30 pounds overweight. If he stands training, he may start during the Tanforan meeting, which opens November 14.

November 18, 1939
SEABISCUIT'S FOALS

Last spring, when Seabiscuit was forced out of action by injuries, he was bred to a few mares. None of them has been examined, but Owner Charles S. Howard believes that Dressage and Smart Agnes, and probably Fair Knightess, are in foal, is rather certain that Illeanna is not.

December 9, 1939
SEABISCUIT'S STATUS

On November 29 Charles S. Howard's Seabiscuit unloaded without incident at Santa Anita Park, for his fourth attempt on the Santa Anita Handicap. In his first two ventures, in 1937 and 1938, he was second to Rosemont and Stagehand respectively. Last winter he went wrong in training shortly before the race, which was won by stablemate *Kayak II. He has been taking slow gallops at Tanforan, and even Trainer Tom Smith has little way of knowing yet whether the Hard Tack horse will stand training again.

December 30, 1939
SEABISCUIT WORKS

In his first public trial since going wrong before the Santa Anita Handicap last winter, Charles S. Howard's Seabiscuit came out at Santa Anita Park December 19, went a fast half-mile in

:48, and apparently cooled out sound. *Kayak II, which may start in the New Year Handicap, worked six furlongs in 1:12, after finishing the first five furlongs in :59.

January 27, 1940
SEABISCUIT'S FOALS

Last year Seabiscuit was bred to seven mares, including such good racing performers as Fair Knightess and Dressage, and Paul Lowry reported, in the Los Angeles *Times* of January 15, that all seven were in foal, were expected to drop their produce in March.

February 3, 1940
SEABISCUIT, IN AND OUT

On January 24 Charles S. Howard's Seabiscuit was entered in an overnight six-furlong race at Santa Anita Park, in which he was given 120 pounds. The track was heavy, he was withdrawn, and the race was declared off. On January 25 the same race was offered again, with Seabiscuit again entered. The track was slow, Seabiscuit was withdrawn, and the race was again declared off. On January 27 the son of Hard Tack, under 128 pounds, was part of an entry in the San Felipe Handicap. The track was fast, but Seabiscuit was again withdrawn, as was his stablemate *Kayak II.

February 3, 1940
SEABISCUIT AND *KAYAK II

As Charles S. Howard's Seabiscuit continues to stand training, two reports of the stable's winter strategy have been circulated. One is that Seabiscuit will be sent to Florida for the Widener Handicap, that *Kayak II will go after a second victory in Santa Anita Park's $100,000 event; another is that *Kayak II will go to Florida, that Seabiscuit will try for the big California race. Apparently neither story has much support from the C.S. Howard stable.

February 17, 1940
SEABISCUIT'S SHOWING

The road back, for Thoroughbreds which have broken down, is an extremely difficult one, but the first attempt this year of Charles S. Howard's Seabiscuit, if not all that had been hoped for, was at least not entirely discouraging to his connections. On February 9 he came out in four bandages, for his first start since February 14 last year, in a seven-furlong race in which the speedy Sun Egret, and the not especially predictable Heelfly seemed the chief competition. He had 128 pounds in the saddle, giving 10 to Heelfly, 13 to Sun Egret, and more to the other five in the field.

He was away rather well, but was hemmed against the rail, and Red Pollard had to take up a little to keep him off the heels of the horses in front. He got through on the rail into the stretch, and with a furlong to go went into third place with Heelfly getting to Sun Egret three lengths ahead of him. He went on steadily, but gained little on the leader, Heelfly winning by a length from Sun Egret, Seabiscuit two lengths farther away. But he gave a decisive beating to the others, which included Arigotal (107), No Competition (105),

Our Mat (110), and two others. The race was run in the fast time of 1:23, and Trainer Tom Smith seemed pleased with the showing.

The race did little toward proving that Seabiscuit was regaining his best form, but it did indicate that he was sound for racing. And it added $200 to his earnings, which now total $341,080, with Sun Beau $35,664 ahead.

March 2, 1940
SEABISCUIT'S HIMSELF AGAIN

Sun Beau's crown as leading money winner of the Turf, which stopped rocking last February when Seabiscuit went out of training with an injury, became considerably less secure February 24 when the Hard Tack horse, essaying the difficult task of coming back as a 7-year-old after a season in the stud and an injury, ran like his old self to win the San Antonio Handicap ($10,000 added, 3-year-olds and up, 1$\frac{1}{16}$ miles) at Santa Anita Park. Ahead of him is his third attempt on the Santa Anita Handicap (he was second in both of his previous starts in it), and a victory would take his earnings far past Sun Beau's. Even a second place, if he remains sound, would almost assure him of the position of leading money winner, for he would be but a few thousand dollars short of the goal, and almost any other victory would take him to the top.

The San Antonio drew 13 starters, including most of the Santa Anita Handicap probables except Whichcee, Specify, and Can't Wait. At the start

Binglin Stock Farm's *Ra II (116), which ran as if short, dashed into the lead. No Competition (108) was just behind him, and *Vino Puro (109) raced into third place. Seabiscuit (124) broke well, was fifth after the first quarter-mile, but his stablemate *Kayak II (128) lacked the speed to keep up and fell back to tenth place. As they went into the back stretch Seabiscuit came up steadily. *Ra II dropped out of it and *Vino Puro tired and fell back. Seabiscuit took the lead in the upper stretch, and drew out steadily. *Kayak II had gradually improved his position and was in contention on the upper turn. Valdina Farm's Viscounty (110) was going steadily in third place, but neither was any match for Seabiscuit, which won by two and a half lengths with Jockey J. (Red) Pollard taking a light hold on him at the finish. *Kayak II came very fast to take second place, a half-length in front of Viscounty, and Binglin Stock Farm's *Preceptor II (112) closed some ground to be fourth, four lengths farther back. In order followed Heelfly (119), which had been outrun early, Wedding Call (110), Anthology (110), No Competition, *Vino Puro, Arjac (104), *Comet II (108), Sun Lover (117), and *Ra II. Time, :23⅕, :46⅘, 1:11⅕, 1:36⅖, 1:42⅖ (equals track record), track fast. Stakes division, $10,000, $2,000, $1,000, $500.

Seabiscuit reached the peak of his fame at Pimlico November 1, 1938, when he defeated War Admiral in a special race, and that success was his last until the San Antonio. Preparing for the 1939 Santa Anita Handicap he went wrong after making one start in which he was second. This year he had started twice, had been third once, unplaced once. In all he has started 88 times, won 32 races, finished second 15 times, third 13 times, and has earned $351,080. Sun Beau's record is 74 starts, 33 wins, 12 seconds, 10 thirds, $376,744.

Seabiscuit's history is now rather well known. Bred by Wheatley Stable, he was campaigned hard as a 2-year-old, beginning in Florida and starting 35 times. He was considered only a fair horse, though he won the Ardsley and

Swing On, dam of Seabiscuit.

Springfield Handicaps, and the Watch Hill Claiming Stakes. He was sold to Charles S. Howard for a reported $7,500 at three, after winning the Mohawk Claiming Stakes. He won several minor stakes for his new owner at three, but did not reach his best form until he was four, when he earned $168,580, winning 10 stakes, including the Massachusetts, Brooklyn, Butler, and Riggs Handicaps. At five he earned $130,995, including some rather easy races on the West Coast.

Swing On did not race. Her first foal died. Her second was Query, a winner at two. Seabiscuit was next. In 1934 she had a full sister to Seabiscuit, which did not win. She was barren in 1935, had Brown Biscuit, a winner at two, in 1936. [Editor's Note: Brown Biscuit produced four stakes winners and Koubis, the dam of 1954 Kentucky Derby winner Determine.] She was barren again in 1937. She has a 2-year-old by Hard Tack which was not started. Swing On did not have a foal last year. Balance produced Flippant (Broadway Stakes, Bayview Handicap), Hornpipe (Amsterdam Stakes), and the winners Scales, Even Up, Abby, and High Wire, and the producer Flutter. *Balancoire II won the Prix La Fleche, and produced six winners, including Swinging (dam of Equipoise, etc.), Distraction (Wood Memorial, Colorado, Flash Stakes, Yonkers, Bay Shore, Edgemere, Champlain, Pierrepont Handicaps and sire), Blondin (Empire City Derby, Long Beach Handicap and sire), and *Escarpolette (dam of the stakes winners Alyssum and Depression), and the producers Wiggle Waggle and *See Saw II (dam of the stakes winner Tonto Rock). *Balancoire II is sister to the stakes winners Night Rider, Melody, and Mediant, their dam being the high-class race mare *Ballantrae, by Ayrshire.

March 2, 1940
PROSPECTS FOR THE HANDICAP

Just as observers were beginning to count out Seabiscuit and *Kayak II as Santa Anita Handicap prospects, the two scored a smart one-two performance in the San Antonio Handicap,

Seabiscuit winning in track record time, so the counting can begin over again, with Seabiscuit and *Kayak II included. If Seabiscuit wins it will be a remarkable feat; twice before he has been leading at the furlong pole, only to be caught from behind by Rosemont in 1937 and Stagehand in 1938. He has 130 pounds, or six more than he carried in the San Antonio, which will hardly stop him if his form is right.

Heelfly, Viscounty, and Sun Lover were in the beaten field, but will probably be starters in the big handicap nevertheless. Whichcee, which won a narrow victory at six furlongs over a fair field on February 24, will start for A.C.T. Stock Farm, and may vie with Specify for pacemaking honors. Can't Wait and War Plumage are also considered probable starters. About eight others, most of them South American, are doubtful prospects, though it seems probable that two or three of them may start. Included in this group are *Ra II, *Preceptor II, *Don Mike, *Beautiful II, *Vino Puro, Wedding Call, Hysterical, and Teddy Kerry.

But it seems quite probable that when the field turns into the stretch on March 2, Specify and Whichcee will be on the head end, with Viscounty somewhere around, and Heelfly, Can't Wait, Seabiscuit, and *Kayak II moving up. The pacemakers will be slowing up and the routers will be coming on, but where the finish post fits into all this is, as usual, debatable. It seems certain that the Howard entry will be favored at the track, with Seabiscuit the sentimental favorite nearly everywhere.

March 9, 1940
THEY CAN COME BACK

The mile and a quarter of the Santa Anita Handicap has been a weary road for the great Thoroughbreds which, past their best form, or recovering from injuries, have tried to make it the occasion of a return to greatness. In the inaugural running, in 1935, such once brilliant racers as Equipoise, Twenty Grand, Mate, Head Play, and Faireno finished in the ruck behind the former steeplechaser *Azucar. Cavalcade was prepared for it the following year but went out of training before the race. Discovery failed that year, as did Singing Wood, which was no longer at his best. In later years Pompoon, Mr.

Bones, Time Supply, Today, and others have gone under in the big race.

But perhaps the stage was never set so appropriately as for the 1940 renewal. Charles S. Howard's Seabiscuit, after racing in the better claiming races at two and three, had rocketed to prominence at four and five as a fine handicapper, a weight carrier, and he had set the seal on his performances with a victory over War Admiral at the end of the 1938 season. Twice he had started in the Santa Anita Handicap, and in both cases he got to the front in the stretch. In 1937 Rosemont came up from behind to win, and in 1938 the 3-year-old Stagehand closed with a great rush to turn him back. Preparing for the 1939

Seabiscuit defeating a first-class field in the 1940 Santa Anita Handicap.

renewal Seabiscuit went out with a tendon injury, was put in the stud.

The number of horses which have returned to first-class form after such a history could almost literally be counted on one's fingers. In his first two attempts under silk this year Seabiscuit showed very little, but on February 24 he came out with a brilliant display to win the San Antonio Handicap in track record time. The field he was to face in the $100,000 race was by no means the best the event has ever drawn, but it was good enough that no horse could make any mistakes with it. It was apparent that Seabiscuit was very close to the victory that had so often escaped him, and to the title of leading money winner of the world which would go with it. But there were 10 dusty furlongs to cover, and a capable, if not a brilliant, field of horses to turn back.

So the question, in the minds of those who had no professional or wagering interest in the other horses, was not what horse would win the Santa Anita Handicap, but whether Seabiscuit would win it. Some 70,000 persons turned out at Santa Anita Park March 2 to see the answer as it was written.

The field was at the post three minutes, with no chances taken on a bad start. Specify was a little the fastest out of the gate, but Whichcee sprinted at once into the lead, and Seabiscuit, breaking from far on the outside, was away with the first flight. Going to the first turn it seemed that he might be caught in close quarters, and Jockey J. (Red) Pollard hustled him forward. Seabiscuit drew clear of possible inter-

ference and dropped in behind Whichcee. Specify had enough in the first half-mile and fell back, and Wedding Call, a 96-to-1 chance, came up into third place. Royal Crusader, a 3-year-old which had been second in the Santa Anita Derby 10 days earlier, got up to fourth. Seabiscuit's stablemate, *Kayak II, winner of the race in 1939 and considered a formidable contender this year, was making heavy weather of it in the middle of the field. He had got off slowly, was gradually making up ground. In the back stretch he moved up with a sustained run and at the end of a mile was in sixth place.

But most of Santa Anita's 70,000 spectators were watching Seabiscuit. Down the back stretch he moved slowly to the leader, and going into the last turn was lapped on him. As the two turned into the stretch Seabiscuit was only a head behind, and a mile and a quarter was never Whichcee's distance. There was a great cheer from the stands as Seabiscuit got his head in front just at the eighth-pole, and the only horse moving from behind was *Kayak II, which got into third place just as Seabiscuit took the lead. The Hard Tack horse drew out, Whichcee fell back, and *Kayak II moved to second. Pollard kept Seabiscuit under a drive, but it was hardly necessary. Leon Haas was in no hurry with *Kayak II once he had only his stablemate in front, and Seabiscuit, going very smartly, came to the finish line a length in front, with *Kayak II the same distance ahead of Whichcee, which he had beaten about the same distance last year. Wedding Call, a Grade

C contender which was given virtually no chance at all, couldn't handle the first three, but he held on doggedly nevertheless and finished fourth, a length and a half farther back. In order followed War Plumage, Heelfly, Viscounty, Can't Wait, Specify, Royal Crusader, *Don Mike, *Ra II, and Kantan, the latter a maiden which got into the race for some reason and ran about as expected.

After the race Basil James, who rode Whichcee, lodged a claim of foul against the winner, saying that Seabiscuit had cut in on him at the sixteenth-pole, but the protest was not allowed.

Seabiscuit had not only run a brilliant race under top weight, but he had run what was probably the second fastest 10 furlongs in American racing history. Whisk Broom II's record of 2:00 remains on the books, but the consensus is that Belmont Park's timer, in 1913, caught him on the wrong one of Belmont Park's two finish posts. The only other faster performance is that of Sarazen, which as a 3-year-old ran the distance at Latonia in 2:00⅘. Seabiscuit shares the honor with Discovery, which ran a mile and a quarter in 2:01⅕ at Arlington Park. The weights carried in these performances were: Whisk Broom II (139), Discovery (135), Sarazen (3, 120), Seabiscuit (130).

Seabiscuit has now raced 89 times, won 33 races, finished second 15 times, third 13 times, and has earned $437,730, and is, by a wide margin, the leading money winner of the world. The record he passed was that of Sun Beau, which also had 33 victories, the last coming in 1931, and total earnings of $376,744.

Howard and Smith basking in Seabiscuit's glory.

Seabiscuit has had a dozen or more riders in his long career. Jockey J. Pollard was up on him for the first time in August, 1936, and the combination proved so effective that Pollard rode him in 26 consecutive starts. But he suffered a broken collar bone at Santa Anita Park when Fair Knightess fell with him, in February, 1938, and just before he was to ride Seabiscuit again, in the Massachusetts Handicap of that year, he broke a leg while exercising a horse at Suffolk Downs. But in all of Seabiscuit's four starts this year Pollard has been in the saddle. In the 11 starts while Pollard was incapacitated, George Woolf rode him nine times, Noel Richardson and Raymond Workman once each.

*Kayak II almost exactly duplicated his 1939 performance in the Santa Anita Handicap, though picking up 19 pounds. Last year he won in 2:01⅖ to set the track record which Seabiscuit broke last Saturday, and, beaten a length in 2:01⅕, just about equaled that time this year. Though far behind Seabiscuit's record, he is twenty-first among American money winners, with earnings of $199,055, the $20,000 which he received in second money moving him forward 10 places on the list.

Whichcee, which was second to *Kayak II last year, and gained some measure of revenge by beating him in the New Year's Handicap this year, has earned $81,325 for his owner.

On Monday, March 4, Mr. and Mrs. Howard received a telegram from the owners of Sun Beau, now in the stud at Willis Sharpe Kilmer's Court Manor, New Market, Va. Mr. and Mrs. Kilmer telegraphed:

The victory of your great horse on Saturday must be a wonderful satisfaction to both of you. It was your faith in his ability and your perseverance in the face of discouraging setbacks which finally won the title. We are elated to think that such a great champion had such splendid and purposeful owners. Your example will be an inspiration. To you and Mr. Tom Smith we offer our sincere congratulations and we are sure that Sun Beau would have us extend his best wishes to his successor, Seabiscuit.

March 16, 1940
AFTERMATH AND
RETIREMENT

The greatest drawing card on the Turf at present, except in Maryland, is Charles S. Howard's Seabiscuit. In Maryland it is of course the Maryland-bred Challedon. So it is quite natural that, immediately after the Santa Anita Handicap, there should be reports of plans for bringing the two together. Most credible of the reports was that Alfred Vanderbilt was trying to get a race for $50,000, between the two at Belmont Park. Mr. Vanderbilt, however,

saw no need of a special race with so many fixtures coming up, and Challedon's owner agreed with him.

On March 4 California papers questioned Leon (Buddy) Haas, who rode *Kayak II into second place, regarding the chances of the South American had not Seabiscuit been his stablemate. Jockey Haas said, "I had the best horse in the race." A good many trainers also believed that *Kayak II, if pressed, could have headed Seabiscuit. Trainer Tom Smith (local reports said he "almost smiled" when Seabiscuit brought to full fruit his months of patience and care in training him) contented himself by saying, "*Kayak II never saw the day he could beat Seabiscuit with the latter at his best." This, of course, was hardly the point, but those who claim *Kayak II could have passed his stablemate seem to forget that only two horses, in all American Turf history, have run 10 furlongs faster than Seabiscuit's Santa Anita Handicap.

There was a good deal of speculation regarding Seabiscuit's future. It was understood that Trainer Smith would like to retire him: "I would like to see Seabiscuit retired now—sounder than he was the first time I brought him to Santa Anita four years ago—and turned into the stud. He has achieved his goal."

On March 11 the speculation ended, with the decision of his owner to retire him permanently. Mr. Howard had, he said, been getting about a hundred letters a day asking him what he was going to do with the horse, and on that day he announced that Seabiscuit would be shipped to his Ridgewood Ranch, near

Willits, Calif., to make the rest of the stud season. Said Mr. Howard:

"He's earned a well deserved rest. He ran well, he's made a lot of money, and from now on he can take it easy."

March 30, 1940
THE SEABISCUIT MYSTERY

Turf writers on the West Coast last week were playing with what they called the "Seabiscuit mystery." There were reports in San Francisco that the Howard horse had broken down, and Mr. Howard was quoted as saying there was nothing the matter with him except a slight quarter-crack. In Los Angeles this was accepted with some skepticism, as not explaining why Trainer Tom Smith had refused to allow photographers to make pictures of the injured hoof. Mr. Smith, told that photographers would refute stories that the horse had broken down seriously while being unwound, said he didn't care what stories went around, that Seabiscuit wasn't to be photographed and neither was Mioland. Said Trainer Smith: "Photographers are not going to 'show' my colt out of the Kentucky Derby like they did with Stagehand two years ago."

Meanwhile Mr. Howard announced that Seabiscuit, which will be quartered at Hollywood Park during the summer and shipped to Mr. Howard's ranch in the fall, will stand at a fee of $2,500.

April 6, 1940
SEABISCUIT'S FIRST FOAL

Less than a month after he became the leading money winner of the world and was retired to stud, Seabiscuit had the first of the foals which will have the task of carrying on his line. On March 28, at Charles S. Howard's Ridgewood Ranch, near Willits, Calif., was foaled a chestnut coal from Illeanna, 8-year-old *Polymelian mare. Illeanna, which raced until the early months of 1939, was a moderate performer which won 13 races and $11,170 in her Turf career. She won one race at two, failed to win at three and seven, won two races at four and six, and in 1937, as a 5-year-old, won eight events.

April 13, 1940
LIFE OF SEABISCUIT

The life of Seabiscuit in book form will be published early next month by Schwabacher, Frey and Company, of San Francisco. The book is now being written by B.K. Beckwith, field secretary of the California Breeders Association, and is being designated as the official life of Seabiscuit by his owner, Charles S. Howard.

The book will run approximately 25,000 words and will include many pictures of Seabiscuit and his greatest races. Marginal drawings are being done by Brodie, San Francisco artist. Grantland Rice [a celebrated American sportswriter] will do the foreword.

Mr. Beckwith, besides being with the California Breeders Association, is connected with racing associations in California, both as an official and in the publicity departments. He is the author of the novels *Galloping Down*, *Mad Breed*, and *Spinning Dust*.

May 11, 1940
SEABISCUIT'S FIRST CROP

When Seabiscuit, now the world's largest money-winning horse, was taken out of training temporarily last year he was bred to seven mares. In keeping with Owner Charles S. Howard's phenomenal good fortune of recent years, the seven mares now have seven foals, and, according to Mr. Howard, they are the standouts among the sucklings at his California ranch.

Last of the Seabiscuit foals to arrive was a bay colt, born April 29, out of the good stakes winner Fair Knightess, by *Bright Knight. There are three other colts, out of Illeana, Lady Riaf, and the stakes winner Lucille K., and three fillies, out of Flying Belle, Sun Frolic, and Coldstream's sister Dressage. All seven of these mares are being bred to Seabiscuit again.

December 28, 1940
MATES FOR SEABISCUIT

In the spring of 1939, before the racing comeback which made him the leading money-winning Thoroughbred of the world, Charles S. Howard's Seabiscuit was bred to seven mares, got seven foals of 1940. After his victory in the Santa Anita Handicap of 1940 he was retired permanently to the stud. In 1941 he will have his first full-time season as a stallion. Hence Mr. Howard has busied himself this year with making additions to his band of broodmares, and now expects to breed between 20 and 25 of his own mares to "The Biscuit" during the coming season. At the W.S. Kilmer estate dispersal he purchased three mares, and from C.V. Whitney he obtained the 3-year-old filly Black Gnat, a three-parts sister to Top Flight. In addition to these, Mr. Howard has recently imported eight mares from England:

*Goldrim, gr. m., 8, by Tetratema—*Golden Araby, by Golden Sun. In foal to *Mahmoud.

*Golden Araby, b. m., 15, by Golden Sun—Sweet Palm, by William Rufus. In foal to *Mahmoud.

*Catherine Glover, b. m., 12, by Gainsborough—Perce Neige, by Neil Gow. In foal to Windsor Lad.

*Heads I Win, gr. m., 7, by Gainsborough—Tete-a-Tete, by The Tetrarch. In foal to Windsor Lad.

*Frivolous, ch. m., 4, by Coronach—Fickle, by Solario. In foal to Windsor Lad.

*Flying Sands, b. m., 4, by Sandwich—Life Belt, by Hurry On. Barren.

*Printemps, ch. m., 9, by Hurry On—Comedienne, by Bachelor's Double. Barren.

*Buskin, b. m., 7, by Blandford—Saffian, by Stornoway. Barren.

1941-Beyond

The Legend Lives

Long before the success of Laura Hillenbrand's book, interest in Seabiscuit continued following his retirement from racing after the 1940 Santa Anita Handicap. Seabiscuit made news in various ways for the next four decades. A total of twenty-nine items relating to him appeared in *The Blood-Horse* during that period. Of modern American racehorses, only Man o' War (his grandsire) and perhaps Secretariat have made such long-lasting impressions.

In 1941 Seabiscuit's statue was unveiled at Santa Anita. That was the year that jockey George Woolf detailed his meticulous preparations for the 1938 match race against War Admiral. Flashlight in hand, Woolf prowled the Pimlico racing strip at night and found the "path" he would put Seabiscuit on the next afternoon. The racing world was hard hit when Woolf succumbed to injuries incurred in a Santa Anita riding accident in January of 1946. Though reported to be 36, Woolf was actually only 35 at the time of his death, having long before added a year to his age so that he could obtain his jockey's license and begin his career a year early.

A year after Woolf's death, Seabiscuit died at age fourteen. His obituary was published in the issue of May 24, 1947. He died of an apparent heart attack on the night of May 17, in his stall at Charles S. Howard's Ridgewood Ranch north of San Francisco. As the obituary noted, "Seabiscuit's story was book-length. It included six seasons of racing during which feats, headlines, incidents, yarns accumulated to great depth...To Californians, Seabiscuit was a hero...To many an enthusiastic admirer, he was 'the best horse in the country.' "

In an earlier story that year in which Santa Anita Handicap winners were assessed, Seabiscuit was termed the only "truly great horse" to have won the race up to that point. In the opinion of John Hervey, writing under his "Salvator" pseudonym, "There is all the difference in the world between a (single) first-class performance and a first-class horse."

Two *Blood-Horse* stories — one in 1951, the other in 1978 — dealt with the nature of the injury Seabiscuit sustained in his career farewell. Trainer Smith shattered his veil of secrecy and silence with a lengthy interview in the 1951 article. David Alexander authored another information-packed piece. His fond remembrance of Seabiscuit and jockey Pollard carried the memorable headline, "Four Good Legs Between Them." Pollard described his feelings as he sweated out the foul claim lodged against him following the finish of the 1940 Big 'Cap. First there was the wave of sound as Seabiscuit crossed the wire in front. Then people held their breaths as the stewards examined the film of the race. As Alexander pointed out, "When 80,000 people are cheering, it's just a great, big noise. When 80,000 people are completely silent, it's damned impressive."

Red Pollard passed away at seventy-one in 1981. His obituary is included in this section, as are those of Charles S. Howard and Tom Smith.

January 4, 1941
COVER PICTURE:
SEABISCUIT

To THE BLOOD-HORSE last week came a Christmas card from the Charles Stewart Howards, with an attractive photograph (actually two photographs pieced together) of Seabiscuit with his seven foals in 1940. It was so fortunate a picture that THE BLOOD-HORSE telegraphed immediately to Mr. Howard, asking his permission to reproduce it on the front cover. Mr. Howard kindly consented, and the first crop by the world's leading money winner is thus presented.

When these foals were conceived, Seabiscuit was still looking up to Sun Beau in the matter of earnings. He had developed, or rather had suffered an increased development of, trouble with one knee. So he went to the stud for what was left of the season and served seven mares, all owned by Mr. Howard.

How he returned to racing in 1940 and won the Santa Anita Handicap is now a

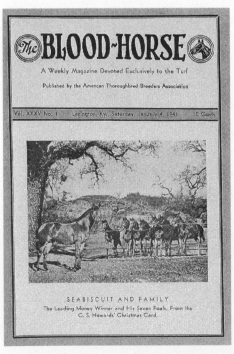

SEABISCUIT AND FAMILY
The Leading Money Winner and His Seven Foals. From the
C. S. Howards' Christmas Card.

standard story among the romances of racing.

Seabiscuit's first crop consists of four colts and three fillies. First to be dropped, last April 29, was a colt from the fine race mare Fair Knightess. There also were colts from Illeana, Lady Riaf, and Lucille K., the latter also a stakes winner. The fillies are from Flying Belle, Sun Frolic, and Coldstream's sister Dressage.

February 1, 1941
SEABISCUIT'S STATUE

A life-size statue of Seabiscuit, the work of Tex Wheeler, will be unveiled in the Santa Anita Park infield February 6. Seabiscuit will be brought briefly out of his retirement to attend the ceremony, will lead the field of the feature race to the post, with Jockey Red Pollard in the saddle.

February 15, 1941
SEABISCUIT'S STATUE

About the only part of Santa Anita Park's February 6 program which went off according to schedule was the unveiling of the statue of Seabiscuit, which the track has purchased at a reported figure of $35,000. Seabiscuit was in attendance, paid no great amount of attention to the ceremony. He was to have led the parade to the post for the featured event, but racing was called off for the day when the grooms struck.

April 5, 1941
NOW IT CAN BE TOLD

The following story comes from George Woolf, but through the

A statue honors the champion at the scene of one of his greatest triumphs, Santa Anita.

Hollywood Park publicity department. Woolf, according to the story, tells this tale of how he beat War Admiral with Seabiscuit in the Pimlico Special:

It had rained around Pimlico. The track was kinda bad. Worried me a little. Biscuit wants to hear his feet rattle. Well, night before the race I stuck around the barn until it was dark. I took a pocket flashlight and went out on the track. Not a soul around. I walked from the half-mile pole to the stretch, looking for holes. Wanted to spot them so I'd miss them next day.

I searched the track pretty thoroughly. Right at the top of the straightaway I saw the track of a tractor. Ten feet out from the rail. I found a hard spot almost a yard wide. I followed it. Saw it was a whole path—clear around the track, lightly covered over with loose dirt from harrows and graders—but still a good firm path.

Jockey George Woolf, who substituted for an injured Red Pollard, flanked by the Howards.

So I figures to myself, "Woolf, get on that lane and follow it." I walked around again so I couldn't make any mistake. I knew it like an airplane pilot knows a radio beam.

Next afternoon they lined us up at the barrier. I flung Seabiscuit away from the break like he was a quarter horse. I landed him on that lane. Didn't get off it until we had finished. The Admiral—well, he was in the soft going.

June 28, 1941
SEA HORSES

Seven colts and fillies, representing the first crop of foals by Seabiscuit, have been given their names. Sea Knight is out of the good race mare Fair Knightess, which did most of her racing for Hobson C. McGehee. Sea Skipper is from Lucille K., and Sea Belle is out of Flying Belle, a daughter of Flying Ebony. The other four yearlings are Sea Convoy, Sea Mite, Sea Patrol, and Sea Frolic. Sea Mite, Sea Belle, and Sea Frolic are fillies.

July 5, 1941
NOW THERE ARE SIX

One of the seven yearlings which represent Seabiscuit's first crop was destroyed last week, after efforts to set a leg broken in a paddock accident had proved unavailing. This was Sea Knight, a colt out of the excellent race mare Fair Knightess.

September 27, 1941
TOURIST ATTRACTION

Joe Hernandez reported recently that the guest book at Seabiscuit's stall contained the names of 33,072 visitors for the 212 days ending July 31, an average of 156 visitors a day. On some days more than a thousand visitors appeared to see the world's leading money winner at C.S. Howard's Ridgewood Ranch in Mendocino County, California.

September 27, 1941
WHEN WHIRLAWAY GOES WEST — WE WANT SEABISCUIT!
By David Alexander

Hollywood, Calif.—When a horse with a tail that resembles the beard of the Smith Brother on the right hand side of the cough drop box comes to California this winter, it is doubtful that he will have much of a rooting section. Whirlaway, under the devil-red jacket of Calumet Farm, made three other Thoroughbreds look like so many stumblebums in the Lawrence Realization, moved into third place on the all-time money-winning list, with only Seabiscuit and Sun Beau pacing him. Whirlaway is a 3-year-old, apparently has no holes in him anywhere, and has overcome his perverse affection for the outside timber, judging from recent races. The winner's pot in the Realization brought Whirlaway's winning total to $347,661, just $90,069 under the world record total of Seabiscuit, which is growing fat and shaggy on a ranch in the hills of northern California. It seems also inevitable that Warren Wright's colt will pass Seabiscuit's money-winning record. It seems likely, indeed, that he will pass Seabiscuit by the time the Santa Anita Park meeting ends on March 16, 1942.

This is something that California's sentimental race-goers do not care to see. California is very proud of its native sons, human and Thoroughbred. And native son is a very elastic term in this State. When any California resident, whether he was born in Iowa or Timbuctoo, achieves fame, he is immediately adopted as a native son. Seabiscuit was bred in Old Kentucky, where the meadow grass is blue, but he trod the glory road under the red and white silks of Charley Howard (also an adopted Californian, born in Georgia).

He ran his greatest race and became the world's greatest money winner in the Santa Anita Handicap of 1940. To California race-goers, Seabiscuit is a California Thoroughbred. A life-size statue of him stands at Santa Anita Park. Californians are jealous of their idols. Furthermore, Californians are die-hards.

Even after old Nathan Bedford Forrest, last of the Confederate leaders to surrender, handed over his sword, hundreds of Southern soldiers rushed to Texas to join the guerrilla Quantrell, in the wild hope of forming an alliance with Mexico and continuing the war. California Turf fans are clutching at a straw almost as fragile. A "draft Seabiscuit" movement is afoot at the moment. Seabiscuit will turn eight years old on January 1. So great is the faith of Californians in their heroes that they believe the round-barreled, rough-coated, still gimpy son of Hard Tack could come back successfully, defend his honors, stem the tide of the invader from Calumet. Such wishful thinking makes Charley Howard smile ruefully.

A total of $205,000 in stake prizes alone awaits *Blenheim II's bushy-tailed son at Santa Anita Park. His main chance, of course, is the $100,000 Santa Anita Handicap. The winner's prize in that event might well put him within a couple of thousand dollars of Seabiscuit's total. And Whirlaway can try for five other stakes during the Santa Anita season. One is the San Juan Capistrano, on the final day of the meeting, which carries $50,000 in added money. A new stakes, the San Marcos, offers a $25,000 added prize. And there are three other events with $10,000 added on the calendar.

It is very doubtful that War Relic, Whirlaway's jinx horse in the East, will come to Santa Anita. At present it seems that Whirlaway should be able to flaunt his plumy tail in the faces of most of the handicap horses he meets out here.

[*Editor's Note: Whirlaway did not race in California because the war forced cancellation of the Santa Anita meeting. He did, however, surpass Seabiscuit's record earnings in 1942 with a victory in the Massachusetts Handicap.*]

November 15, 1941
LITTLE BISCUITS' NAMES

Charles S. Howard has received approval from The Jockey Club for names submitted for his three colts and three fillies comprising the first crop of yearlings by Seabiscuit.

Sea Convoy, ch. c. by Seabiscuit—Illeanna, by *Polymelian.

Sea Patrol, br. c. by Seabiscuit—Lady Riaf, by *War Cry.

Sea Skipper, b. c. by Seabiscuit—Lucille K., by Whiskalong.

Sea Mite, ch. f. by Seabiscuit—Dressage, by *Bull Dog.

Sea Frolic, b. f. by Seabiscuit—Sun Frolic, by *Sun Briar.

Sea Belle, b. f. by Seabiscuit—Flying Belle, by Flying Ebony.

About the first of the year the six yearlings will be transferred from Mr. Howard's Ridgewood Ranch at Willits, Calif., to his place at San Ysidro near the Mexican border, where they will be given their early training.

November 22, 1941
RISING BISCUITS
By David Alexander

Seabiscuit's first crop of foals, three colts and three fillies, are being shipped from the Willits ranch in the hills of northern California, to the Howard subsidiary farm at San Ysidro, just across the border from Tia Juana, where there is more sunshine at this time of year. Weather has set them back in their training in the north. Trainer Silent Tom Smith will give them intensive schooling at the southern ranch. They are reported a good-sized, round-barreled lot of youngsters, and high-spirited.

The half dozen rising Biscuits are definitely going to Santa Anita. Whether they will be sent out in early 2-year-old dashes down the straightaway there depends upon their advancement. They will probably be saved for Hollywood Park.

One other foal, which Charley Howard believed would be the star of the crop, was killed last summer in an accident at the farm. The colt ran into a fence while romping in a pasture, broke his leg.

The debut of the get of no stallion was ever awaited here with more impatience, for Seabiscuit, world's greatest money-winner, Santa Anita Handicap winner, conqueror of War Admiral in the Pimlico match, was the all-time Thoroughbred hero of the State.

January 10, 1942
SHELTER FOR SEABISCUIT

California newspapers last week reported that Charles S. Howard had written friends in England asking for specifications for a bombproof shelter for Seabiscuit.

December 2, 1944
ALMOST AND QUITE

Charles S. Howard, whose Seabiscuit is California's No. 1 equine hero, was an enthusiastic supporter of the Haggin

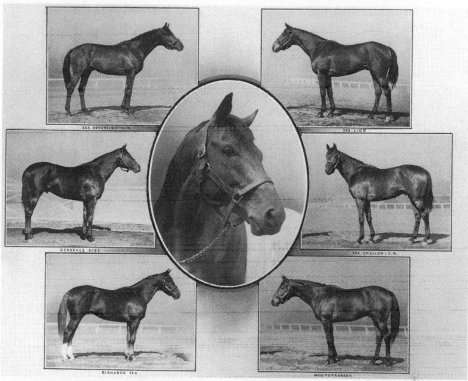

Seabiscuit with his sons (clockwise from top right) Sea Lion, Sea Swallow, Mediterranean, Bismarck Sea, General's Aide, Sea Sovereign, four of whom ran in the two divisions of the Haggin Stakes.

Stakes. In the overnight entries he put four of his "Little Biscuits," as he sometimes calls them, hoping that one of these would become the first stakes winner among the get of the former world's leading money winner. But other California owners were also enthusiastic with their entries, and so many horses were named that Hollywood Park split the race into two divisions. Mr. Howard's horses were divided evenly, two in each division. In the first they finished second and third, but in the second division, run two-fifths of a second faster than the first, the Howard colors were home first.

It appeared during the early running of the first division that Mr. Howard's stable was likely to be the winner, as his Bismarck Sea took over the lead from Blue Agent after the first quarter and Mediterranean began moving up third behind the favored War Allies. Norman Church's Realization, however, loomed up dangerously on the turn, moved into second place entering the stretch and wore down the leading Bismarck Sea for victory by half a length. War Allies went wide on the turn, and Mediterranean stood off another bid of Blue Agent to take the show money, several lengths back of his stablemate.

Louis B. Mayer's Hemisphere, winner of the Sequoia Stakes, earlier in the meeting, was a 3-to-1 second choice, but showed little.

In the second division Sea Swallow forced the pace of Gold Bolt all the way and wore down the leader in the closing yards to gain the victory by a neck. Louis B. Mayer's Pater, a son of his Australian stallion *Beau Pere and the stakes-winning Halcyon mare Sweet Patrice, came from far back to earn show money, a length and a half behind Gold Bolt. Fourth was Father Neptune, another son of *Beau Pere, which had won the first division of the Hawthorne Juvenile Handicap in the colors of Mrs. Emil Denemark, but ran in the name of R. F. Chambers in the Haggin. The partnership of Coward and Dupuy had purchased Father Neptune from Mrs. Denemark and sold him to Mr. Chambers. Originally he raced for Mr. Mayer.

Foaled February 3, 1942 at Mr. Howard's Ridgewood Ranch, Willits, Calif., Sea Swallow had won in the East for his only victory before the Haggin. The colt has started 14 times, won three races, finished second once, third once, and has earned $13,694.50.

[*Editor's Note: The above paragraph contains an error. In addition to his win in the East, Sea Swallow had also won an allowance race at Hollywood Park before the Haggin, accounting for the three victories.*]

March 15, 1947
AFTER TEN YEARS

After ten years and a day, Seabiscuit's record of 1:48⅕ for 1⅛ miles at Santa Anita Park was broken on March 7 when Cum Laude, a 6-year-old Canadian-bred stakes winner, ran the distance in 1:48⅗, under 108 pounds. As a 4-year-old, Seabiscuit carried 120 pounds.

Beaten in the $10,000 Lake Arrowhead overnight handicap, in which the new record was established, were Stitch Again, Texas Sandman, El Lobo, and Be Faithful. The victory was the fourth in six starts this season for the son of *By-Pass 2nd—Silver Dime, by Vandergrift. He finished second in his two other efforts. His breeder and owner is L.H. Appleby; G.C. Campbell is his trainer.

March 29, 1947
THE SANTA ANITA HANDICAP—ITS START, ITS DEVELOPMENT, ITS SIGNIFICANCE
By "Salvator"

The "richest race in the world" now has been run ten times, and it would seem appropriate to sum up what has been accomplished. In the beginning the race was avowedly an experiment— a try-out of a project for the purpose of ascertaining how the sport and the public would react to such a daring departure from precedent in a depression era.

It was to be "make or break." If the results were favorable, all would be well for the projectors. If they were not, the probability was that the undertaking would go into Turf history as a flash in the pan, a wildcat scheme such as American promoters are too prone to conceive and perpetrate. It would be deplored as something that had done racing no good, and it would be said

Statistics on 10 Santa Anita Handicaps

Year	Winner/Age	Wt.	Time	Odds to $1	Strs.	Attn.	Mutuel Handle	Value to Winner
1935	*Azucar (7)	117	2:02⅕	$16.40	20	52,000	$300,000	$108,400
1936	Top Row (5)	116	2:04⅕	6.40	13	60,000	350,000	104,600
1937	Rosemont (5)	124	2:02⅘	3.90	18	63,000	396,553	90,700
1938	Stagehand (3)	100	2:01⅗	3.60	18	67,000	406,994	91,450
1939	Kayak 2nd (4)	110	2:01⅖	3.00	16	73,000	375,685	91,100
1940	Seabiscuit (7)	130	2:01⅕	.70	13	74,000	328,700	86,650
1941	Bay View (4)	108	2:05⅖	59.20	16	50,000	325,600	89,360
1945	Thumbs Up (6)	130	2:01⅕	1.00	13	55,000	791,837	84,025
1946	War Knight (6)	115	2:01⅗	6.65	23	80,200	805,082	101,220
1947	*Olhaverry (8)	116	2:01⅘	15.35	22	85,500	1,044,351	98,900
	Averages	**116½**	**2:02⅖**	**$10.62**	**17**	**65,900**	**$512,802**	**$94,640**

that those who had attempted to put it over had overleapt themselves and set a bad example.

However, big-time racing had come back to California. Its first concrete manifestation had been the formation of the Los Angeles Turf Club, Inc., and the building of the most elaborate racing plant that the Pacific Coast—and, in some ways, the whole United States—had ever beheld. It was located on a portion of what had been the Rancho Santa Anita of once-so-famous Lucky Baldwin, in the township of Arcadia, a suburb of the City of Angels. The course was almost precisely ten miles from the center of that metropolis.

Vast and unbelievable changes had taken place there since the days of glory for Lucky Baldwin and the Maltese cross that was borne to victory in so many great events by the members of his stable. Back in the eighties, Los Angeles had been a rather sleepy, sequestered, but seductive town whose mild climate had made it a favorite resort. By padding the census returns a bit—an always pardonable stratagem—its population had reached the proud altitude of 50,000. One of its newer suburbs, a village called Hollywood, had several hundred inhabitants, and was clamoring loudly for a postoffice of its own. There was a race track—there had been one of one sort or another almost from the beginning of things—and a jockey club, and in the year 1887, the Derby, feature of the program, had $500 in added money, while the regular line of purse events were worth $100.

Seabiscuit the Great

If we look down the list of winners we will discover the name of just one truly great horse—Seabiscuit. He not only won under the top weight of 130 pounds, but had previously twice run second, on one of these occasions also

Six of Seabiscuit's sons visit the bronze statue of their celebrated sire in the paddock at Santa Anita.

carrying 130 pounds, giving the winner 30 pounds and being beaten by a head only. He set the record for the race and for the track at 2:01⅗, which still stands. Such a series of performances cannot be discounted, though an endeavor was made to do so by the claim that *Kayak 2nd, his stable companion, could have beaten him in his final triumph had it been so desired. This, however, is merely an opinion and—"opinions die, only the records live." *Kayak 2nd was doubtless a high-class horse—but if he was a great one, what, oh what, was Challedon, who beat him every time they met, with maddening regularity?

Rosemont, first of the two horses to leave the 'Biscuit in second place, just escaped greatness. Had not Nature, in a fit of ill-nature, given him an unsound foot his record might look far differently. As it is, only seven wins in 23 starts will not qualify him for any list of "greats."

The same thing is true of Stagehand, which doubled the dose that Rosemont had administered. It required a concession of 30 pounds for him to win by a head under the feather of 100 pounds, and his complete record is but nine wins in 25 starts—which again will not pass him into the "great" enclosure. We must render a similar account when considering Thumbs Up, winner also under 130 pounds in time equaling Seabiscuit's. At intervals capable of splendid feats, when we see that out of 45 races he was able to win but 17, he too must be "given the gate."

The above verdicts are rendered not in any spirit of hypercriticism. Far from it, though such may be thought the case. They are merely an expression of the old, old racing maxim, now little held in mind, that there is all the difference in the world between a first-class performance and a first-class horse. Turf history, like human history, is full of wonderful things done by individuals that otherwise never rose above mediocrity—"single-speech Hamiltons" whose one big day was followed by no others.

May 24, 1947
SEABISCUIT DIES IN CALIFORNIA

A groom sleeping in the stables at Charles S. Howard's sprawling Ridgewood Ranch in the hills some two hundred miles north of San Francisco was awakened on the night of May 17 by noises coming from Seabiscuit's stall. He found the horse had fallen, apparently with a heart attack. He called the ranch veterinarian, Dr. John W. Britton, but no treatment was enough. About midnight Seabiscuit died.

To Californians in general, Seabiscuit was a hero comparable with his grandsire, the great Man o' War, though he gained fame and affection in vastly different fashion. To his owner, Charles S. Howard, he was "one of the family." To many an enthusiastic admirer he was "the best horse in the country."

Seabiscuit's story was book-length. It included six seasons of racing during which feats, headlines, incidents, yarns accumulated to great depth.

Foaled May 23, 1933, at A.B.

Hancock's Claiborne Stud, Paris, Ky., he was by the incorrigible Hard Tack out of Swing On, by Whisk Broom 2nd out of Balance, by Rabelais, third dam the French-bred *Balancoire 2nd, grandam of Equipoise. Swing On, foaled in 1926, had been one of the yearlings which the Wheatley Stable had obtained from Harry Payne Whitney in 1927 as the nucleus for its racing and breeding venture. She was very small as a foal, developed later into a mare of great width and substance, but was never raced. Seabiscuit was the second of her seven foals, all winners but none of the others distinguished.

Despite his lack of size (he was about 15:2½ when he was retired from racing) and his late foaling date, Seabiscuit ran 35 times as a 2-year-old, sometimes in claiming races, his five wins including three small stakes. Rugged and speedy, but too small and chunky to look like the classic material to which his trainer, the veteran Jim Fitzsimmons, was accustomed, he was turned, as a 3-year-old, into a working mate for the massive, great-striding Omaha, the year's champion.

He sharpened Omaha's speed, and conceivably dulled his own, for besides working with the top horse of the year he also ran frequently. He was available at a claiming price of $6,500 August 3 at Saratoga, but no one took him. Mr. Howard bought him privately, about August 10, for about $7,500.

Tom Smith, then training the Howard horses, found Seabiscuit restless and irritable, gave him a goat and a pony for companions, took him to Detroit. In

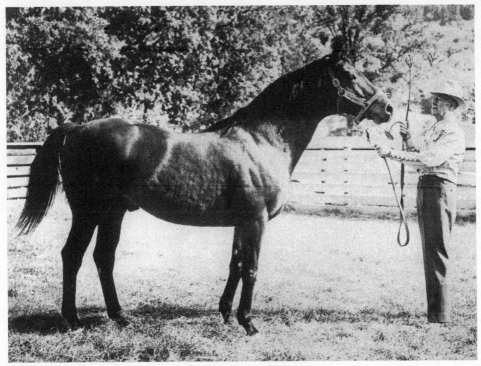

Seabiscuit with C S. Howard in 1946.

Seabiscuit's last two races of the 23 he ran that year, both at Bay Meadows, he ran a mile in 1:36 and then set a track record of 1:55⅗ in the 1⅛-mile World's Fair Handicap.

In March he missed the Santa Anita Handicap by a nose (Rosemont's), but he went on to win $168,580 during the season, his richest win being in the Massachusetts Handicap, 1⅛ miles in 1:49, under 130 pounds. The next year (1938) he again missed the $100,000 Santa Anita race by a nose (Stagehand's). His legs were none too firm now, but he finished worse than second only once during the season, ending up with a four-length victory over the favored War Admiral in the Pimlico Special, the most talked-of race of the year.

An injury suffered in a spectacular race with Today at Santa Anita Park, in February, held his racing for 1939 to one start, but the next year Tom Smith brought him back and held the sickness out of his ailing legs long enough for him to climax his career with a third try for the Santa Anita Handicap. This time, in his last start, he won, under 130 pounds, going 1¼ miles in 2:01⅕, a new track record, with his stablemate *Kayak 2nd next behind him. In a little while there was a statue of Seabiscuit between the stands and the paddock at Santa Anita Park, and in California no name is known better than his.

His last race made Seabiscuit the world's leading money winner—until Whirlaway displaced him in 1942. Altogether he started 89 times, won 33 races, was 15 times second, 13 times third, and earned $437,730. After his 3-year-old season he was only twice unplaced.

In his winning races, he carried up to 133 pounds.

In 1939, when he was out of racing because of his injury, he got seven foals, and after his victory in the 1940 Santa Anita Handicap, he was retired permanently. Mr. Howard, much too fond of him to consider sending him to Kentucky, where his chances of stud success would have been far better, made him "one of the family" at Ridgewood Ranch, began to build a stud about him.

There, through 1944, he was credited with 66 registered foals, many of which have given high promise, only a few of which have gained special distinction. His only stakes winners to date are Sea Swallow, a 1942 foal, son of the *Polymelian mare Illeana, and Sea Sovereign, of the same crop, out of Queen Helen, by *Light Brigade. His get through 1946 had won a total of $261,313.

It had been a sad year for the Howard family. *Kayak 2nd and Seabiscuit were dead. George Woolf, who rode Seabiscuit in some of his greatest races, had died in a racing accident early in January of last year. In the jockey room at Suffolk Downs John M. (Red) Pollard, a great jockey when Seabiscuit was a great horse, remembered wistful- ly the day they won the hundred grand. "It seems only yesterday," he said.

September 13, 1947
FLICKER

Warner Brothers have obtained from C.S. Howard the right to film the story of Seabiscuit. Sea Sovereign is being considered for the role of his famous father.

November 15, 1947
THE SONS

Of Man o' War's six or seven sons with enough class to justify high expectation as sires, War Admiral was the first to gain distinction. American Flag, Crusader, and Mars had gone back to stand at Faraway, where the best mares—and none too good, at that— were reserved for Man o' War. Crusader was a failure, Mars an abysmal failure. American Flag—which Miss [Elizabeth] Daingerfield [Faraway Farm's manager] described as the son of Man o' War most like his sire—indicated that with full opportunity he would have been

M an o'W ar, grandsire of Seabiscuit and sire of W ar A dm iral.

highly successful. His get included Gusto, winner of the American Derby, Classic Stakes, and Jockey Club Gold Cup, and the excellent filly Nellie Flag, which became a foundation mare of the fantastically successful Calumet Farm and stud of Warren Wright.

Scapa Flow died, Clyde Van Dusen was a gelding. Boatswain spent a few years at Faraway, got nothing, and quietly went away to Cuba. Genie got a chance at W.S. Kilmer's Court Manor Stud in Virginia and muffed it.

It remained for Hard Tack to sire Man o' War's best grandson, the stout-hearted Seabiscuit, which was the world's leading money winner when he left off racing. Hard Tack on the race track was a scoundrel who would stop at nothing to put an assistant starter out of the way. It was difficult to tell, after all his carryings on, just what his racing class was, but as far as the record went there was nothing in it to suggest that he would father a Seabiscuit. After the latter's performances had gained him a fair opportunity, Hard Tack got a good number of stakes winners, but not enough to keep him from going finally to the Remount.

War Admiral, which shares with Crusader the honor of *best* among the get of Man o' War, was the first to have advantage of a wide-open book and the patronage of numerous successful breeders. He was—perhaps consequently—the first of the sons of Man o' War to gain outstanding distinction as a sire. He remains at Faraway Farm, the best hope for the survival of a male line which has held high distinction in American racing

ever since it was established at the old Woodburn Farm of the Alexander family in Woodford County, Kentucky, during the Civil War.

On the West Coast the handsome War Glory has sired several good horses. Out of Annette K., grandam of War Admiral, he was one of the leading 3-year-olds in the lean year of 1933. In Virginia, Battleship devotes his efforts largely to siring jumping prospects, at which he has proved very good, despite the fact that he stands only 15:2. In Kentucky one of the still undeveloped prospects of the line is Sky Raider, by Man o' War out of C.V. Whitney's noted race mare Top Flight. Like other foals of this mare, he suffered an injury early in his racing career (in his third start, after two wins), so that his actual class was never thoroughly revealed. The results he has produced from modest opportunities apparently have gained him a better chance.

June 10, 1950
OBITUARY OF CHARLES STEWART HOWARD

Charles S. Howard, who in the course of a few years achieved the pinnacle of success in racing, died of a heart attack June 6 at his home in the San Francisco suburb of Hillsborough. He was stricken and died at 8:20 a.m., shortly after he had risen for his day's work. The 69-year-old sportsman had been ill on several occasions in the last few years, but his sudden death came as a quite unexpected shock. He was among the best known and most popular figures in racing.

Charles Stuart [sic] Howard was born in Georgia and lived there as a boy, but it took a much larger portion of the world to contain his energy and ambition. While still in his teens he was one of Teddy Roosevelt's Rough Riders in the Spanish-American War, and here perhaps is a leading clue to his later fondness for Thoroughbreds and other types of horses—he was a good horseman himself.

He became the representative of a New York bicycle firm, and for some time was a bicycle racer. Early in the century he took off for California, arriving there with 31 cents in his pocket, as he later recalled. Soon he was operating a bicycle repair shop in San Francisco, and when it became apparent that the horseless carriage had "come to stay" he turned to selling automobiles in 1905.

Later his "luck" on the Turf was to become proverbial, but nothing he ever did in racing was comparable to the choice he made in business. Among the numerous makes of cars in the new industry he chose Buick, one of the few which lasted out the years. He became the distributor for California and a few counties in Nevada, and his agency in time became one of the largest in the world.

As his wealth accrued into the millions he became one of the largest landowners in California, with several ranches totaling many thousands of acres. His earlier sporting interests included yachts and big game hunting. Always fond of horses, he played polo into his later years and kept a considerable stable of ponies for himself and others in his family.

Howard achieved racing fame with Seabiscuit.

Mr. Howard turned his attention to racing in 1934, operating at first on a small scale, with the horses trained by M. (Buster) Millerick and racing in the name of Mrs. Howard. Expansion came soon, and in 1937 Mrs. Howard was the leading owner, with 60 wins and $214,559 in earnings. Beginning in 1938, the stable raced in the name of Mr. Howard, and for four years in succession he ranked first (in 1940), second, or third on the list of leading money-winning owners.

Those were the years of Seabiscuit, *Kayak 2nd, *Sorteado, Porter's Cap, and Mioland. He had bought Seabiscuit as a 3-year-old for $7,500 at the Saratoga meeting of 1936. *Kayak 2nd was bought for about $7,500 from the Palermo sales in Argentina as a result of a suggestion from his son Lin, who was

M rs.H ow ard on Seab iscu it, accom pan ied by M r.H ow ard ,at R idgew ood R anch .

in Buenos Aires playing polo. Lin had telephoned his father that three good Congreve colts were to be sold next day, and had received instructions to go as high as $10,000. The two which Lin preferred went above that figure, and he was left with *Kayak 2nd—which earned $213,205.

*Sorteado, a triple crown winner in Argentina, was bought for $20,000 and had established himself as the country's leading stayer when he suffered an injury which made it necessary to destroy him. Mioland was obtained in 1940 for $15,000, Mr. Howard getting the horse because he used the telephone to close the deal while another owner was sending his acceptance by telegraph. Porter's Cap, one of the top

2-year-olds of 1940, was a $1,300 bargain from the Saratoga yearling sales.

These and other purchases skyrocketed the Howard Turf fortunes at a rate of which most owners can only dream. They gave Charles Howard the reputation for a sort of magic touch. Actually, of course he bought many other horses on which he took considerable losses. In his earlier, so-called "lucky" years, it was his practice to buy most of his racing stock at modest prices. His first good stakes winner, the mare Coramine, was bought as a yearling at Saratoga for $500 in 1935, a year in which he bought 19 yearlings for $15,550.

In recent years he has invested large sums in the purchase of high-class stock. After the death of Seabiscuit he purchased the Australian champion *Ajax for a reported $100,000 to take the place of his favorite in the stud. He paid about $40,000 for the English *Fast and Fair in 1946, and in 1948 spent, by newspaper guesses, about $175,000 for the Aga Khan's *Nathoo and *Noor. The latter repaid him in good measure this year by beating Citation in the Santa Anita Handicap and the San Juan Capistrano Handicap. It was his third victory in the Santa Anita Handicap, and he was narrowly beaten on three other occasions, twice with Seabiscuit and once with Mioland.

Seabiscuit was the great horse of Mr. Howard and for California. After a hard season at two (35 starts) and a modest performance in the first half of his 3-year-old year, he passed from the Wheatley Stable into the hands of Mr. Howard, and under the direction of Tom Smith became the largest money winner up to that time (1940), with earnings of $437,730. Twice beaten a nose in the Santa Anita Handicap, he came back from a year of unsoundness and won the big race in 1940, setting a new track record of 2:01⅕ under 130 pounds. As a 5-year-old in 1938 he had run one of his best remembered races, winning the Pimlico Special from War Admiral.

C.S. Howard (center) and trainer Hurst Philpot (far right) schooling some of the stable's runners in Santa Anita's paddock area.

Seabiscuit was retired to the stud at a fee of $2,500 after his Santa Anita Handicap victory. Though he stood at Ridgewood Ranch in northern California, far from the centers of racing, thousands of tourists stopped to see him, as he was the most famous horse in the West. He died in May, 1947, and a statue of him stands at Santa Anita Park as a memorial to his courage and class.

At Ridgewood Ranch, a sprawling, mountainous 16,000 acres near the village of Willits, north of San Francisco, Howard established his Thoroughbred nursery. The horses were kept, for the most part, near the residence, where the land is comparatively flat. The stud was built up rapidly, and at the time of his death included about 75 mares and the stallions *Ajax, Mioland, *Fair Truckle, Sea Sovereign, and Sabu. Last year a *Daily Racing Form* columnist reported that Howard had taken a census of the horses he owned and that the count was 474, a figure which presumably included several different types and breeds.

As a complement to his northern ranch, Mr. Howard maintained another establishment, including a training track, at San Isidro, just above the Mexican border. There he sent his yearlings when they were ready to go into training.

Among the trainers who handled the Howard horses were Major Sven Christensen and M. (Buster) Millerick in the early, exploratory period, and Tom Smith, J. H. (Bud) Stotler, Hurst Philpot, and Burley Parke in the years of the stable's ascendancy. Parke is the present trainer.

Mr. Howard is survived by his wife, Mrs. Marcella Howard, and three sons, Lindsey, Robert S., and Charles S. Howard, Jr. All the children were in southern California at the time of his unexpected death. Lindsey and Robert have been interested in racing for several years.

October 28, 1950
SEABISCUIT STATUETTE

A ten-inch statuette of Seabiscuit was presented to the Keeneland race course in a between-races ceremony on October 18. In the absence of W. Arnold Hanger, donor, the statuette was presented by Mary Jane Gallaher, Turf columnist for the Lexington *Leader*. The gift was accepted by Louis L. Haggin 2nd, president of Keeneland race course, who said the statuette would be placed in the Keeneland library. Mrs. Charles S. Howard, widow of Seabiscuit's owner, witnessed the presentation. The statuette was made by June Harrah, of New York.

February 24, 1951
*KAYAK II AND THE 'BISCUIT; A NAMESAKE TURNS OUT WELL
By Robert Hebert

A good man at keeping a secret is Silent Tom Smith, the man who made a career of training such horses as Seabiscuit, *Kayak II, *Sorteado, and Jet Pilot. Now that there is no necessity to keep this particular secret any longer, Silent Tom has just added a most interesting footnote on the career of the game little Seabiscuit.

"I told you once," Tom began, "that

Seabiscuit could never have raced again after winning the 1940 Santa Anita Handicap. But I never told you why. The reason was that he fractured a bone in his fore leg. Now that Mr. (C.S.) Howard is dead, and Seabiscuit is gone, too, there is no reason why the story should not be told. That race was going to be the last for Seabiscuit. As it turned out, it had to be his last race, and it was a good thing that on that afternoon he became the money-winning champion of the world at the time. That was his goal, and he made it.

"But for the next five weeks," Tom said, "Seabiscuit did not leave his stall. We put a cast on his leg, and the cracked bone mended perfectly. But photographers kept dropping by, anxious to get pictures of Seabiscuit, and I had to tell them he had just had his exercise and I could not take him out of the stall again."

As you know there has always been a lot of conjecture about the finish of that 1940 Santa Anita Handicap. *Kayak II was second to his stablemate that afternoon, and Mr. Howard always maintained that the black horse from South America would never have caught Seabiscuit even if they had gone another mile and a quarter. Most of the observers in the press box, including this reporter, saw the race differently, and thought *Kayak II could have won had he been ridden out. So I put the question to Tom, and asked him what he thought: Could *Kayak II have beaten Seabiscuit that afternoon? Tom Smith's answer was an emphatic "Sure!"

"But that doesn't take any credit away from the 'Biscuit that day," Tom added. "*Kayak II may not have been able to win, if Seabiscuit had not been in there. Seabiscuit was bulldogging the leaders all the way, running them into the ground, and he really set up the race there in the stretch for *Kayak II."

When you talk to Tom Smith you learn a number of astonishing things that bring these fine Thoroughbreds parading through your memories once again. For example, Tom's pet of all was not Seabiscuit; it was the black *Kayak II. I think the reason for this was that Tom's son, Jimmy, broke the South American, and he was a part of the family from his first lesson to his last race. On the other hand, Tom Smith thinks that Seabiscuit was the gamest race horse he has ever seen. In a match race, Tom said, he would have to take the 'Biscuit against any horse that ever lived.

Tom Smith had one other pet, too, and that was *Sorteado. This was really a great horse, in Tom's opinion, and had it not been for an untimely accident that ended his career, *Sorteado might have proven himself the finest of all the horses that ever carried the famous red and white triangle silks of the Howards.

One of the noted horsemen at Santa Anita whose name does not escape me now, but who shall be nameless, anyway, was discussing his fellow trainers the other morning. "You know," he said, "we are all pretty much copycats in this business. If we see another trainer do something, and it succeeds, we all try it. We play a game of follow the leader, trying to do what the man does who is winning races. To my mind, there has been only one original man in our time, and that is Ben Jones."

It sounds like pretty good sense to this reporter, but I would like to add the name of Tom Smith. Each horse was something new and challenging to Tom. I don't think he ever trained two alike. Tom would look at a horse for hours, without saying a word, but when he finally turned away he had a pretty good idea of what was in that horse and what he could do. Tom likes to keep busy, and now is training a 2-year-old filly by Wild Chicle named Miss Honor. He thinks she might make a runner. Tom Smith has been looking at her quite a while, and if he thinks she may do, that is good enough for me.

December 24, 1955
FOUR GOOD LEGS
BETWEEN THEM
By David Alexander

The phone in my New York apartment rang, and the operator said it was a long-distance call from Pawtucket. A man named John Pollard came on the line. He said, "I'm hanging up my blouse for good. I wanted you to be the first to know." There was a pause, and then Pollard added, with his usual flair for the dramatic, "You can't first-past Father Time."

I made some flippant reply that seemed appropriate for the occasion. I said it was about time. Pollard, who will be 46 his next birthday, has ridden race horses for more than 30 years. He has been one of the oldest active jockeys this side of England's Sir Gordon Richards, now retired. In recent years he

has been riding mostly at tracks such as Sunshine Park in Florida and Lincoln Downs in Rhode Island. He began booting horses when he was 14 at the leaky-roof courses of the West which horsemen call "bull rings." Pollard can't remember the name of the first horse he rode or the name of the track where he accepted the mount. "It was a fair meet in Montana or Western Canada," he says, "and the horse was a short-coupled chestnut with a wide blaze on his face."

I didn't take Pollard's announcement too seriously. This was the third time in 15 years he had retired. The first time he announced his retirement was on the evening of his day of greatest glory back in 1940 when he told representatives of press and radio, "I'll never throw a leg over another horse unless it's for a canter in the park."

He got a job as trainer, but a few months later he was back in the saddle. He retired again, in a burst of patriotism, in 1942. The Army, Navy, and Marines had rejected him, so he volunteered for work in a defense plant. "They found out I knew how to screw a light bulb in a socket, so they made me an electrician," he says. "I complained to the boss because I had nothing to do. 'Just walk around,' he told me. 'You're an inspector.' A few days later I went to the boss and told him they were on to me because a little man was following me everywhere I went. The boss said, 'Don't be silly. He's your assistant.' I figured if I needed an assistant I must be overworked, so I quit and went back to riding."

Pollard comes from Butte, Montana. He was a teen-age ranch wrangler and,

Seabiscuit with regular jockey Red Pollard.

besides riding Quarter Horses in his youth, he was a ham-and-egg fighter in preliminaries at cow town clubs. He says he had 20 or 30 fights and "lost a lot of 'em." In the ring he was known as The Cougar. On the tracks he was Red. His oldest friends still call him Cougar.

Pollard claims every bone in his body was broken at least once during his riding career. "The only reason I'm alive is that Satan has no stall for me." He talks like that. He has little formal education, but he'll quote you a quatrain from Omar or an aphorism from Emerson at the flick of a whip. He says he read the *Rubaiyat* and Emerson's essays during one of his long stays in a hospital. He calls Emerson "Old Waldo."

Physically, Pollard is matchstick-thin, though heavy-muscled, and tall for a jockey, about 5 feet 7. He has a Puckish freckled face, and his hair is as red as the racing silks of the late Charles S. Howard, which he once carried to the money-winning record of the world on a horse named Seabiscuit. Even today, Pollard makes me think of Huckleberry Finn.

Pollard had been riding on the Big Apple with only moderate success for about 10 years before he found the road that led to sportspage headlines. This

103

happened when he was at Detroit in 1937 with his agent, Yummy Allen, a dumpy little man with sleepy eyes. Pollard and Allen had 27 cents and a half a pint of brandy between them at the time. Allen, who is still around the horse parks, is a gregarious sort. If he sees an interesting-looking stranger at the track, he's likely to walk up to him, extend a stubby hand and say, "My name's Yummy, not Dummy. Let's you and me have a drink and pick a winner." Yummy had just signed Pollard on to ride for Howard.

Howard's trainer at the time was Tom Smith, a wiry, bespectacled fellow like one of those New England characters who sit around the cracker barrel in a general store. He started out as a Western ranch hand. They call Smith "Silent Tom" for good reason. One day Seabiscuit, by then a champion, was limping to the post and a friend said to Smith, "Tom, that horse of yours can't walk."

"Runs, though," Tom replied.

I once happened to be a witness to another example of Silent Tom's taciturnity in the stable area of Santa Anita. Tom was a famous trainer by then, but he liked to perform menial tasks around the barn. On this day he was chopping wood. The ax slipped and slit his boot. Smith took the boot off, turned it upside down. He pointed to a small object on the ground. "That's my toe," he said.

Smith persuaded Howard to buy Seabiscuit for $7,500 at Detroit at about the same time he engaged the services of Pollard. Seabiscuit was notoriously bad-legged. I have heard him described as a champion which never took a sound step in his life, though he ran 35 times as a 2-year-old. But 2 years later, with Pollard as his rider, the son of Hard Tack was being mentioned in the same breath with his paternal grandsire, Man o' War. By 1937 a serious challenger for Seabiscuit had come over the horizon. This was Man o' War's son War Admiral. Repeated efforts on the part of race track managements failed to bring the 2 champions together, but by the fall of 1938 Alfred Gwynne Vanderbilt had arranged a match for them in the Pimlico Special.

I had sought out Pollard, not only because he was the regular pilot of one of the great horses of the century, but because he had a reputation around the race tracks as a "character." I've always had a weakness for rugged individualists. My favorite story about Pollard concerned the time he was one of the leading riders of the old Tijuana track in Mexico. A little Indian apprentice jockey had developed a hero-worship for Pollard and followed him around like a pet dog. One day the Cougar rode into the stretch dead last. The only horse directly in front of him was ridden by the Indian apprentice, who had a very high seat. Red couldn't resist the target and cracked the Indian's backside with his whip. When the little fellow demanded an explanation, Pollard told him, "I was getting even for what you guys did to Custer."

During the summer of 1938, when Seabiscuit was training at Suffolk Downs in Boston for the Maryland match, I was staying at a seaside hotel near the track. Very early one morning my phone rang. It was Yummy Allen, and his voice was full of tears. "The Cougar just got throwed off a horse he was working and busted his leg," he said. I visited Pollard in the hospital that evening and encountered Yummy in the corridor. "How's he?" I asked.

"He's okay, I guess," Yummy answered. "I snuck him in a crock of bow-wow wine, and he's quoting Old Waldo to the nurses."

George Woolf, a nerveless rider who was called "The Iceman," was assigned the mount on Seabiscuit in the War Admiral match after Pollard broke his leg. A few days before the race a national network asked me to conduct a 2-way radio program between Woolf, in a Boston broadcasting studio, and Pollard in his hospital room. I gave Pollard, whose leg was in traction, a carefully prepared script, but he dropped it to the floor at the crucial point of the broadcast. As I scrambled frantically for the scattered papers, an evil gleam came into Pollard's eye. Woolf had just asked the Cougar how he should ride Seabiscuit in the match. "Why, Georgie-boy," Pollard ad-libbed, "just ride your usual race. Get left at the post and louse it up from there on in." Woolf and Seabiscuit beat War Admiral despite Pollard's advice.

Pollard's leg failed to heal. It was broken and reset twice, and he underwent several operations. He lay on a hospital cot for months, quoting Omar and Old Waldo to a pretty nurse named Agnes. When he could walk, he married Agnes. "I got something out of one of my bro-ken bones, anyway," he says.

No one thought the Cougar would ever ride gain. But by the late winter of 1939 he was galloping horses at Santa Anita, determined he would ride Seabiscuit in the last race of his career. Howard had his heart set on winning the 1940 Santa Anita Handicap in March, then the world's richest race. The $100,000 prize would make Seabiscuit the greatest money-winning horse of all time, putting him well ahead of Sun Beau's long-standing $376,744 record. After that, Seabiscuit was to go to stud.

A week before the race Pollard came to my house in Hollywood. He wasn't his usual flip self and I could tell that he was worried. He went into the den and I gave him a drink of brandy.

"How's Pops?" I asked. They called Seabiscuit "Pops" around the barn.

"Pops' leg is no worse than usual," Pollard said. "But how's the Cougar?"

He rolled up his pants leg. The leg he showed me looked like a charred, knobby broomstick. It was eggplant color. "One little tap," said Pollard. "Just one."

He shrugged. "Oh, well. Pops and I have got four good legs between us," he said.

Pollard then told me Howard had brought Buddy Haas, a good jockey, to the West Coast. Pollard was worried. Maybe Haas was going to ride Seabiscuit's stablemate, *Kayak II. Or maybe Howard planned to take Red off Seabiscuit.

"I've got to ride that horse," Pollard said. It was one of the few times I ever saw him completely serious.

I saw Howard next day and asked him if he was taking Pollard off Seabiscuit. "What would you and the other newspaper boys do to me if I rode Haas?" he asked. I told him I didn't know about the others. I said I would crucify him and use a whole keg full of nails for the job.

"If Red breaks that leg again, it will cripple him for life," Howard said.

I said maybe it was better to break a man's leg than to break his heart. I don't know if what I said had any effect on Howard. Anyway, Pollard rode Seabiscuit and Haas rode *Kayak II.

I encountered Yummy Allen in the Santa Anita paddock just before the race that could make Seabiscuit the greatest money-winner in the world. He sidled up to me mysteriously and said, "I've got it." When I asked what he had, he showed me a tiny bottle of brandy he had hidden in his coat pocket.

"I promised the Cougar I'd give him a drink of bow-wow wine before he ever got off the horse if he wins this one," he said. "And I'm going to."

As the field filed down the lane to the track, I saw Charley Howard and wished him luck. I had always regarded him as a rather cold and imperturbable man. He was trying to light a cigarette and he already had used 3 matches. "You're shaking like a leaf," I said.

Howard grinned sheepishly. "I guess I'm a little nervous," he replied. I'd heard he had bet $15,000 on Seabiscuit in the winter book at 10 to 1. Between the bet and the purse, he stood to win about a quarter of a million in the next few minutes.

The Cougar was coming by us, perched high over the Biscuit's neck. The race meant more to him than it did to Howard, I thought. He'd just been married a few months before, Agnes was carrying her first child, and he was flat broke. He'd get at least $10,000 if he won. He needed it so much he was risking a leg for it.

Mrs. Howard couldn't stand to watch the race from her box. She went to the backstretch and climbed up on a water tower with some stablehands, but she closed her eyes tight when the field was off and kept them closed until the finish. "I'd seen Johnny's leg," she said. "I couldn't bear to watch."

For three-quarters of a mile it was just another horse race. Then, at the half-mile pole, Seabiscuit moved, hugging the rail. A horse named Whichcee, ridden by Basil James, a smart, tough boy, came over on Seabiscuit sharply. The crowd of 80,000 seemed to hold its breath. For an instant the 4-legged horse and the 2-legged boy with 4 good legs between them seemed certain to go down. But Pollard had learned the hard way—in the Western bull rings—and he managed to ease off.

They came into the stretch and Pollard was outside and James was inside now, and Pollard was squeezing the frantic James closer and closer to the rail. "I wanted to see if he could take it," the Cougar said later. "He made me take it."

The Biscuit drew off to win by a length, withstanding a final challenge from his own stablemate, *Kayak II. But it wasn't over yet.

James climbed into the stewards' stand and for 2 minutes Pollard sat uncertainly on Seabiscuit. The red board that signaled a claim of foul was up.

The stewards disallowed the claim. They threw a wreath of roses over Seabiscuit's neck, and he was officially the greatest money-winning Thoroughbred in the history of the Turf.

Yummy went up and shook Red's hand as the cameras clicked. I wondered if he'd passed Red the little bottle. Pollard ducked down as if he were smelling the flowers. I wondered if he were drinking the brandy.

Later the Cougar told me he had gulped the brandy under cover of the flowers. "Best smelling drink I ever tasted," he said.

That night, after Pollard had issued his first statement about retiring from the saddle, I sat with him and his agent and his lovely wife in a fancy saloon owned by George Woolf, the jockey who had won the Maryland match on Seabiscuit. Pollard had switched from brandy to Scotch, I remember.

I said, "Cougar, how'd you feel when the red board went up?"

The freckled flesh beneath Pollard's eyes crinkled and he gave me a snaggle-toothed grin.

"I'll tell you how I felt," he said. "I felt just fine. I thought, if those dudes call me up in the stand and ask me questions, I'll sass 'em. This is one time I can get away with sassing 'em. There are 80,000 people here and they all love me and Pops. If those dudes take our number down, the crowd will burn the stand—with those dudes in it." Pollard

sipped his drink and looked off into space. "You know," he said, "not a single one of those 80,000 people was making a sound."

I thought about it, and he was right. The real drama hadn't been the 121⅕ seconds it had taken Seabiscuit to run the mile and a quarter. The drama had been the 120 seconds that a crippled boy sat on a crippled horse waiting for 3 men to decide whether he was, temporarily, the most famous figure in sports or just another jock who'd ridden foul.

When 80,000 people are cheering, it's just a great, big noise. When 80,000 people are completely silent, it's damned impressive.

February 2, 1957
OBITUARY OF TOM SMITH

Tom Smith, 78, one of America's leading trainers from 1938-48, died in a Glendale, Calif., sanitarium on January 23 of a stroke he suffered late last year.

Born in the hill country of Georgia, Mr. Smith's family moved to Colorado when he was a young boy. His first experience with horses was as a ranch hand, and he participated in some of the last of the great western cattle drives. He later joined the wild west show of the late C.B. (Cowboy) Irwin, working as a blacksmith and trainer. He went with Irwin's racing stable in 1923 and served as assistant trainer for more than 10 years. Twice during that period Irwin was America's leading trainer, saddling 147 winners in 1923 and 92 winners in 1930.

When Irwin died in 1934, Mr. Smith went with the late Charles S. Howard, for whom he trained numerous good horses. He developed Seabiscuit, which Howard had purchased from Wheatley Stable for $7,500, into the world's leading money-winning horse with earnings of $437,740 at the time of his retirement in 1940. Seabiscuit won many of the top handicaps in America during the years he was in the Howard barn, including the Santa Anita, San Juan Capistrano, Bay Meadows (twice), Brooklyn, Butler, Yonkers, Massachusetts, Continental, Riggs, Hollywood Gold Cup (under 133 pounds), Agua Caliente, Havre de Grace, and San Antonio Handicaps and the 1938 Pimlico Special. The Special was a match race with War Admiral,

Tom Smith

and Seabiscuit, usually a come-from-behind horse, led all the way to win by 4 lengths. Twice Seabiscuit lost the Santa Anita Handicap by a nose.

Mr. Smith also handled *Kayak II and Mioland for Howard. *Kayak II was one of the country's leading handicap horses in 1939, when he won 8 of 11 starts, including the San Carlos, Santa Anita, American, Hollywood Gold Cup, Continental, and Bowie Handicaps and finished second in the Narragansett and Pimlico Specials. In 5 of his 6 stakes successes he set new track records. Mioland was a top performer in 1939 and 1940. In 1939 he won the San Juan Capistrano, Westchester, and Potomac Handicaps and the American Derby; in 1940 he won the San Juan Capistrano, San Pasqual, San Antonio, and American Handicaps and was beaten a head in the Santa Anita Handicap.

In 1940 the Howard outfit was the leading American stable with earnings of $334,120.

During his years with the Howard stable Mr. Smith became known as "Silent Tom" by Turf writers because of his reluctance to discuss the progress of his horses. He replied to his critics in a newspaper column in 1940:

"In my estimation more harm can be done by overworking a horse than by going easy with him. That's why I guess I have appeared mysterious; why stories have been spread of how I sneak horses out at night and work them, or work them in a fog.

"The fairy stories about 'mystery' shoes and 'magic' salves are other things I would like to correct. I wish I could take a horse and make him win stakes simply by rubbing a magic salve on his ankles, knees, or feet. What a joke!

"If I tried, however, to rush here and there to correct every wrong story spread about me or the horses I train I would have time for nothing else."

After Howard died, Mr. Smith took over the stable of Mrs. Elizabeth N. Graham's Maine Chance Farm, and he had one of the longest tenures in the job. In 1945, his first full season with Maine Chance, he had the good stakes winners Beaugay, Star Pilot, War Jeep, Lord Boswell, and Colony Boy. He led American trainers for the second time, with $589,170.

In November, 1945, Mr. Smith was suspended by The Jockey Club for the alleged stimulation of Magnific Duel, a cheap claimer. The case became the most widely discussed stimulation case since the advent of chemical tests. Smith was charged with having sprayed the nose of Magnific Duel with a 2.6 per cent solution of ephedrine. Magnific Duel's urine test was negative, but a Jockey Club investigator said he had seen a groom administer the spray before a race.

Mr. Smith was given an open hearing before the New York State Racing Commission. After several days of testimony, during which several pharmacologists said that it would be impossible to stimulate a horse with the dosage reportedly used, the one-year suspension was upheld.

Returning to Maine Chance immediately after his reinstatement, Mr. Smith trained Jet Pilot for his 1947 Kentucky

Derby win over Phalanx, Faultless, and Fervent. A few months later he left Maine Chance for the stable of Mrs. Ada L. Rice, for whom he trained Model Cadet and Admiral Lea.

In December, 1949, Mr. Smith returned to Maine Chance, but this time his stay was brief. He trained his own stable for several years, in 1954 took over the Maine Chance horses for the third time. He and Mrs. Graham soon parted company again, and he retired.

Survivors include his wife, Mrs. Janet Smith; a son, James William Smith; and 2 daughters, Mrs. Erline Talbot and Miss Vera Smith.

January 9, 1965
FITZSIMMONS EDGES JONES IN HIALEAH 40-YEAR POLL

Venerable Sunny Jim Fitzsimmons, now 90 and in the second year of his retirement after one of racing's most illustrious careers, edged the late Ben A. Jones in polling to determine "Hialeah's Famous 40," and has taken rank alongside Citation, jockey Eddie Arcaro, and Calumet Farm as the most famous in the 40 years of the Miami track.

Behind Mr. Fitz and "Plain Ben" in voting on the leading trainers associated with Hialeah came Max Hirsch, Hirsch Jacobs, H.A. (Jimmy) Jones, George M. Odom, Bert Mulholland, Preston Burch, Woody Stephens, and Carl Hanford, in that order.

Citation, owned by Calumet Farm and trained by the Jones father-son team, took rank as the leading horse to figure in Hialeah's 40 years of racing.

Kelso, designated Horse of the Year for the last five seasons, was second in the voting. In order behind those two were ranked Nashua, Whirlaway, Round Table, War Admiral, Armed, Seabiscuit, Bold Ruler, and Carry Back.

Arcaro, who rode Citation in 17 of his races and has since retired from the saddle, won out over Ted Atkinson in voting on the track's leading jockey. In order behind them were Bill Shoemaker, Bill Hartack, Steve Brooks, Manuel Ycaza, John Adams, Robert Ussery, Jack Westrope, and Walter Blum.

Calumet headed the owner rankings, followed by Greentree Stable, Brookmeade Stable, Alfred G. Vanderbilt, Belair Stud, Col. E.R. Bradley, King Ranch, George D. Widener, Wheatley Stable, and Maine Chance Farm.

Coming closest to the consensus choices and thus winners among the racing writers and radio-TV commentators who voted in the poll were Whitney Tower of *Sports Illustrated*, Fred Neil of Baltimore's Station WCBM, Fred Russell of the Nashville *Banner*, and James Anderson of the Greenville, S.C., *News*.

July 23, 1966
30 YEARS OF SURF AND TURF
By Giles E. Wright

A superior racing idea called the Del Mar Turf Club was foaled 30 years ago in the mind of crooner Bing Crosby. The cross of a money-plagued county fairgrounds project and the return of racing to California actually sparked the idea into life, but there was plenty of nourishment to flesh it out with details.

Crosby was living in near-by Rancho Santa Fe when a WPA project designed to erect permanent buildings for the San Diego County Fair began to run out of money at the quarter pole.

Seemed a shame, too…lovely weather…within easy reach of several million persons…100 miles south of Los Angeles and only 20 north of San Diego…not much more than a long iron shot from the blue Pacific…perfect spot for summer months…Hmmm.

Before long the idea grew strong enough to lead Bing before directors of the 22nd District Agricultural Association, guiding body of the fair. His proposition in those depression-ridden days stood out like Native Diver would stand out in a field of $2,500 claimers.

He proposed to loan the association $600,000, at no interest, if horse racing facilities were included at the fairgrounds. The loan could be repaid out of the Turf Club's rent—12½ per cent of the track's share of the pari-mutuel handle.

It sounded almost like too much of a good thing, but the board was game and the idea really began to take on substance.

On May 6, 1936, Crosby was elected president and Pat O'Brien vice president of the Del Mar Turf Club Association. The meeting was held at Warner Brothers Studio in Burbank, appropriately enough, since movie folk have figured largely in the track's activities and still do. (A thoroughfare at the track is called Jimmy Durante Boulevard.) A Del Mar stock issue was quickly subscribed, much of it snapped up by members of the movie colony.

When the first racing fans arrived on July 3, 1937, the grandstand and club-house left some punters slightly agog. Spanish tile roofs and walls of adobe brick suggested old Franciscan missions rather than a place where one could enjoy running horses and invest in judgment of their speed, but everything was impressive, even grand...

During the second meeting of 25 days, Bing and Lin Howard, who raced as Binglin Stable, had an Argentinean runner called *Ligaroti which could really scamper. They talked of its prowess considerably within earshot of Lin's father, C.S. Howard, owner of Seabiscuit. The almost inevitable happened—a betless match race was arranged.

The purse was $25,000, winner take all, Seabiscuit to carry 130 pounds, *Ligaroti 115 at 1⅛ miles. A crowd estimated between 18,000 and 25,000 was on hand that Friday, Aug. 12, 1938, when George (The Iceman) Woolf guided Seabiscuit and Noel (Spec) Richardson took *Ligaroti to the start. Both Bing and Pat were at the microphone to describe the scene and race to a nationwide radio audience.

Woolf got Seabiscuit out of the gate a half-length ahead, but by the time the horses went past the stands the first time Richardson had his mount within a head of the leader. They ran that way throughout, with Seabiscuit winning by a nose in 1:49. The huge crowd was limp from watching the dramatic contest, and the nation remembered that this memorable event took place at a track called Del Mar...

April 18, 1970
SEABISCUIT (58th in a Series on THE GREAT ONES)
By Kent Hollingsworth

Luck. It was said that Charles Stuart [sic] Howard was the luckiest guy to come on the race track since Elias J. Baldwin. It might be noted, however, that lucky success is seldom sustained without some acumen and diligence.

Be that as it may, Howard seemed to be blessed with good luck in the horse business. His first good stakes winner, Coramine, was purchased as a $500 yearling at Saratoga in 1935; he bid $1,200 to get Porter's Cap, one of the top 2-year-olds of 1940. He was looking for a nice allowance horse that might win some change in California when he paid $7,500 for Seabiscuit, which became the world's greatest money winner. When Seabiscuit went lame, before the 1939 Santa Anita Handicap, Howard happened to have a substitute winner in *Kayak II, which his son had managed to pick up for about $7,500 while in Argentina playing polo. Before anybody in America had thought much about *Nasrullah, Howard imported *Noor and beat Citation.

Such good fortune in racing was a carryover from Howard's business activities. Born in Georgia, Howard rode up San Juan hill with Teddy Roosevelt's Rough Riders, took up bicycle racing, quickly ascertained he was no Frank L. Kramer, became a representative of a New York bicycle firm and opened a repair shop in San Francisco. In 1905 he decided the horseless carriage was here to stay and started sell-

111

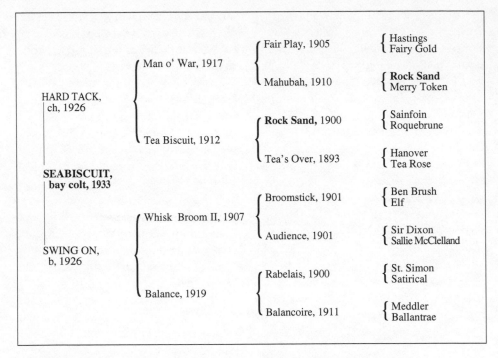

	Fair Play, 1905	{ Hastings { Fairy Gold
Man o' War, 1917		
	Mahubah, 1910	{ **Rock Sand** { Merry Token
HARD TACK, ch, 1926		
	Rock Sand, 1900	{ Sainfoin { Roquebrune
Tea Biscuit, 1912		
	Tea's Over, 1893	{ Hanover { Tea Rose
SEABISCUIT, bay colt, 1933		
	Broomstick, 1901	{ Ben Brush { Elf
Whisk Broom II, 1907		
	Audience, 1901	{ Sir Dixon { Sallie McClelland
SWING ON, b, 1926		
	Rabelais, 1900	{ St. Simon { Satirical
Balance, 1919		
	Balancoire, 1911	{ Meddler { Ballantrae

ing automobiles, picking one that did stay—Buick. He became the sole distributor for California and a few counties in Nevada, his agency at one time being the largest in the world. As his storied, original stake of 31 cents was multiplying into several million dollars, Howard became one of the largest landowners in California and he turned again to sports—yachting, polo, big-game hunting, and in 1934 to Thoroughbreds trained by M.E. (Buster) Millerick.

Seabiscuit was not much to get excited about until after Howard bought him as a 3-year-old. He was by a hot-tempered son of Man o' War, Hard Tack, which had won two minor stakes at three for the Wheatley Stable of Mrs. Henry Carnegie Phipps and her brother,

Ogden Mills. Leased as a stallion to Horace N. Davis Sr., Hard Tack sired only four foals in his first crop. Seabiscuit was one of these, out of Wheatley's unraced Swing On, a half-sister to three stakes winners whose dam was a half-sister to the dam of Equipoise. Swing On later was to produce Brown Biscuit, founder of a marvelous family from which descend Brownian, Hail to Patsy, Alecee, Isa, Inbalance, Lebkuchen, Espea, Noureddin, Pit Stop, and Determine.

Seabiscuit was on the smallish side, as a 4-year-old measuring 15.2 hands and weighting 1,040 pounds, but he was sturdy. Sunny Jim Fitzsimmons started him 35 times at two (in 1969, all 2-year-old starters averaged 6.2 races). Beginning in January, Seabiscuit started

18 times—once with a $2,000 claiming price, twice for $2,500, and once for $4,000—in Maryland, New York, and New Hampshire before he broke his maiden at Narragansett Park on June 22. He equaled the five-furlong track record, 1:00⅗, and four days later lowered the mark by a full second in winning the Watch Hill Claiming Stakes (entered to be claimed for $5,500). He was to win the Springfield Handicap at the old Agawam meeting in Massachusetts, the Ardsley Handicap at Empire City, and an overnighter, earning $12,510 at two. John Blanks Campbell in compiling his first Experimental Free Handicap thought there were at least 27 other 2-year-olds better than Seabiscuit and assigned him 114 pounds, 10 less than champion Tintagel, six under Bold Venture, but one pound above Granville.

As a 3-year-old, Seabiscuit may not have commanded much of Mr. Fitz' attention. While he was winning two overnighters in his first 10 starts, Granville was putting together a string of victories in the Belmont, Arlington Classic, Kenner, Travers, Saratoga Cup, and Lawrence Realization en route to Horse-of-the-Year honors.

At Saratoga on Aug. 3, Seabiscuit won the Mohawk Claiming Stakes (entered to be claimed for $6,000) by six lengths and a week later won a graded handicap by four lengths. When Howard came around looking for a nice allowance horse, Mr. Fitz let him have Seabiscuit for $7,500. Seabiscuit by then had started 47 times, had won nine, and had earned $18,465; he was to start another 42 times, win another 24 races, and earn an additional $419,265, becoming champion handicapper at four, Horse of the Year at five.

Howard shipped Seabiscuit to Silent Tom Smith in Detroit, where he won the Governor's and Hendrie Handicaps; then down to Cincinnati, where he placed in two stakes; then to New York, where he won the Scarsdale Handicap; then to San Francisco, where he set two track records, a mile in 1:36 in taking the Bay Bridge Handicap and 1¹⁄₁₆ miles in 1:55⅘ in winning the World's Fair Handicap. At season's end, Seabiscuit had won himself out for Howard three times over.

At four, Seabiscuit lost his first Santa Anita Handicap by a nose, won seven stakes in a row, set four track records, was voted champion handicapper, and emerged as the year's leading money earner.

He started with an overnight handicap victory over William du Pont Jr.'s Rosemont, then lost to Rosemont in the San Antonio. Rosemont was a horse whose injuries permitted only brief glimpses of his extraordinary class. He won only one stakes at three, upsetting Triple Crown winner Omaha in the Withers; he won only once at four, upsetting champion Discovery in the Narragansett Special, and he won only twice at five, beating Seabiscuit in the San Antonio and coming back the next week to catch Seabiscuit in the final stride by a nose on the post.

Seabiscuit then took the San Juan Capistrano by seven lengths, setting a track record for 1⅛ miles in 1:48⅖. At

Tanforan he took the Marchbank in identical time and five days later added the Bay Meadows Handicap before shipping east.

For the Brooklyn, Seabiscuit was assigned 122 pounds, equal with John Manfuso's Aneroid, fresh from victories in the Carter and the Suburban, while Rosemont drew top weight of 127 pounds. John (Red) Pollard sent Seabiscuit to the front immediately and stayed there, winning by a nose from Aneroid, with Rosemont seventh and lame again.

Seabiscuit next took the Butler, then the Yonkers, setting a track record for 1 1/16 miles (1:44⅕), and then the Massachusetts, setting a track record for 1⅛ miles (1:49) with 130 pounds.

Assigned 132 pounds for the Narragansett Special, he was beaten back to third by E.K. Bryson's Calumet Dick (115) and a former stablemate, Wheatley's speedy Snark (117). Given a month's rest, he easily won the Continental at Jamaica, then finished in a dead heat with Heelfly in the Laurel Stakes. Bypassing War Admiral in the Washington Handicap, Seabiscuit took the Riggs Handicap under 130 pounds, setting a track record for 1 3/16 miles (1:57⅖). In his final start he tried to give William Ziegler Jr.'s champion mare, Esposa, 15 pounds and missed by a nose as she lowered Pimlico's 1⅝-mile record to 2:45⅕.

At five, Seabiscuit proved to be the best horse in America—on a dry track. Aiming for the Santa Anita Handicap, he lost the San Antonio by a nose to Aneroid, which was getting 12 pounds. Pollard was injured in a spill and Georgie (The Ice Man) Woolf rode Seabiscuit for the first time, in the 1938 Santa Anita Handicap. He had the lead in the stretch, but was hooked by Maxwell Howard's presumptuous 3-year-old, Stagehand, which at 100 pounds was getting 30 from Seabiscuit and beat him a nose on the post. Thus by two noses in successive runnings of this race, Seabiscuit missed a net of $142,150.

Seabiscuit returning to be unsaddled following the match race with Ligaroti at Del Mar.

Three weeks later, Seabiscuit was dropped below the border and picked

War Admiral and Seabiscuit in the post parade prior to the match race at Pimlico.

up easy money in winning the Agua Caliente Handicap, by seven lengths, then shipped up to San Francisco and lowered the nine-furlong record to 1:49 in taking the Bay Meadows Handicap.

Meanwhile, War Admiral had won the Widener and a clamor arose for a match. Belmont Park hung out $100,000 to be run for on May 30. War Admiral was ready, but Seabiscuit was not and Howard withdrew his horse. Then it was revealed the two might meet in the Massachusetts Handicap on June 29, but late on the day of that race Howard again scratched his horse; Hal Price Headley's 3-year-old Menow beat War Admiral pointless, ending his winning streak at 11.

Howard shipped his horse out of Boston to Chicago under a cloud of bad press and decided to go in the Stars and Stripes Handicap despite the high burden of 133 pounds and rain; he was beaten 3½ lengths by an ordinary gelding, War Minstrel. That put him back on the train again, headed for Hollywood Park's inaugural meeting, at which he took the Gold Cup in a gallop, setting the 1¼-mile track record at 2:03⅗.

About this time Bing Crosby had come up with an exotic 6-year-old named *Ligaroti, which he owned in partnership with his trainer, Lin Howard, son of Seabiscuit's owner. Del Mar, with which Crosby was largely identified, put up $25,000, winner take all, for a match between Seabiscuit (130 pounds) and *Ligaroti (115). The race was characterized by the press as a setup, a gift to Seabiscuit, and the racing commission prohibited wagering on the event. It proved a rouser.

Noel Richardson hustled *Ligaroti into a slight lead at the quarter and held it at the half. Woolf pushed Seabiscuit into the lead on the backstretch and held it rounding the final turn on the rail, but the two were together again after a mile in 1:36, two seconds under the Del Mar record. Then it started: Richardson grabbed Seabiscuit's saddle cloth and Woolf rapped him with his whip; Richardson snatched Seabiscuit's bridle and Woolf whipped Richardson repeatedly all through the stretch. Meanwhile, Seabiscuit and *Ligaroti continued on with their business and Seabiscuit managed to win by a scant nose in the incredible time of 1:49—a full four seconds faster than the track record. The stewards worried about this for a while and finally decided to let the finish stand and set down both riders for the meeting.

Seabiscuit then was shipped to Chicago for the Hawthorne Gold Cup, but it rained and he went on to New York, taking the weather with him. He was started in the 1½-mile Manhattan Handicap despite the off track and weight concessions of 20-28 pounds, and got third money for his trouble. This defeat prompted Howard to forego a scheduled meeting with War Admiral in the two-mile Jockey Club Gold Cup, and Seabiscuit was shipped to Maryland, where he won the Havre de Grace Handicap easily from Menow and top mares Marica and Esposa.

Howard no longer could take the public charges that he was ducking War Admiral. Alfred Vanderbilt arranged the match, to take place at Pimlico on Nov.

1 if the track was right, $15,000 winner take all. In the interim, Seabiscuit was to pick up the Laurel Stakes, but Mrs. Edward Friendly's Jacola, best of the 3-year-old fillies, got 24 pounds from Seabiscuit and beat him easily, setting a mile record of 1:37.

Thus, for the famous match race, 4-year-old War Admiral, victor in 16 of his last 17 races, was installed a heavy favorite at 1-4 odds, with Seabiscuit at 2-1. War Admiral, which routinely broke like a shot, was expected to scamper to the lead immediately and thereafter improve his position. Such was not the case, however, Woolf started whipping Seabiscuit the moment the flag fell and Charley Kurtsinger sat flabbergasted as Seabiscuit spurted to the front. Passing the finish line the first time with a two-length lead, Woolf looked back and laughed. Kurtsinger got into War Admiral entering the backstretch, thought better of trying to go along the rail as Woolf drifted out, and sent War Admiral up on the outside. The 4-year-old drew alongside the 5-year-old at the half-mile pole and then War Admiral's head showed in front. Woolf was still grinning. With the advantage of the rail, Seabiscuit slowly regained the lead around the turn. At the top of the stretch, Kurtsinger asked War Admiral for all he had; it was not enough. Seabiscuit began to draw away and at the end was three lengths on top, his ears pricked, in new track-record time of 1:56⅗ for 1³⁄₁₆ miles. Seabiscuit had met a champion head on and beaten him.

At six, Seabiscuit was only $36,000 shy of Sun Beau's record earnings mark and Howard figured the Santa Anita

Handicap on March 4 was the place and time to send him over the top. He put Seabiscuit in an overnighter on Feb. 15 against Marica and an old gelding, Today, which promptly ran a record mile for him. Seabiscuit came out of the race lame, and Howard sent him to his Ridgeway Farm at Willits, about 125 miles north of San Francisco, where he was bred to seven mares. Meanwhile, Howard won the Santa Anita Handicap with *Kayak II, which was voted champion handicapper of 1939. In October, Seabiscuit was returned to the racing stable. He was being sent after that money record.

At seven, Seabiscuit was assigned top weight of 130 pounds for the Santa Anita Handicap; *Kayak II had 129 and Horse of the Year Challedon was allotted 128. Rain postponed his debut four times, but on Feb. 9 Seabiscuit finally got to the post; to little effect, for Heelfly beat him by three lengths at seven furlongs. This next week Seabiscuit and *Kayak II finished sixth and eighth in the San Carlos and it was generally agreed that Howard was not going to make it with either horse.

The following week, however, everybody did an about-face as Seabiscuit came down in the San Antonio in track-record time for 1¹⁄₁₆ miles, with *Kayak II 2½ lengths back in second place. Suddenly, incredibly, Howard appeared to have lucked into a lock on the big race. His entry was 7-10.

Pollard was back. He said he was known as The Cougar during his stint in the ring ("15 or 20 fights; I lost a lot of 'em"). Pollard's right leg was badly scarred; he said he and Seabiscuit had only four good legs between them, but they were enough. Pollard kept Seabiscuit within a length of pace-setting Whichcee until the final eighth, then went past easily and galloped home, lowering the track record for 1¼ miles to 2:01⅕. *Kayak II came from last place and was a restrained second by a half-length.

And that was how Seabiscuit became the first horse to earn more than $400,000. In 89 starts, he won 33 races, 27 of which were stakes. That was the end, really. Seabiscuit was retired to Howard's Ridgeway Farm and sired only four stakes winners, none of consequence, and compiled a moderate Average-Earnings Index of 1.25 with 327 year-starters. He is remembered not as a sire, but as a race horse, a champion, a patched-up champion, a great one.

January 8, 1973
SANTA ANITA 1973— NOSTALGIA, AND A FAST START
By Robert Hebert

On a crystal-clear afternoon, when the temperature was 92 degrees at the association gate and the San Gabriel Mountains in the background seemed closer than ever, Santa Anita opened its winter racing season before an enthusiastic crowd of 43,431.

The 36th inaugural had its nostalgic moments. In midafternoon, there was a pause while Santa Anita paid tribute to Joe Hernandez, the track's first and only announcer until his sudden death last winter. Hernandez had called 15,587 consecutive races at the track.

"This is the first opening day at Santa Anita that Joe Hernandez has not been here in person," director of public relations Alan Balch reminded the crowd.

Highlight of the ceremonies was the playing of a recording over the public-address system of Hernandez' call of the 1940 running of the Santa Anita Handicap, and the crowd once again was thrilled by his exciting description of the battle between Seabiscuit and Kayak II. It was obvious that Hernandez himself had been caught up in the drama of the occasion. At the exuberant shout of "It's Seabiscuit on top," in the stretch, fans began cheering and the excitement—spanning almost 33 years—continued long after the recording had ended.

In the winner's circle were Joe's son, Frank Hernandez, and a granddaughter, Liz Cunningham, who was in tears. They were accompanied by board chairman Robert P. Strub, president Fred H. Ryan, and Mrs. John K. Seidel, a friend of the Hernandez family.

February 4, 1974
MEMORIES OF SANTA ANITA—THE GHOSTS OF THE SAN GABRIELS
By Robert Hebert

Johnny Longden's legendary ride on George Royal to win the 1966 San Juan Capistrano Handicap in the last race of his career...The Noor-Citation duel in the San Juan Capistrano of 1950...and the storybook comeback by Seabiscuit, after a year on the sidelines, to win the 1940 Santa Anita Handicap and become the money-winning champion of racing.

Those are the top thrills that Santa Anita has provided in 36 years of racing, but there have been other wonderful, exciting moments, as well as some sad ones at the stately course in the shadow of the San Gabriel foothills, and it is appealing to look back.

Some of the moments that never will be forgotten by this reporter include those unbelievable come-from-behind victories by Silky Sullivan in 1958. He brought out fans by the thousands, and introduced a new phrase—a Silky Sullivan finish—into the sport's vocabulary.

Stagehand, a 3-year-old, upsetting Seabiscuit in the 1938 Santa Anita Handicap with Nick Wall and 100 pounds in the saddle.

War Knight's surprising victory in the 1946 Santa Anita Handicap when there were four noses on the wire, and the winning nose belonged to a member of the mutuel field owned by Mrs. Ethel Hill, a scenario writer. Unable to find the gate to the winner's circle in all the excitement after the race, Mrs. Hill was lifted over the fence by trainer C.B. Leavitt. The night before the race, Mrs. Hill had had a dream that War Knight would win the Big 'Cap. She could not have written a scenario that would have been as exciting.

The pulse-quickening call of "Here comes Malicious" by the late Joe Hernandez. Joe's call became so famous that fans made a hero of Malicious.

The amazing riding skill of Bill Shoemaker in the 1950s...and of Laffit Pincay Jr. in the 1970s.

Azucar's victory in the inaugural run-

The San Gabriel Mountains provide a spectacular backdrop for racing at Santa Anita.

ning of the Santa Anita Handicap in 1935, with the iceman, George Woolf, in the saddle.

Eddie Arcaro's relentless stretch drive aboard Talon in the 1948 Santa Anita Handicap. Arcaro truly was the master that day as he weaved in and out of horses, finding racing room like a magnificent broken field runner picking his holes.

C.V. Whitney's Bug Brush the afternoon that she set what was then a world's record of 1:46⅗ for 1⅛ miles in winning the San Antonio, and Whitney's Silver Spoon, which dominated the 3-year-old division and won the Santa Anita Derby. What a grand pair they were in 1959.

Just as remarkable, and memorable, were Alfred Vanderbilt's game Bed o' Roses and the spectacular Next Move. They were one-two in the Santa Margarita of 1952, after Next Move narrowly missed winning the Santa Anita Handicap of 1951.

Your Host, crippled by a spill during the running of the 1951 San Pasqual Handicap, then winning a fight for his life; he was to sire five-time Horse of the Year Kelso.

That classic dead heat between Fiddle Isle and Quicken Tree in the San Juan Capistrano of 1970, with Fort Marcy only a nose away.

Hillsdale's triumph over Round Table in the San Carlos of 1959—a victory that heralded the arrival of another exciting star on the scene.

The training genius of Bill Winfrey and the late Bill Molter, and the gentleness and warmth of the late Bill Finnegan.

The heartbreaking fatal accident to Lamb Chop, when she broke down so badly in the Strub Stakes of 1964.

Buckpasser's lagging starts followed by dramatic outbursts of speed near the finish to win the Malibu and San Fernando Stakes in 1967.

Busher and Honeymoon, two magnificent fillies owned by the late Louis B. Mayer; both beat top colts on many occasions.

Stuart Hamblen, who later ran for president of the United States, standing in the winner's circle and tossing El Lobo's blinkers to the crowd following his victory in the 1947 San Antonio Stakes.

Olhaverry, a ham and a crowd pleaser, showing off with his customary kick as he came onto the track, then going on to win the 1947 Santa Anita Handicap before a crowd of 83,768, the largest in Santa Anita's history.

Majestic Prince slipping out of his bridle in the paddock before the Santa Anita Derby, starting to run away—then stopping dead in his tracks when he heard the voice of trainer Johnny Longden calling him.

Page, at the age of eight and with enough ailments to fill a veterinarian's notebook, equaling the six-furlong track record of 1:08⅕.

The great mare Two Lea. After winning the Santa Margarita in 1950, she finished third to Noor and Citation in the Santa Anita Handicap, and trainer Jimmy Jones admitted later that she might have won if he had realized how good she was and trained her for the race. Instead, she was used only to set the pace.

Susan's Girl and Pincay, a picture of coordination between horse and rider as they thundered down the stretch to victory in the 1973 Santa Margarita.

Apple Valley's upset victory on a holding track to win the Maturity of 1954 with Merlin Volzke in the saddle.

The brilliant filly Blue Norther, which had everything to become a great champion—except soundness.

Native Diver, a sprinter which ran so effortlessly that he sometimes forgot to stop.

Unconscious' victory over Triple Bend and Good Counsel in the 1972 Strub, a truly outstanding race.

The frequent duels between On Trust and Yankee Valor, two of the best California-breds of all time.

Ralph Neves winning the Santa Anita Derby aboard Sweepida, then while still aboard the horse in the winner's circle reaching down and plucking a diamond stickpin from owner-breeder Dutch Hill's cravat as his reward.

Those are only a few of the exciting moments, and there will be more.

March 13, 1978
THE SEABISCUIT COVER-UP
By Jane Goldstein

The curious case of the Seabiscuit cover-up has come to light, 38 years after the fact.

It has to rank as one of racing's most successful conspiracies, although unlike many another there was nothing particularly underhanded or harmful and nothing unlawful about it.

Seabiscuit was retired to stud at owner Charles S. Howard's California farm following his third try—and heroic victory—in the Santa Anita Handicap of 1940. He was at the pinnacle of a distinguished career and was seven-years-old. He had won 33 of 89 races, and his Santa Anita Handicap score made him the all-time leading earner, with $437,730.

Retirement then seemed a logical move. Hardly anyone—few of the horsemen and certainly none of the racing press—questioned Seabiscuit's retirement. Yet until recently, it seems that no one except those who worked around Seabiscuit knew for sure that he was retired because of a fractured pastern bone.

One of those people, Dr. John Peters, now tells the tale. He feels there is no reason any longer to keep it quiet. Those who cared to perpetuate the cover-up are gone.

"At that time, I think the Santa Anita Handicap was run rather late in the race meeting," recalled Peters, who was Seabiscuit's personal veterinarian. "He pulled up fine, no problem then at all, and walked good the next day. A couple of days later Tom (trainer Tom Smith) began galloping the horse, just unwinding him, because they were going to go to Hollywood Park. There was a month or six weeks interval between the two meetings.

"One morning, the horse was galloping. I was standing, watching with Tom—he wanted me to be around whenever Seabiscuit was on the race track. He had gone around the track and had pulled up pretty lame about the finish line. The boy got off of him there, and the horse hobbled back to the barn. Immediately, we noticed that he wouldn't put his foot down to the ground and that some swelling was beginning to show in the pastern area."

Peters had his X-ray machine there and made pictures immediately.

"The first phalanx, which is the first bone below the ankle in the pastern area, was split in the center longitudinally from top to bottom, clear through," Peters recalled. "The crack looked like the crack in the table right here—you could stick a knife blade through the whole crack. It was just as straight as if you'd hit it with a cleaver.

"That was the end of him, as far as his racing career went, and even as far as coming out of the stall, for a while."

Then the subterfuge began.

Howard had insurance on Seabiscuit,

and the company's representatives were called.

"They saw the pictures and said, 'You cannot move this horse, absolutely,' " said Peters. The Howard horses, and most others stabled at Santa Anita, were about to move across town to Hollywood Park. Days passed.

"Now all the horses had shipped out from Santa Anita," Peters went on. "The Howard stable was the only one left on the grounds. Dr. (Charles H.) Strub (head of the track), kept coming down about every two or three days.

"He'd say, 'Tom, when are you going to move out?' Tom said, 'We've got a few things here we've got to do. We'd like to clean the barn, we want to do this, we want to do that. We're going to move just as soon as we can.'

"Mr. Howard was a great individual, one of the nicest men I've ever known in racing, and there was nobody at that time, I'm sure, that would have put any pressure on Mr. Howard unless absolutely necessary. But still no one, beyond those involved with the stable, knew that there was a problem with Seabiscuit. Nothing was ever said about it."

Six weeks after the accident, the insurance people said Seabiscuit could be moved in a narrow and padded van. He was shipped to Howard's Ridgewood Ranch at Willits, Calif., 135 miles north of San Francisco, in Howard's own van.

Alfred Shelhamer, a jockey of Seabiscuit's era and now a steward at Santa Anita and other Southern California tracks, arranged for Peters to tell the story and sat in on the interview.

"Now, how did they keep this away from the press?" he asked.

"Just nothing was ever said about it," Peters replied. "Nobody knew it except Tom Smith, Mr. Howard, the groom, and myself."

Why was it kept a secret?

"You'd have to know Tom Smith and Mr. Howard," Peters said. "I think it was just something they thought wasn't necessary to be told. There was quite a lot of talk about the horse being retired to stud anyway. He had come back and won the handicap. I think in Mr. Howard's mind that would have been the last race for him, anyway, but this put the finishing touch to the racing career of the horse."

Seabiscuit's temperament contributed to his recovery.

"The horse had a great disposition," said Dr. Peters. "He carried that leg around. He just put it down like a dog with a sore foot—he wouldn't put any weight on it at all. When he moved around the stall he kind of went on three legs, hopping around. We kept a tight cast on him, practically to his knee."

The injury was not connected with that which had put Seabiscuit out of action the year before his comeback and third try in Santa Anita's Big 'Cap, the first $100,000 race established in the United States.

In February of 1939, Seabiscuit had been in a three-horse race at Santa Anita, finished second and pulled up lame.

"The rider (George Woolf) got off at the seven-eighths pole and walked Seabiscuit back to the barn," said

Peters. "They didn't put him in the ambulance—it wasn't that bad. It was a suspensory problem. Mr. Howard couldn't go on with the horse, obviously, so I said 'Let's send him back to the ranch and fire him or blister him, or both, and get him back to the races here next year—give him a year.' That was agreeable to Tom Smith and Mr. Howard."

Seabiscuit had the year off, missing the Santa Anita Handicap of 1939 after running second in the race in both 1937 and 1938.

Shelhamer picked up the story when Seabiscuit was ready to go back to the track: "When the horse was back to where he was able to train, he was placed in Buster Millerick's hands—he was second-string trainer for Howard at the time—and Buster brought him along carefully until he knew he was ready to go to the races. He brought him to Santa Anita and turned him over to Tom Smith, the first-string trainer.

"The next day, Tom sent Seabiscuit to the track, with Buster there, and told the boy to send him for three-eighths of a mile, to stand him on his head. As I got the story, he went in :34.

"Buster Millerick was petrified, because here the man was deliberately trying to break his horse down, or so it appeared. After he worked, Tom said, 'Well, if the so-and-so will stand up under that, he'll stand up under anything,' so he went on to the races."

Before the Big 'Cap on March 2, Smith asked Peters to be at the track one Sunday at noon. He was going to work Seabiscuit a mile in company with Howard's stakes winner Kayak II.

"Red Pollard was on one of the horses, and I've forgotten what jockey was on the other, but anyway, they broke the two horses off at the finish line and worked an easy mile. The time I don't think makes any difference. The horses ran like a team until they hit the head of the stretch, about the eighth pole, and Seabiscuit pulled off from him. Kayak II quit. He pinned his ears. He quit. Tom said Seabiscuit broke his (Kayak II's) heart right there."

Shelhamer continued, "And more than that, Ted Kingsley, who galloped Seabiscuit all the time, said that when they got back and were unsaddling, Kayak II made a run at Seabiscuit."

Seabiscuit defeated that same stablemate when he won the subsequent Big 'Cap, though some thought—and the chart footnotes corroborate—that second-place Kayak II was not pushed to challenge sentimentally favored Seabiscuit as he set a track record of 2:01⅛ in the 1¼-mile race. Seabiscuit carried 130 pounds and Kayak II, winner of the handicap in 1939, carried 129.

"Doc flew his own plane up every week to take an X-ray of this horse," said Shelhamer, recalling the period when Seabiscuit was retired to the ranch, his leg still in a cast.

"Mr. Howard was a loyal individual," said Peters, "and expected loyalty and the best attention and care given by all his help to his horses. I had my own airplane, so about once a week or every 10 days I took my X-ray machine and flew up to the ranch. This went on for about 3½ months. Finally, the bone healed completely.

"We took the cast off in 3½ or four months. The horse was sound, but still we kept him in the stall as a protective measure. He was in the stall about six months' total time."

Charles S. Howard owned so many horses that he decided to breed Seabiscuit to his own mares and to no outside mares. As Peters put it, it was all right with the owner "whether or not he got runners." The horse truthfully never had a fair chance to prove himself at stud.

Seabiscuit died of a heart attack at the age of 14. He also had survived an earlier heart attack.

Before Seabiscuit's death and burial at Ridgewood Ranch, Howard commissioned Tex Wheeler to sculpt a life-size statue.

"Mr. Howard got me to help him," Peters remembered. "We measured Seabiscuit by the fraction of an inch— the length of his ears, his head, his legs, the distance around his ankle, knee, elbow, foot. Seabiscuit would have fit within the statue like a glove, if he could have walked in.

"He had two bronze casts made, one for the ranch and one for Santa Anita. If you look at one closely, you'll see how realistic it is—even to the arteries extending down over the ankle. Mr. Howard said, 'I don't care what it costs. I want this to be an exact duplicate of the horse.' "

Hubert Jones, another Santa Anita steward and a riding contemporary of Shelhamer, recalled that he helped break the first crop of Seabiscuit's offspring. Jones' father worked with Howard's cattle and saddle horses at Ridgewood for 15 years.

"Did you ride Seabiscuit at all?" Shelhamer asked Jones.

"Up at the ranch," Jones confirmed. "During the breeding season, I'd ride him to keep him fit. They didn't want me to gallop him too much. I don't know if it was you, Doc, but someone told me. 'Don't turn him to the right too sharp.' I never did know why."

Peters laughed: "Now, you see, Jonesey didn't even know."

He turned to Jones, "Because he had had a broken leg, we didn't want any sharp turning on the horse at all."

"That's all I was told—just don't turn him sharp," Jones said. "I did herd cattle on him, moved cattle on him slow. He always struck me as being a very intelligent horse. He enjoyed doing things. For example, if you were moving cattle with him—slow I'm talking about—he enjoyed getting up and making the cattle do what they were supposed to do. He like to reach out and nip them and make them get up with the bunch."

It is a slightly incongruous picture, Seabiscuit, a legend of Thoroughbred racing, herding cattle in his retirement, making no sharp turns to protect the hushed-up injury that prompted the end of his racing career; but if Hubert Jones is right, Seabiscuit enjoyed it, and so it is nice to think of the great race horse ending his days that way.

March 21, 1981
OBITUARY OF RED POLLARD

One of the many talents attributed to jockey John (Red) Pollard was the knack for telling a good story. He frequently made himself subject of his own jokes, as was the case when he recounted the occasion during World War II when he hung up his tack to volunteer for his country.

The Army, Navy, and Marines rejected him, so he volunteered for work in a defense plant.

"They found out I knew how to screw a light bulb in a socket, so they made me an electrician," he recalled. "I complained to the boss because I had nothing to do. 'Just walk around,' he told me 'you're an inspector.' A few days later I went to the boss and told him they were on to me because a little man was following me everywhere I went. The boss said, 'Don't be silly. He's your assistant.' I figured if I needed an assistant I must be overworked, so I quit and went back to riding."

Born in Edmonton, Alberta, Canada, in 1909, Pollard rode Quarter Horses in his youth, and he also boxed in preliminaries at cow town clubs. He fought in perhaps 20 or 30 fights, and he recalled that he "lost of lot of 'em." Pollard rode his first Thoroughbred winner in 1926 and competed primarily at smaller tracks during the early years of his riding career.

The first stakes win for Pollard came in 1931, when he piloted a horse named Up to Victory in the Agua Caliente Derby, and in 1933 he won the King Edward Gold Cup at Woodbine aboard Dis Dat.

In 1936 Pollard and his agent, Yummy Allen, found themselves in Detroit, and the story went that they had 27 cents and a half-pint of brandy between them.

Red Pollard

Shortly thereafter Allen signed Pollard on to ride for owner Charles S. Howard, whose trainer, "Silent" Tom Smith, also was in Detroit at the time. At about the same time that Smith had engaged Pollard, Howard had purchased a 3-year-old named Seabiscuit for $7,500 that Sunny Jim Fitzsimmons had been training at Saratoga.

The team of Red Pollard and Seabiscuit (Hard Tack—Swing On, by Whisk Broom II) became one of the most popular and successful duos on the racing scene of the day. Seabiscuit became a champion handicapper at four, Horse of the Year at five, and the world-leading money earner at seven. In 1937 Pollard rode him to win the San Juan Capistrano, San Antonio, Bay Meadows, Brooklyn, and Massachusetts Handicaps, among other races.

Injuries dogged Pollard throughout his riding years and several prevented him from riding Seabiscuit at important points in the colt's career. In the fall of 1938 Alfred G. Vanderbilt had arranged a match race between Seabiscuit and Man o' War's celebrated son, War Admiral, for the Pimlico Special. While Seabiscuit was in training at Suffolk Downs for the Maryland match, Pollard, as a favor to a friend, was galloping a 2-year-old. The youngster was green and bolted, and Pollard re-injured his bad leg. He had to sit as an observer as his friend George Woolf rode Seabiscuit to victory over War Admiral.

While Woolf and Pollard shared what one writer called "a mutual admiration society such as the Turf has seldom seen before," they loved to trade barbs in public and through the press. Pollard claimed that prior to the match race between Seabiscuit and War Admiral, he sent Woolf a telegram which read, "There is one sure way of winning with the Biscuit. You ride War Admiral."

Woolf often grabbed opportunities for his own pot shots. Once when praised for being a remarkably strong finisher on a horse, Woolf replied, "Nuts... Strength doesn't mean anything in riding a horse. A good jockey rides with his head, not his muscles. Why, Red Pollard is one of the smartest jockeys in the country today, and he hasn't the strength to blow out a candle."

Following his injury, Pollard was sent to Howard's farm in California to convalesce, and not long thereafter he was joined by Seabiscuit, which also had an ailing leg.

"Our wheels went wrong together," Pollard said, "but we were good for each other, and out there among the hootin' owls we both got sound again." Pollard and Seabiscuit made their return in the 1940 Santa Anita Handicap—the year Seabiscuit was seven years old—and Pollard rode him in a one-length victory over stablemate Kayak II, in track-record time, and withstood a foul claim to take home the winner's prize of $86,650. The victory clinched the earnings record for Seabiscuit, and Howard soon announced the retirement of his champion.

More injuries forced Pollard to consider retirement again. Seriously hurt in a spill in 1945, Pollard lay immobile for a long time, and he later recalled his first conversation when he awakened.

"When I woke up the parish priest leaned over me and whispered, 'The devil has no stall for you,' so here I am. And I guess I'll be here forever, me and Methuselah."

During his recuperation from that particular spill, Pollard turned to training for a time, but found it was not to his liking.

"It's too hard on the nerves; no wonder all trainers have ulcers. As a trainer," he added, "I am a barnacle on the wheels of progress."

Back to the saddle he went, although he never rode another mount to rival

Seabiscuit. He finally hung up his tack in 1955, after more than 30 years in the saddle. "You can't first-past Father Time," he said.

Red Pollard died on March 7 in East Boston, Mass., following a long illness. He was 71 years old.

November 14, 1981
RETROSPECT

The Nov. 7 Seabiscuit Invitational Handicap at Bay Meadows honors the late Charles S. Howard's 1938 Horse of the Year. Sired by Man o' War's son Hard Tack and produced from the unraced Whisk Broom II mare Swing On, Seabiscuit raced from age two through age seven, and from 89 career starts he won 33 times. With career earnings of $437,730, he ranked as the world's leading money-earner after his retirement in 1940 until Whirlaway displaced him in 1942.

Seabiscuit did not attract much attention early in his career. Bred by the Wheatley Stable of Mrs. H.C. Phipps and her brother Ogden Mills, he was trained initially by Sunny Jim Fitzsimmons. Although a smallish colt and a late foal, he made 35 starts at two, winning five races. He competed in claiming company that year, but he also won two small stakes and set a track record for five furlongs at Narragansett Park.

After Seabiscuit had won a claiming stakes and a graded handicap at Saratoga at three, Howard went to Fitzsimmons' barn looking for a nice allowance horse, and the trainer sold him Seabiscuit for $7,500. Howard turned the colt over to trainer Tom Smith in Detroit, where Seabiscuit won two stakes. From there, the colt's campaign included stops in Cincinnati, New York, and San Francisco, where he set two more track records, and by the end of the season he had won himself out three times over for Howard.

Things got better, as his career thereafter had an ascent similar to that of current campaigner John Henry.

At four, Seabiscuit won seven stakes in a row, set four track records, was voted champion handicap male, and completed the season as the year's leading money-earner. The following year, his most-publicized efforts came in two match races. The first was at Del Mar against Bing Crosby's 6-year-old Ligaroti, with Seabiscuit winning by a nose, and the next match was against champion War Admiral, with Seabiscuit again the winner.

Seabiscuit pulled up lame in his only start at six, a prep race for the Santa Anita Handicap. Turned out until October of that year, he was returned to win the Santa Anita Handicap the following year in track record time, defeating stablemate Kayak II. He was retired after that victory, with 27 stakes wins to his credit.

January 2, 1982
DISPATCHES — CLAIM OF GREATNESS
By Dan Mearns

Horse of the Year John Henry's appeal stems in part from his achievements as a runner, in part from his background. The fact that racing's first $3-million earner could have been purchased for $1,100 as an auction yearling somehow enhances his triumphs, reinforcing the peculiarly American notion that major success is possible for the rank-and-file, that the average Joe can take on the system and beat it.

John Henry as a 3-year-old raced four times in claiming company, and his ascent to Horse of the Year recalls the career of Seabiscuit, which also started in claiming races. In 1978, John Henry raced for claiming prices of $20,000 and $25,000 in Louisiana in February and March, finishing no better than third in those outings. In May and June, he won under tags of $25,000 at Aqueduct and $35,000 at Belmont. John Henry's current owners, Sam and Dorothy Rubin, bought him privately for $25,000.

Seabiscuit as a young horse may have been held in even less esteem than was John Henry at two and three, although unlike John Henry, Seabiscuit was not gelded. A son of Hard Tack—Swing On, by Whisk Broom II, foaled in 1933, Seabiscuit was trained initially by Hall of Fame conditioner Sunny Jim Fitzsimmons, who started the Wheatley Stable colt 35 times as a 2-year-old.

Racing in Maryland, New York, and New Hampshire, Seabiscuit at two started once with a $2,000 claiming tag, twice for $2,500, and once for $4,000. He set a track record at Narragansett Park in winning the Watch Hill Claiming Stakes, in which he was entered with a $5,500 claiming price, and he also won stakes that year at Empire City in New York and at the Agawam meeting in Massachusetts.

John Henry at two did not race at any track as obscure as Agawam, although he started on the lower rungs in Louisiana. He broke his maiden at Jefferson Downs and won in allowance and stakes company at Evangeline Downs.

Seabiscuit was purchased from Wheatley by Charles S. Howard for $7,500 in the summer of his 3-year-old campaign; the colt earlier had won the Mohawk Claiming Stakes while racing under a $6,000 tag. By the end of the season, Seabiscuit had won himself out for Howard three times over. The following year at four, Seabiscuit was named champion male handicapper, an honor he reclaimed at five in 1938, when he also was named Horse of the Year.

Seabiscuit raced on, to age seven, Howard wanting him to surpass Sun Beau's earnings record and become the first horse to earn more than $400,000. Seabiscuit did it, setting a track record of 2:01⅕ in the Santa Anita Handicap and bringing his earnings total to $437,730. He had won 33 of his 89 starts.

Past Performances

Seabiscuit — b. c. 1933, by Hard Tack (Man o' War)–Swing On, by Whisk Broom II — Lifetime record: 89 33 15 13 $437,730

Own.– C.S. Howard
Br.– Wheatley Stable (Ky)
Tr.– T. Smith

2Mar40- 6SA	fst	$1\frac14$	:47^1 1:11^1 1:36 2:01^1	3↑ S Anita H 121k	12	5	2^1	2^{hd}	1^{hd}	$1^{1\frac12}$	Pollard J	130wb	*.70e	101-11	Seabiscuit130$^{1\frac12}$Kayak II129^{1}Whichcee114$^{1\frac12}$		13
	Avoided trouble first turn																
24Feb40- 6SA	fst	$1\frac{1}{16}$	:23^1 :46^4 1:11^1 1:42^2	3↑ S Antonio H 13k	10	5	$2^{\frac12}$	$2^{\frac12}$	$1^{\frac12}$	$1^{2\frac12}$	Pollard J	124wb	*1.70e	100-07	Seabiscuit124$^{2\frac12}$Kayak II128$^{\frac12}$Viscounty110^4	Much best	13
17Feb40- 6SA	fst	7f	:22^3 :45^3 1:10^3 1:23^2	3↑ San Carlos H 12k	1	2	9^4	$8^{5\frac14}$	6^9	$6^{6\frac34}$	Pollard J	127wb	*.80e	88-14	Specify115$^{1\frac34}$Lassator105^{hd}Viscounty109^3	Close quarters	11
9Feb40- 6SA	fst	7f	:22^4 :45^4 1:10^3 1:23	4↑ Handicap 2000	2	5	$5^{2\frac14}$	$6^{3\frac34}$	$4^{3\frac14}$	3^3	Pollard J	128wb	*1.00	94-13	Heelfly118^{1}Sun Egret115^{2}Seabiscuit128^3	Close quarters	8
14Feb39- 6SA	fst	1	:22^3 :45^3 1:10^2 1:35^3	4↑ Alw 1900	1	3	2^{nk}	2^3	2^3	$2^{2\frac14}$	Woolf G	128wb	*.20	99-06	Today104$^{2\frac14}$Seabiscuit128^{6}Marica113	Went lame	3
1Nov38- 6Pim	fst	$1\frac{3}{16}$	:47^3 1:11^4 1:36^4 1:56^3	3↑ Pim Spl 15k	2	1	1^1	1no	$1^{\frac12}$	1^4	Woolf G	120wb	2.20	101-08	Seabiscuit120^{4}War Admiral120	Driving,best	2
15Oct38- 5Lrl	fst	1	:23^1 :47^2 1:12^1 1:37	2↑ Laurel 10k	6	8	$6^{3\frac12}$	$4^{1\frac14}$	$2^{1\frac12}$	$2^{2\frac12}$	Woolf G	126wsb	*.60	98-12	Jacola102$^{2\frac12}$Seabiscuit126^{3}The Chief116^4	Second best	12
28Sep38- 5HdG	fst	$1\frac18$	:47^2 1:12^2 1:37^2 1:50	3↑ Havre de Grace H 11k	6	5	$3^{2\frac12}$	$2^{\frac12}$	1^1	$1^{2\frac12}$	Woolf G	128wb	*.55	99-16	Seabiscuit128$^{2\frac12}$Savage Beauty103^{1}Menow120$^{1\frac12}$	Going away	8
20Sep38- 5Bel	my	$1\frac12$	:49 1:14 2:05^1 2:31	3↑ Manhattan H 6k	4	1	$5^{2\frac34}$	$5^{3\frac12}$	$3^{4\frac14}$	3^3	Woolf G	128wb	*1.20	85-12	Isolater108^{hd}Regal Lily108^{3}Seabiscuit128^{10}	Forced wide	5
12Aug38- 5Dmr	fst	$1\frac18$	:46^2 1:10^4 1:36^1 1:49	3↑ Match Race 25k	1	2	2^{hd}	1^{hd}	1^{hd}	1no	Woolf G	130wb	-	124-02	Seabiscuit130^{no}Ligaroti115	Driving	2
16Jly38- 7Hol	fst	$1\frac14$	:47^1 1:11^2 1:37^3 2:03^4	3↑ Hol Gold Cup 55k	7	8	9^{12}	4^8	2^4	$1^{1\frac12}$	Woolf G	133wb	*.70	- -	Seabiscuit133$^{1\frac12}$Specify109^{no}Whichcee114^5	Going away	10
4Jly38- 6AP	sl	$1\frac18$	:48^4 1:14^3 1:41 1:54^1	3↑ Stars & Stripes H 12k	10	7	$9^{7\frac34}$	6^7	$4^{2\frac12}$	$2^{3\frac12}$	Woolf G	130wb	*.90	72-30	WarMinstrel107$^{3\frac12}$Seabiscut130$^{\frac12}$Arb'sArrow111^4	Closed fast	10
16Apr38- 7BM	fst	$1\frac18$	:47^4 1:11^4 1:37 1:49	3↑ Bay Meadows H 16k	7	2	2^1	2^{hd}	1^1	1^3	Woolf G	133wb	*.20e	107-10	Seabiscuit133^{3}Gosum113$^{1\frac34}$Today112^{no}	Going away	7
27Mar38- 8AC	fst	$1\frac18$	:47 1:11^4 1:37 1:50^2	3↑ Agua Caliente H 13k	1	1	$1^{\frac12}$	$1^{1\frac12}$	1^3	1^2	Rich'son N	130wb	*.30	97-13	Seabiscuit130^{2}Gray Jack103^{hd}Little Nymph98$^{4\frac12}$	Eased up	8
5Mar38- 6SA	fst	$1\frac14$	:46^1 1:11^1 1:36^4 2:01^3	3↑ S Anita H 126k	12	14	$12^{7\frac12}$	1^{hd}	1^{hd}	2no	Woolf G	130wb	*1.90	103-12	Stagehand100^{no}Seabisct130^{6}Pmpoon120^2	Impeded,game try	18
26Feb38- 6SA	fst	$1\frac18$	:47 1:11^3 1:37^1 1:50	3↑ San Antonio H 9.2k	5	5	4^6	$4^{2\frac12}$	$3^{\frac12}$	2no	Workman R	130wb	*.40e	94-12	Aneroid118^{no}Seabiscuit130$^{1\frac12}$IndianBroom108^{hd}	Just missed	13
11Nov37- 6Pim	fst	$1\frac58$	:50^1 1:41 2:06^2 2:45^1	3↑ Bowie H 12k	8	3	$5^{2\frac34}$	$4^{1\frac14}$	1^{hd}	2no	Pollard J	130wb	*1.25	107-11	Esposa115^{no}Seabiscuit130$^{1\frac14}$Burning Star114^1	Game try	8
5Nov37- 5Pim	fst	$1\frac{3}{16}$	:47 1:11^3 1:37 1:57^2	3↑ Riggs H 12k	11	4	$5^{5\frac12}$	$4^{\frac34}$	$1^{\frac12}$	1^{nk}	Pollard J	130wb	*.40e	103-11	Seabiscuit130^{nk}BurningStar114$^{\frac34}$CaballroII116$^{\frac12}$	Hard drive	11
	Previously owned by Mrs C.S. Howard																
16Oct37- 5Lrl	fst	1	:24 :47^1 1:12^1 1:37^2	2↑ Laurel 9.6k	7	3	2^{hd}	2^{nk}	1^{hd}	$1^{1\frac12}$	Pollard J	126wb	*.70	99-14	[DH]Seabiscuit126[DH]Heelfly114$^{1\frac12}$Deliberator116^1	Gamely	7
12Oct37- 5Jam	fst	$1\frac{1}{16}$	:24 :48 1:12^4 1:44^4	3↑ Continental H 12k	2	1	1^{hd}	1^{nk}	1^2	1^5	Pollard J	130wb	*.80	89-20	Seabiscuit130^{5}Caballero II117^{2}Moon Side112^1	Easily	12
11Sep37- 5Nar	sly	$1\frac{3}{16}$	:47^3 1:12 1:38 1:57	3↑ Nar Spl H 33k	5	4	$4^{6\frac12}$	$2^{1\frac12}$	$3^{3\frac12}$	$3^{2\frac12}$	Pollard J	132wb	*.85	87-16	Calumet Dick115^{1}Snark117$^{1\frac12}$Seabiscuit132^4	Weakened	6
7Aug37- 5Suf	fst	$1\frac18$	:47 1:11 1:36 1:49	3↑ Mass H 70k	3	3	$2^{2\frac12}$	2^1	1^{nk}	1^1	Pollard J	130wb	*1.00	102-06	Seabiscuit130^{1}CaballeroII108^{1}FairKnghtss108$^{2\frac12}$	Drove out	13
24Jly37- 5Emp	fst	$1\frac{1}{16}$	:23^3 :47^2 1:11^3 1:44^1	3↑ Yonkers H 10k	2	2	2^2	1^{hd}	$1^{1\frac12}$	1^4	Pollard J	129wb	*1.00	102-12	Seabiscuit129^{4}Jesting108^{3}Corinto109^3	Going away	6
10Jly37- 5Emp	fst	$1\frac{3}{16}$	:48 1:12 1:38^2 1:58^3	3↑ Butler H 25k	1	2	$1^{\frac12}$	$1^{\frac12}$	$1^{1\frac12}$	$1^{1\frac12}$	Pollard J	126wb	*.90	98-08	Seabiscuit126$^{1\frac12}$Thorson107^{3}Corinto109^1	Driving,best	6
26Jun37- 5Aqu	fst	$1\frac18$	:47 1:11^2 1:37 1:50^1	3↑ Brooklyn H 25k	1	1	1^1	$1^{\frac12}$	1^{hd}	1no	Pollard J	122wb	3.20	90-14	Seabiscuit122^{no}Aneroid122^{5}Memory Book114^3	Hard drive	9
22May37- 7BM	fst	$1\frac{1}{16}$	:24 :47^3 1:11 1:44^3	3↑ Bay Meadows H 11k	8	2	2^{nk}	2^1	$1^{\frac12}$	$1^{1\frac14}$	Pollard J	127wb	*.10e	87-15	Seabiscuit127$^{1\frac14}$Exhibit105^{no}Watersplash103^1	Going away	8
17Apr37- 6Tan	fst	$1\frac18$	:45^2 1:10^3 1:36 1:48^4	3↑ Marchbank H 11k	7	1	1^5	1^2	1^4	1^3	Pollard J	124wb	*.40	94-08	Seabiscuit124^{3}Grand Manitou110^{hd}Sobriety109^5	Easily	7
6Mar37- 6SA	fst	$1\frac18$	:46^3 1:11 1:36^1 1:48^4	3↑ S Juan Capistrano H 12k	2	2	$2^{1\frac12}$	2^{hd}	1^4	1^7	Pollard J	120wb	*1.50	103-08	Seabiscuit120^{7}GrandManitou108$^{\frac34}$SpecialAgent116^{nk}	Easily	10
27Feb37- 6SA	gd	$1\frac14$	:45^4 1:10^4 1:36^4 2:02^4	3↑ S Anita H 125k	3	9	$4^{4\frac12}$	$4^{1\frac12}$	1^{hd}	2no	Pollard J	114 w	6.40	97-13	Rosemont124^{no}Seabiscuit114^{1}Indian Broom116$^{2\frac12}$	Nosed out	18
20Feb37- 6SA	fst	$1\frac18$	:46^4 1:11 1:37^2 1:50^1	3↑ San Antonio H 9.4k	11	14	$12^{8\frac34}$	$12^{9\frac14}$	$9^{8\frac34}$	$5^{3\frac34}$	Pollard J	115wb	2.30	92-11	Rosemnt122$^{\frac34}$StarShadow106$^{\frac12}$SpecialAgent117^1	Forced wide	16
9Feb37- 6SA	fst	7f	:22^4 :45^2 1:10^4 1:23^1	4↑ Handicap 1545	5	1	$1^{\frac12}$	1^1	$1^{\frac12}$	$1^{4\frac12}$	Pollard J	112wb	3.20	96-13	Seabiscuit112$^{4\frac12}$Sir Emerson104^{nk}Time Supply118^5	Easily	6
12Dec36- 7BM	fst	$1\frac{3}{16}$	:47 1:11^2 1:36^4 1:55^4	2↑ World's Fair H 11k	4	3	1^5	1^3	1^3	1^5	Pollard J	113wb	*1.10	- -	Seabiscuit113^{5}Wildland101$^{2\frac12}$GiantKiller107$^{1\frac12}$	Easily best	7
28Nov36- 7BM	fst	1	:23^2 :46^4 1:11^2 1:36	2↑ Bay Bridge H 2.7k	6	8	$5^{1\frac34}$	2^2	1^{hd}	1^5	Pollard J	116wb	*2.20	106-07	Seabiscuit116^{5}Uppermost114$^{\frac12}$Velociter107^{nk}	Eased up	8
31Oct36- 4Emp	fst	$1\frac18$	:49^1 1:14 1:39^2 1:52	3↑ Yorktown H 6.5k	7	6	5^4	$6^{6\frac12}$	$3^{3\frac12}$	$3^{1\frac34}$	Pollard J	119wb	8.00	93-11	Thorson112^{nk}Piccolo107$^{1\frac12}$Seabiscuit119^3	Closed fast	8
24Oct36- 4Emp	fst	1 70	:23^3 :47^3 1:12^1 1:44	3↑ Scarsdale H 7.3k	2	7	$8^{4\frac34}$	$8^{8\frac34}$	$6^{3\frac34}$	1no	Pollard J	116wb	12.00e	90-13	Seabiscuit116^{no}Jesting112^{hd}Piccolo105.5^3	Just up	11
17Oct36- 6RD	my	$1\frac{1}{16}$	:26 :51 1:18 1:56^2	3↑ East Hills H 2.7k	4	2	2^2	2^4	2^3	$3^{2\frac12}$	Pollard J	116wb	3.20	29-59	MuchoGusto111$^{1\frac12}$SafeandSound103^{1}Sebscut116$^{2\frac12}$	Closed well	6
3Oct36- 5RD	fst	$1\frac{1}{16}$	:23^2 :46^4 1:11^3 1:44	3↑ Western Hills H 2.8k	7	4	$5^{2\frac14}$	$5^{3\frac12}$	$4^{3\frac12}$	$3^{1\frac12}$	Pollard J	116wb	4.90	92-16	Marynell100$^{\frac12}$Cristate108^{1}Seabiscuit116^1	Closed fast	8
26Sep36- 6Det	fst	$1\frac{1}{16}$	:24^3 :48^3 1:13 1:44^2	3↑ Hendrie H 2.8k	2	2	$2^{\frac12}$	1^1	1^2	1^4	Pollard J	115wb	2.10	98-12	Seabiscuit115^{4}Cristate114$^{2\frac12}$Safe and Sound108^3	Easily	6
19Sep36- 6Det	fst	$1\frac{1}{16}$	:24^3 :48^3 1:13^3 1:46	3↑ De La Salle H 2.8k	7	1	1^1	3^1	$6^{3\frac12}$	$6^{3\frac34}$	Pollard J	115wb	*1.60	86-13	Cristate106^{hd}Professor Paul105^{hd}Paradisical109$^{1\frac12}$	Quit	8
7Sep36- 6Det	fst	$1\frac18$	:47 1:12 1:38 1:50^4	3↑ Governor's H 5.6k	12	3	2^{hd}	2^{hd}	$1^{\frac12}$	1^{nk}	Pollard J	109wb	4.90	96-13	Seabiscuit109^{nk}Professor Paul99$^{1\frac12}$Azucar112^3	Driving	12
2Sep36- 6Det	sl	1 70	:24^3 :48^4 1:14 1:44	3↑ Handicap 1200	3	1	1^{hd}	$4^{1\frac14}$	3^1	$3^{\frac12}$	Pollard J	114wb	3.90	89-18	ProfessorPaul104^{no}SafeandSound102$^{\frac12}$Seabsct114$^{2\frac12}$	Impeded	8
22Aug36- 6Det	fst	$1\frac{1}{16}$	:24 :47 1:11^3 1:43^2	3↑ Motor City H 5.7k	3	1	3^3	7^8	6^5	$4^{4\frac14}$	Pollard J	110wb	13.20	99-08	Myrtlewood122^{3}Professor Paul95^{nk}Cristate106^1	Tired	11
	Previously owned by Wheatley Stable; previously trained by J. Fitzsimmons																

Seabiscuit 1124 Trefari 110 — Easily 2

Seabiscuit 1096 Ann O'Ruley 1122 Balkan Land 1092 — Easily 7

Kearsarge 99ns Tatterdemalion 113 5⁴⁶ Brown Top 109no — Faltered 7

Seabiscuit 1151½ Deliberate 115 Liberal 1153 — Handily 12

Party Spirit 1071⁴k Indomitable 1052⁵ Speed to Spare 1141⁴ — Outrun 13

Gallant Prince 1161 Brown Twig 114no Gillie 114nk — Stumbled 6

Faust 1032no Gallant Gay 110 5no Party Spirit 1112 — Outrun 15

Seabiscuit 1113 Piccolo 1063 Swamp Angel 1113⁴ — Easily 7

Tugboat Frank 1102 Piccolo 108no Gallant Gay 109⁴ — No excuse 8

Gleeman 1101⁴ Wha Hae 1131 Stubbs 116nk — Finished fast 7

Goldeneye 1053 Chancer 105no Seabiscuit 1203 — No excuse 4

Tintage 1181½ Seabiscuit 1054 Hollyrood 1198 — Good effort 5

Ned Reigh 116½ Challenphen 1074no Wise Duke 1123 — No excuse 10

Clocks 1111½ Seabiscuit 11721½ Crossbow 11121 — Finished fast 5

Seabiscuit 1129 Neap 1072 Wha Hae 115½ — Easily 6

Infidox 110no Clocks 110no Sparta 109⁴ — Ridden out 8

Seabiscuit 1091 Bright Plumage 117no Infidox 1171½ — Outrun 10

The Fighter 122no Teufel 1122 Postage Due 124⁴½ — Off slowly 11

Postage Due 172½ Wise Duke 1154 Material 1201 — Forced wide 14

Seabiscuit 1159 Count Morse 1059 Dark Wizard 1122 — Easily 8

Phantom Fox 1086no Pullman 1145 Seabiscuit 110nk — Finished well 7

Ned Reigh 1166no Speed to Spare 1159no Granville 1145 — No excuse 7

Bold Venture 1151½ Grand Slam 1223 Valvctorn 152 — Dropped back 9

Maerial 1181 Lovely Girl 104⁴ Speed 109no — Off slowly 13

Black Highbrow 1113 Nouveau Riche 1086no SLouis 108no Faltered 7

Black Highbrow 1151½ Seabiscuit 1159 Nedvive 1123 — Gamely 5

Maerial 1233 Jari 1111½ Tugboat Frank 1111½ — No excuse 6

Bright and Early 1141½ swashbuckler 1143 Chilpain 1121 — No excuse 6

Seabiscuit 1082 Infidox 1081 Zowie 1022 — Easily 9

Winter Sport 1051 Postage Due 124nk Seabiscuit 1103½ — Good effort 12

Swashbuckler 1163 Seabiscuit 1181½ Sobriety 1163 — Good effort 12

Sandy Mack 1161 Browbeat 1131 Tugboat Frnk 116no — Closed gap 11

Microbe 114nk Black Mistress 111no Seabiscuit 1061 — Closed fast 7

Pullman 1151 Knowing 1151½ Royal Fox 1155 — Shuffled 8

Galsac 116½ Seabiscuit 110no Transit Lady 110no — Finished fast 6

Cherry Stone 115no Hiatus 110no Prosy 113½ — Finished fast 11

Hiatus 113½ Deliberate 114 Seabiscuit 1161½ — Close quarters 13

Parquqay Tea 1124 Parsey Begone 1123 Sebscui 1151½ — Off slowly 9

Victorious Ann 112no Winter Sport 1151½ SteLouise 121 — Outrun 12

Borsa 1151½ Seabiscuit 1134 Green Mist 1151 — Finished gamely 8

Victorous Ann 1182 Wllw Wood 113no Two E.egd 1131½ — Finished fast 14

James City 1191½ Grand Slam 1086no Bright Light 114no — Impeded 13

Black Bess 100no Transit 110no Edri 1051½ — No excuse 11

Clapping Jane 1072 Seabiscuit 110no Sport 107nk — Finished fast 12

Wha Hae 1131 Wise Duke 1109 Blue Donna 1073 — Good effort 10

Watch Hill Claiming Stakes
Purse: $2,500 Added

Fifth Race   Narragansett Park - June 26, 1935
Purse $2,500 added. Two-year-olds. 5-8 Mile. Main Track. Track: Fast.
Net value to winner $2,795; second, $500; third, $250; fourth, $125.

Horse	A	Wgt	Eqp	Odds	PP	St	1/4	1/2	Str	Fin	Jockey
Seabiscuit	2	108	wb	1.70	6	5	$2^{11/2}$	$1^{11/2}$	1^1	1^2	F Horn
Infidox	2	108	wb	3.05	8	7	$4^{1/2}$	$3^{11/2}$	$2^{11/2}$	2^1	J Lynch
Zowie	2	102	wb	7.05	2	1	$3^{1/2}$	4^3	$3^{1/2}$	3^2	N Wall
Challephen	2	108	w	†10.70	4	4	$6^{1/2}$	$6^{1/2}$	$6^{1/2}$	4^h	H Schutte
The Hare	2	105	w	†	3	3	$5^{1/2}$	5^2	$5^{1/2}$	$5^{1/2}$	R Howell
Herondas	2	108	w	11.00	7	6	$7^{1/2}$	8	7^2	$6^{11/2}$	L Fallon
Sandy Mack	2	105	w	5.85	1	2	$1^{1/2}$	2^h	4^2	$7^{1/2}$	C Hanford
Royal Ballad	2	105	wb	15.25	5	8	8	7^{nk}	8	8	C Corbett

†Coupled as Branncastle Farm Stable entry.

Off Time: 4:43   **Time Of Race:** :22⅖ :45⅘   :59⅗ (new track record)
Start: Good and slow   **Track:** Fast
Equipment: w for whip; b for blinkers

Mutuel Payoffs

Seabiscuit	$5.40	$3.10	$2.50
Infidox		3.80	3.00
Zowie			3.70

Winner: Seabiscuit, b. c. by Hard Tack—Swing On, by Whisk Broom II (Trained by G. Tappen).
   Bred by Wheatley Stable in Ky. Winner entered to be claimed for $5,500.

Start good and slow. Won easily; second and third driving.
SEABISCUIT moved up leaving the back stretch, wore down SANDY MACK for the lead and, drawing out, was never threatened. INFIDOX moved up on the outside rounding the far turn, was placed under punishment in the stretch and held on well. ZOWIE, away fast, dropped back, lacked speed, but closed with good energy. CHALLEPHEN was racing stoutly at the finish. THE HARE tired through the last three-sixteenths. HERONDAS was never a factor. ROYAL BALLAD, away slowly, was outrun throughout.
Scratched—The Flankman, 105.
Overweight—Royal Ballad, 3 pounds.

Owners: (6) Wheatley Stable; (8) Mrs G W Ogle; (2) Labonte & Seguin; (4) Branncastle Farm Stable; (3) Branncastle Farm Stable; (7) B N Kane; (1) J U Gratton; (5) C T Grayson

©DAILY RACING FORM/EQUIBASE

See page 14 for related story

Springfield Handicap
Purse: $2,500 Added

Fifth Race   Agawam Park - October 16, 1935
Purse $2,500 added. Two-year-olds. 3-4 Mile. Main Track (Out of chute). Track: Fast.
Net value to winner $2,030; second, $500; third, $250; fourth, $100.

Horse	A	Wgt	Eqp	Odds	PP	St	1/4	1/2	Str	Fin	Jockey
Seabiscuit	2	109	wb	8.00	8	1	1^2	$1^{11/2}$	1^1	1^1	J Stout
Bright Plumage	2	117	wb	3.40	1	2	6^h	7^1	5^2	2^h	A Robertson
Infidox	2	117	w	1.10	6	4	3^2	2^h	2^2	$3^{11/2}$	J Lynch
Aboveboard	2	107	wb	5.80	3	5	4^2	4^3	$3^{1/2}$	4^1	J Mattioli
Professor Paul	2	102	wb	48.60	2	8	8	8	6^1	5^1	J Rosen
Bereit	2	95	w	58.40	4	7	7^3	6^1	7^1	6^3	G Watson
Black Mistress	2	96	wb	26.10	5	6	5^1	5^1	8	7^3	A Jolley
Sandy Beach	2	118	w	10.20	7	3	2^h	3^2	$4^{1/2}$	8	J O'Malley

Off Time: 4:13   **Time Of Race:** :23⅖   :46   1:11⅖
Start: Good and slow   **Track:** Fast
Equipment: w for whip; b for blinkers

Mutuel Payoffs

Seabiscuit	$18.00	$8.00	$3.80
Bright Plumage		4.20	3.20
Infidox			2.60

Winner: Seabiscuit, b. c. by Hard Tack—Swing On, by Whisk Broom II (Trained by T. Driscoll).
Bred by Wheatley Stable in Ky.

Start good and slow. Won ridden out; second and third driving.
SEABISCUIT. away in motion, soon took command, drew clear under pressure and was hard ridden all the way to hold his advantage.
BRIGHT PLUMAGE, well back in the early stages, was forced to race on the outside entering the stretch, but closed with a fine burst
of speed to pass the tiring INFIDOX. The latter, always close to the pace, shook off SANDY BEACH, but tired in the last eighth.
ABOVEBOARD raced evenly. PROFESSOR PAUL, a trailer for five-eighths, made up ground. SANDY BEACH tired after displaying
some early speed. BLACK MISTRESS, fractious at the post, had no excuse.
Scratched—Piccolo, 110.

Owners: (8) Wheatley Stable; (1) C V Whitney; (6) Mrs G W Ogle; (3) W Hartman; (2) Mrs J Chesney; (4) W F Lutz; (5) H T
Archibald; (7) Mrs D Melanson
©DAILY RACING FORM/EQUIBASE

See page 15 for related story

Ardsley Handicap
Purse: $2,500 Added

Fifth Race Empire City - October 23, 1935
Purse $2,500 added. Two-year-olds. 5 3-4 Furlongs. Main Track. Track: Fast.
Net value to winner $2,835; second, $500; third, $250; fourth, $125.

Horse	A	Wgt	Eqp	Odds	PP	St	1/4	1/2	Str	Fin	Jockey
Seabiscuit	2	112	wb	4.00	4	3	2^h	$2^{1\,1/2}$	1^1	1^3	F Kopel
Neap	2	107	w	6.00	1	5	5^4	4^3	4^3	2^2	A Pascuma
Wha Hae	2	115	w	2.00	5	2	$3^{1\,1/2}$	3^1	$2^{1/2}$	$3^{1/2}$	T Malley
Tatterdemalion	2	114	wb	3.50	6	6	6	6	6	4^2	R Workman
Knowing	2	110	w	2.00	3	1	1^h	1^h	3^2	5^4	C Watters
Holdum Brown	2	108	w	20.00	2	4	4^2	5^1	$5^{1/2}$	6	C Eye

Off Time: 4:21   **Time Of Race:** :23 :47 1:08⅖
Start: Good and slow   **Track:** Fast
Equipment: w for whip; b for blinkers

Winner: Seabiscuit, b. c. by Hard Tack—Swing On, by Whisk Broom II (Trained by J. Fitzsimmons, Jr.).
Bred by Wheatley Stable in Ky.

Start good and slow. Won easily; second and third the same.
SEABISCUIT, after following the pace closely, readily drew out in the final eighth to win going away. NEAP slipped through on the inside going to the stretch turn, came to the outside in the stretch and finished stoutly. WHA HAE forced to race on the outside, lost ground in the stretch. TATTERDEMALION was outrun early, closed some ground. KNOWING had no excuse and quit badly in the stretch.
Scratched—Fair Stein, 107; **Sheknows,** 100.
Overweight—Tatterdemalion, 2 pounds.

Owners: (4) Wheatley Stable; (1) Brookmeade Stable; (5) W Ziegler Jr; (6) C V Whitney; (3) Mrs C O Iselin; (2) G S Preece
©DAILY RACING FORM/EQUIBASE

See page 15 for related story

1936
Race Charts

Mohawk Claiming Stakes
Purse: $2,000 Added

Fifth Race Saratoga - August 3, 1936

Purse $2,000 added. Three-year-olds and upward. 1 Mile. Main Track. Track: Fast.

Net value to winner $2,960; second, $400; third, $200; fourth, $100.

Horse	A	Wgt	Eqp	Odds	PP	St	1/4	1/2	3/4	Str	Fin	Jockey
Seabiscuit	3	109	wb	4.00	1	1	$1^{1/2}$	$1^{1\,1/2}$	1^{1}	1^{3}	1^{6}	J Stout
Ann O'Ruley	4	112	wb	4.00	3	4	5^{nk}	5^{1}	$5^{1\,1/2}$	$3^{1/2}$	2^{2}	J Gilbert
Balkan Land	3	109	wb	5.00	6	2	$2^{1/2}$	4^{5}	$3^{1/2}$	2^{h}	3^{2}	S Renick
Goldeneye	3	109	wb	5.00	2	3	7	$6^{1/2}$	6^{3}	5^{2}	4^{nk}	I Hanford
Kate	6	112	wb	2.00	7	5	$3^{1\,1/2}$	2^{h}	4^{1}	6^{4}	5^{4}	R Merritt
Jair	3	100	wb	8.00	5	7	$4^{1/2}$	$3^{1\,1/2}$	2^{2}	4^{nk}	6^{2}	R Kastner
Captain Jinks	3	102	w	15.00	4	6	6^{2}	7	7	7	7	I Anderson

Off Time: 5:08 **Time Of Race:** :24 3/5 :48 1/5 1:12 4/5 1:38 3/5
Start: Good and slow **Track:** Fast
Equipment: w for whip; b for blinkers

Winner: Seabiscuit, b. c. by Hard Tack—Swing On, by Whisk Broom II (Trained by J. Fitzsimmons, Jr.). Bred by Wheatley Stable in Ky. Winner entered to be claimed for $6,000.

Start good and slow. Won easily; second and third driving.
SEABISCUIT was rated along under steady restraint, shook off opposition in the stretch and drew away, winning with speed in reserve. ANN O'RULEY was taken under restraint when outrun and was steered to the outside rounding the stretch turn, then finished well to outlast BALKAN LAND. The latter, close up on the inside in the early running, was eased back passing the half-mile post and was placed under urging through the stretch. GOLDENEYE, outrun early, was steered through on the inside in the stretch and finished well. KATE was rushed into contention, made a determined bid when called upon and then tired from her early efforts. JAIR was close up from the start, then quit in the stretch run. CAPTAIN JINKS had no mishaps and was outrun.
Scratched—Purple Knight, 111; Quel Jeu, 108; Chatmoss, 111; Treford, 114.
Overweight—Captain Jinks, 2 pounds.

Owners: (1) Wheatley Stable; (3) Mrs A A Baroni; (6) A G Vanderbilt; (2) Mrs F A Clark; (7) Howe Stable; (5) Mrs A Phillips; (4) H W Jackson

©DAILY RACING FORM/EQUIBASE

See page 16 for related story

Governor's Handicap
Purse: $5,000 Added

Sixth Race Detroit - September 7, 1936

Purse $5,000 added. Three-year-olds and upward. 1 1-8 Miles. Main Track. Track: Fast.

Net value to winner $4,290; second, $800; third, $400; fourth, $200.

Horse	A	Wgt	Eqp	Odds	PP	St	1/4	1/2	3/4	Str	Fin	Jockey
Seabiscuit	3	109	wb	4.90	12	5	3^3	2^3	$2^{11/2}$	$1^{1/2}$	1^{nk}	J Pollard
Professor Paul	3	99	wb	†4.20	3	11	10^5	8^h	8^1	2^h	$2^{11/2}$	C Hanauer
Azucar	8	112	wb	7.90	9	9	$9^{1/2}$	10^{10}	$6^{1/2}$	4^1	3^3	L Hardy
Biography	5	104	wb	§9.80	1	1	$2^{1/2}$	1^h	1^h	$3^{1/2}$	$4^{1/2}$	F Grill
Paradisical	4	108	w	8.70	11	6	$6^{11/2}$	5^2	3^1	5^1	5^h	G Smith
Safe and Sound	5	103	w	24.10	10	8	$7^{11/2}$	6^3	7^h	$7^{1/2}$	$6^{1/2}$	F Chojnacki
Cristate	4	106	w	†	5	10	8^6	$7^{1/2}$	9^1	$8^{1/2}$	7^h	C Mojena
Marynell	5	104	w	18.40	7	4	5^h	4^h	4^h	6^h	$8^{1/2}$	J Nolan
Woodlander	5	100	w	§	2	12	12	1^{12}	$1^{11/2}$	$9^{1/2}$	$9^{1/2}$	R Morris
Finance	4	120	w	2.40	8	3	1^h	$3^{1/2}$	5^h	10^1	10^1	J Mattioli
Heart Break	6	101	w	30.90	4	2	4^1	9^h	10^h	11^1	11^3	T Meloche
Alsang	3	95	wb	45.20	6	7	$1^{11/2}$	12	12	12	12	A Schmidt

† Coupled as Mrs. J. Chesney entry; § B. Hernandez entry.

Off Time: 5:40   Time Of Race: :23⅗ :47 1:12 1:38 1:50⅗

Start: Good and slow   Track: Fast

Equipment: w for whip; b for blinkers

Mutuel Payoffs

Seabiscuit	$11.80	$5.80	$3.80
Mrs. J. Chesney entry		4.40	3.20
Azucar			4.80

Winner: Seabiscuit, b. c. by Hard Tack—Swing On, by Whisk Broom II (Trained by T. Smith). Bred by Wheatley Stable in Ky.

Start good and slow. Won driving; second and third the same.

SEABISCUIT, a strong factor from the start, responded to strong urging when reaching the lead in the stretch and withstood PROFESSOR PAUL. The latter, far back early, moved up fast after five-eighths, was forced to lose ground at the stretch turn, was put to strong urging when straightened and finished strongly. AZUCAR, outrun for three-quarters, moved up fast thereafter. BIOGRAPHY, used up in the pace, tired under pressure. PARADISICAL tired after improving her position. SAFE AND SOUND made up ground. CRISTATE had no mishaps. MARYNELL showed little.

Scratched—Myrtlewood, 126.

Overweight—Paradisical, 3 pounds; Marynell, 3; Woodlander, 2; Heart Break, 5; Alsang, 3.

Owners: (12) Mrs C S Howard; (3) Mrs J Chesney; (9) F M Alger Jr; (1) B Hernandez; (11) I J Collins; (10) H W and W J Young; (5) Mrs J Chesney; (7) Long Run Stable; (2) B Hernandez; (8) Mrs E Denemark; (4) Coward & Coffey; (6) A C Ernst

©DAILY RACING FORM/EQUIBASE

See page 17 for related story

Hendrie Handicap
Purse: $2,500 Added

Sixth Race Detroit - September 26, 1936
Purse $2,500 added. Three-year-olds and upward. 1 1-16 Miles. Main Track. Track: Fast.
Net value to winner $2,010; second, $450; third, $200; fourth, $150.

Horse	A	Wgt	Eqp	Odds	PP	St	1/4	1/2	3/4	Str	Fin	Jockey
Seabiscuit	3	115	wb	2.10	2	2	2^1	2^1	1^1	1^2	1^4	J Pollard
Cristate	4	114	w	†3.50	1	4	4^1	3^h	3^1	$2^{1/2}$	$2^{21/2}$	E Rodriguez
Safe and Sound	5	108	w	6.70	3	5	5^6	5^8	$2^{1/2}$	3^3	3^3	A Fernandez
Paradisical	4	114	w	2.00	5	1	3^h	$4^{1/2}$	5^8	4^h	4^2	L Hardy
Marynell	5	106	w	7.90	4	3	$1^{1/2}$	$1^{1/2}$	4^h	5^3	$5^{1/2}$	H Manifold
Professor Paul	3	113	wb	†	6	6	6	6	6	6	6	J Nolan

† Coupled as Mrs. J. Chesney entry.

Off Time: 5:19   **Time Of Race:** :24⅘ :48⅘ 1:13 1:38⅖ 1:44⅖
Start: Good and slow   **Track:** Fast
Equipment: w for whip; b for blinkers

Mutuel Payoffs

Seabiscuit	$6.20	$4.40	$2.80
Mrs. J. Chesney entry		3.40	2.40
Safe and Sound			2.80

Winner: Seabiscuit, b. c. by Hard Tack—Swing On, by Whisk Broom II (Trained by T. Smith).
         Bred by Wheatley Stable in Ky.

Start good and slow. Won easily; second and third driving.
SEABISCUIT, saved when outrun, responded fast after five-eighths, took command when ready, drew out steadily and won easily.
CRISTATE, never far back and on the inside, finished strongly. SAFE AND SOUND taken back when outrun, moved up fast on the
outside and tired after offering a mild bid approaching the stretch. PARADISICAL tired. MARYNELL was done after three-quarters.
PROFESSOR PAUL was outrun.
Scratched—Gyral, 110; Alsane, 95; Sir Michael, 104; Lookabout, 98.
Overweight—Marynell, 1 pound.

Owners: (2) Mrs C S Howard; (1) Mrs J Chesney; (3) H W and W J Young; (5) I J Collins; (4) Long Run Stable; (6) Mrs J Chesney

©DAILY RACING FORM/EQUIBASE

See page 18 for related story

Scarsdale Handicap
Purse: $5,000 Added

Fourth Race   Empire City - October 24, 1936

$5,000 added. Three-year-olds and upward. 1 Mile and 70 Yards. Main Track. Track: Fast.

Net value to winner $5,570; second, $1,000; third, $500; fourth, $250.

Horse	A	Wgt	Eqp	Odds	PP	St	1/4	1/2	3/4	Str	Fin	Jockey
Seabiscuit	3	116	wb	†8.00	2	1	7^3	$8^{1/2}$	8^1	6^3	1^n	J Pollard
Jesting	6	112	wb	5.00	8	8	6^{nk}	1^h	1^3	1^2	2^h	S Renick
Piccolo	3	105½	wb	8.00	9	9	10^2	10^1	7^1	2^h	3^3	I Anderson
Steel Cutter	4	106	w	7.00	1	2	8^1	6^1	$5^{1/2}$	5^h	4^h	H Dabson
Wha Hae	3	109	wb	††8.00	5	3	1^2	$2^{1/2}$	$2^{11/2}$	3^h	5^h	S Rossi
Prince Abbot	6	112½	wb	15.00	7	11	$1^{11/2}$	1^1	9^2	9^3	$6^{1/2}$	E Arcaro
Emileo	3	116	wb	5.00	3	7	5^h	4^{nk}	4^{nk}	$4^{11/2}$	7^1	A Cooper
Esposa	4	115	wb	§	4	10	9^1	9^1	$6^{11/2}$	8^2	8^5	R Kastner
Sgt. Byrne	5	119	wb	3.50	6	4	$4^{11/2}$	3^2	3^1	7^1	9^2	F Horn
Exhibit	4	113	wb	†	10	6	3	7^{nk}	10	10	10	C Hanford
Snow Fox	3	116	wb	2.50	11	5	2^h	5^h	Broke down.			W D Wright

†Coupled as Mrs. C.S. Howard entry; § W. Ziegler, Jr. and Middleburg Stable entry.

Off Time: 4:00   **Time Of Race:** :23¾ :47½ 1:12¼ 1:39½ 1:44
Start: Good and slow   **Track:** Fast
Equipment: w for whip; b for blinkers

Winner: Seabiscuit, b. c. by Hard Tack—Swing On, by Whisk Broom II (Trained by T. Smith).
Bred by Wheatley Stable in Ky.

Start good and slow. Won driving; second and third the same.
SEABISCUIT, clear of interference, worked his way up steadily, responded gamely when straightened out in the stretch and wore down JESTING in the final strides. The latter moved up with a rush nearing the far turn, bore over and caused a jam, in which SGT. BYRNE and SNOW FOX were the principal sufferers, drew away and then faltered in the final drive. PICCOLO, from a slow start, improved his position on the inside, saved much ground coming for home and finished well. STEEL CUTTER was eased back at the first turn, improved his position and finished well after being bothered near the far turn. WHA HAE was rushed into command after the break, showed speed under restraint, but quit badly at the end. EMILEO was moving up gamely near the far turn when bothered and forced back. ESPOSA lost ground rounding the stretch turn. SGT. BYRNE was knocked off his stride at the far turn and then quit badly thereafter. EXHIBIT quit under urging. SNOW FOX was going strong when interfered with and knocked back. He broke down and was pulled up.
Scratched—Thorson, 109.
Overweight—Piccolo, 1½ pounds; Prince Abbot, 2½.

Owners: (2) Mrs C S Howard; (8) Mrs E D Jacobs; (9) C V Whitney; (1) T B Townsend; (5) W Ziegler Jr; (7) J B Partridge; (3) Orienta Stable; (4) Middleburg Stable; (6) J Simonetti; (10) Mrs C S Howard; (11) H W Jackson

See page 18 for related story

Bay Bridge Handicap
Purse: $2,500 Added

Seventh Race   Bay Meadows - November 28, 1936
Purse $2,500 added. All ages. 1 Mile. Main Track. Track: Fast.
Net value to winner $1,970; second, $500; third, $200; fourth, $100.

Horse	A	Wgt	Eqp	Odds	PP	St	1/4	1/2	3/4	Str	Fin	Jockey
Seabiscuit	3	116	wb	2.20	6	8	8	5^h	2^h	1^h	1^5	J Pollard
Uppermost	4	114	w	2.40	8	3	4^h	3^h	$3^{11/2}$	$2^{1/2}$	$2^{1/2}$	S Young
Velociter	5	107	wb	8.30	2	1	2^1	$2^{11/2}$	1^2	$3^{11/2}$	3^{nk}	A Gray
Noble Count	3	108	w	3.40	4	2	1^1	1^h	$4^{11/2}$	4^3	$4^{11/2}$	B James
Wildland	3	105	wb	17.60	3	7	$5^{11/2}$	4^h	5^1	5^2	$5^{11/2}$	R Neves
Watersplash	4	104	w	23.60	7	4	6^h	8	8	8^2	6^h	V Thompson
Coldwater	5	106	wb	17.90	5	5	7^2	7^2	$7^{11/2}$	6^h	7^{34}	R Jones
Arson	5	108	wb	18.60	1	6	3^h	$6^{11/2}$	6^1	7^h	8	C Rosengarten

Off Time: 4:15   **Time Of Race:**   :23⅖   :46⅘   1:11⅘   1:36 (new track record)
Start: Good and slow   **Track:** Fast
Equipment: w for whip; b for blinkers

Mutuel Payoffs

Seabiscuit	$6.40	$3.60	$3.20
Uppermost		3.40	2.80
Velociter			3.60

Winner: Seabiscuit, b. c. by Hard Tack—Swing On, by Whisk Broom II (Trained by T. Smith).
Bred by Wheatley Stable in Ky.

Start good and slow. Won eased up; second and third driving.
SEABISCUIT, shuffled back at the start, was last around the first turn and in close quarters when he attempted to get through rounding the turn, was forced to take up, then moved up with a rush when clear in the back stretch and, although carried wide on the stretch turn, easily headed UPPERMOST at midstretch to draw out and was taken in hand in the last fifty yards to win eased up. UPPERMOST ran a strong race to take command in the stretch, but was no match for the winner, although carrying her weight well to the end. VELOCITER followed NOBLE COUNT under restraint to the stretch turn, then dashed into a good lead and went gamely to the end. NOBLE COUNT was used up making the pace and tired. COLDWATER bore out on the back stretch and carried WATERSPLASH with him. WILDLAND and ARSON seemed outclassed.
Scratched—Wacoche, 109.
Overweight—Arson, 1 pound.

Owners: (6) Mrs C S Howard; (8) H C Hatch; (2) Hynes & Beezley; (4) Mrs M C Rush; (3) F M Carr; (7) Childs & Walker; (5) Mrs R
F Carman Jr; (1) T Donley
©DAILY RACING FORM/EQUIBASE

See page 19 for related story

World's Fair Handicap
Purse: $10,000 Added

Seventh Race   Bay Meadows - December 12, 1936
Purse $10,000 added. All ages. 1 3-16 Miles. Main Track. Track: Fast.
Net value to winner $8,000; second, $2,000; third, $1,000; fourth, $500.

Horse	A	Wgt	Eqp	Odds	PP	St	1/2	3/4	1	Str	Fin	Jockey
Seabiscuit	3	113	wb	1.10	4	3	1^5	1^3	1^6	1^3	1^5	J Pollard
Wildland	3	101	wb	14.80	1	1	7	5^1	$3^{11/2}$	2^3	$2^{21/2}$	R Neves
Giant Killer	3	107	wb	†1.60	3	6	6^2	6^h	$4^{1/2}$	$3^{1/2}$	$3^{11/2}$	J Longden
Noble Count	3	106	w	12.90	2	2	2^h	2^1	2^h	4^2	$4^{11/2}$	B James
Watersplash	4	101	wb	44.80	5	4	4^h	$4^{1/2}$	5^4	5^5	$5^{21/2}$	C Swain
Tick On	7	115	wb	6.90	6	5	3^h	7	7	6^8	6^{10}	R Jones
Infantry	3	117	wb	†	7	7	5^2	3^h	$6^{1/2}$	7	7	C Corbett

† Coupled as Millsdale Stable entry.

Off Time: 4:36   **Time Of Race:** :23 :47 1:11⅗ 1:36⅖ 1:55⅘ (new track record)
Start: Good and slow   **Track:** Fast
Equipment: w for whip; b for blinkers

Mutuel Payoffs

Seabiscuit	$4.20	$3.40	$2.20
Wildland		8.20	3.00
Giant Killer			2.20

Winner: Seabiscuit, b. c. by Hard Tack—Swing On, by Whisk Broom II (Trained by T. Smith).
Bred by Wheatley Stable in Ky.

Start good and slow. Won easily; second and third driving.
SEABISCUIT raced to the front when ready to make a show of his opposition and, never menaced, was well in hand. WILDLAND, showing a strong effort, moved up in courageous fashion after leaving the back stretch and, while no match for the winner, acquitted himself creditably. GIANT KILLER was well up from the start and had no excuses. NOBLE COUNT tired when the real racing began. TICK ON did not appear to be in his best form and never threatened. INFANTRY was done after making a brief bid in the back stretch. WATERSPLASH was outclassed.
Scratched—Coldwater, 102.
Overweight—Giant Killer, 1 pound; Watersplash, 1.

Owners: (4) Mrs C S Howard; (1) F M Carr; (3) Millsdale Stable; (2) Mrs M C Rush; (5) Childs & Walker; (6) N S McCarthy; (7) Millsdale Stable

©DAILY RACING FORM/EQUIBASE

See page 20 for related story

1937

Race Charts

Santa Anita Handicap
Purse: $100,000 Added

Sixth Race Santa Anita Park - February 27, 1937

Purse $100,000 added. Three-year-olds and upward. 1 1-4 Miles. Main Track (Out of Chute). Track: Good
Net value to winner $90,700; second, $20,000; third, $10,000; fourth, $5,000.

Horse	A	Wgt	Eqp	Odds	PP	St	1/2	3/4	1	Str	Fin	Jockey
Rosemont	5	124	wb	†3.90	17	11	11^{3}	10^{h}	6^{1}	4^{3}	1^{n}	H Richards
Seabiscuit	4	114	w	6.40	3	9	4^{h}	4^{2}	4^{3}	1^{h}	2^{1}	J Pollard
Indian Broom	4	116	wb	††9.60	6	7	8^{h}	$6^{1/2}$	$5^{1 1/2}$	$3^{1 1/2}$	$3^{2 1/2}$	B James
Special Agent	5	113	w	††	9	2	1^{1}	$1^{1 1/2}$	1^{1}	2^{2}	4^{1}	C Corbett
Time Supply	6	122	w	6.90	14	12	12^{h}	11^{h}	$8^{1 1/2}$	5^{2}	5^{5}	A Robertson
Don Roberto	4	104	w	§12.20	16	6	3^{2}	3^{1}	3^{h}	6^{6}	$6^{1/2}$	G Burns
Red Rain	4	116	wb	9.00	4	13	$14^{1 1/2}$	$13^{1 1/2}$	$12^{1/2}$	$8^{1/2}$	$7^{1/2}$	R Workman
Grand Manitou	4	114	w	§	1	1	6^{h}	8^{1}	$7^{1/2}$	$7^{1 1/2}$	8^{h}	A Gray
Gold Seeker	4	110	wb	†	8	17	18	18	17^{1}	9^{3}	9^{5}	M Peters
Watersplash	5	103	w	§	7	16	16^{1}	16^{h}	14^{1}	10^{2}	$10^{1 1/2}$	R Dotter
Goldeneye	4	109	w	§§5.50	12	14	$15^{1 1/2}$	15^{1}	$13^{1 1/2}$	11^{1}	11^{2}	T Luther
Chanceview	5	109	wb	10.60	2	8	$9^{1/2}$	$9^{1 1/2}$	10^{h}	$12^{1 1/2}$	12^{2}	L Knapp
Mr. Bones	4	120	wb	14.80	11	3	$7^{1 1/2}$	$7^{1 1/2}$	$11^{1 1/2}$	13^{h}	13^{h}	L Balaski
Star Shadow	5	113	wb	§§	5	18	17^{h}	$17^{1/2}$	15^{2}	$15^{1/2}$	14^{10}	G Woolf
Accolade	7	116	wb	46.20	13	5	$5^{1/2}$	5^{h}	9^{h}	14^{1}	15^{h}	J O'Malley
Rushaway	4	113	wb	22.30	10	10	$10^{1 1/2}$	$12^{1/2}$	$16^{1 1/2}$	16^{5}	16^{8}	J Longden
Boxthorn	5	112	wb	61.00	15	4	$2^{1 1/2}$	2^{1}	$2^{1/2}$	17^{3}	17^{6}	N Richardson
Sablin	5	109	w	§	18	15	13^{h}	14^{1}	18	18	18	S Young

† Coupled as Foxcatcher Farms entry; †† A.C.T. Stock Farm entry; §Mutuel field; §§ Silver State Stable entry.

Off Time: 4:22 **Time Of Race:** :22⅖ :45⅘ 1:10⅘ 1:36⅘ 2:02⅘
Start: Good and slow **Track:** Good
Equipment: w for whip; b for blinkers

Mutuel Payoffs			
Foxcatcher Farms entry	**$9.80**	**$6.00**	**$4.00**
Seabiscuit		**8.40**	**6.80**
A. C. T. Stock Farm entry			**5.80**

Winner: Rosemont, b. h. by The Porter—Garden Rose, by Colin (Trained by R. E. Handlen).
Bred by Foxcatcher Farms.

Start good and slow. Won driving; second and third the same.
ROSEMONT, well rated in the early running, gained steadily when called on and in a brilliant finish caught SEABISCUIT in the closing strides. SEABISCUIT was in close quarters at the start, but responded quickly and, taken to the rail gained a prominent position rounding the first turn, then followed the pace under steady rating to the stretch, where he went to the front, but, although going gamely to the end and saving ground, could not resist the winner. INDIAN BROOM was on the inside through the back stretch and was lucky to escape serious interference, but came gamely in the run home and was going well at the end. SPECIAL AGENT wore down BOXTHORN in the early running to open up a good lead but tired in the stretch. TIME SUPPLY was slow to get in stride and was in rather close quarters in the back stretch but moved up strongly after rounding the stretch turn and was going well at the end. DON ROBERTO showed good speed and held on well to show a fine effort. RED RAIN was slow to get going and was never a serious contender. STAR SHADOW broke slowly and never threatened. GOLD SEEKER made up some ground. GRAND MANITOU ran a good race. WATERSPLASH, although outclassed, performed fairly well. CHANCEVIEW broke out at the start to interfere with SEABISCUIT and was never a serious contender. MR. BONES could not keep up. ACCOLADE tired in the stretch.
Overweight—Watersplash, 1 pound; Star Shadow, 3.

Owners: (17) Foxcatcher Farms; (3) Mrs C S Howard; (6) A C T Stock Farm; (9) A C T Stock Farm; (14) F A Carreaud; (16) Why Worry Farm; (4) C V Whitney; (1) R Walsh; (8) Foxcatcher Farms; (7) M C Walker; (12) Silver State Stable; (2) A G Vanderbilt; (11) J H Whitney; (5) Silver State Stable; (13) D Christmas; (10) A G Tarn; (15) E & W Janss; (18) Estate E F Seagram

©DAILY RACING FORM/EQUIBASE

See page 22 for related story

San Juan Capistrano Handicap
Purse: $10,000 Added

Sixth Race   Santa Anita Park - March 6, 1937
Purse $10,000 added. Three-year-olds and upward. 1 1-8 Miles. Main Track. Track: Fast
Net value to winner $9,200; second, $2,000; third, $1,000; fourth, $500.

Horse	A	Wgt	Eqp	Odds	PP	St	1/4	1/2	3/4	Str	Fin	Jockey
Seabiscuit	4	120	wb	1.50	2	1	2^6	$2^{11/2}$	$2^{41/2}$	1^4	1^7	J Pollard
Grand Manitou	4	108	w	46.60	10	6	$4^{11/2}$	4^h	4^4	3^h	2^{34}	A Gray
Special Agent	5	116	w	†1.70	9	2	1^2	$1^{11/2}$	1^h	2^4	3^{nk}	C Corbett
Indian Broom	4	118	wb	†	7	9	6^6	3^h	$3^{11/2}$	4^3	4^3	G Woolf
Red Rain	4	114	wb	12.90	4	4	5^h	$6^{11/2}$	$5^{1/2}$	5^h	5^2	R Workman
Goldeneye	4	107	wb	§10.50	3	7	9^6	8^h	7^2	7^6	$6^{1/2}$	C Schultz
Silk Mask	5	105	w	19.50	6	3	3^h	5^2	6^h	6^h	7^4	L Guymon
Star Shadow	5	110	wb	§	5	8	8^h	$7^{11/2}$	8^5	8^2	8^2	R Dotter
Gold Seeker	4	110	wb	12.60	8	10	10	10	10	9^2	9^8	M Peters
Chanceview	5	112	wb	16.10	1	5	7^h	9^5	9^1	10	10	L Knapp

† Coupled as A. C. T Stock Farm entry; § Silver State Stable entry.

Off Time: 4:42   Time Of Race: :22⅖   :46¼   1:11   1:36½   1:48⅘ (new track record).
Start: Good and slow   Track: Fast
Equipment: w for whip; b for blinkers

Mutuel Payoffs

Seabiscuit	$5.00	$4.00	$2.80
Grand Manitou		35.00	5.60
A. C. T. Stock Farm entry			2.40

Winner: Seabiscuit, b. c. by Hard Tack—Swing On, by Whisk Broom II (Trained by T. Smith).
Bred by Wheatley Stable in Ky.

Start good and slow. Won easily; second and third driving.
SEABISCUIT followed the pace of SPECIAL AGENT closely through the back stretch while under restraint and, taking command when ready around the stretch turn, opened up as he pleased in the stretch to finish well in hand. GRAND MANITOU was always close to the pace and showed an exceptionally game effort to finish well. SPECIAL AGENT showed fine speed in pacemaking, but tired in the stretch. INDIAN BROOM was close enough in the early part, but failed to display his usual closing dash. RED RAIN was never a dangerous contender. The others were outrun all the way and seemed outclassed.

Owners: (2) Mrs C S Howard; (10) R Walsh; (9) A C T Stock Farm; (7) A C T Stock Farm; (4) C V Whitney; (3) Silver State Stable; (6) Rosedale Stable; (5) Silver State Stable; (8) Foxcatcher Farms; (1) A G Vanderbilt

©DAILY RACING FORM/EQUIBASE

See page 24 for related story

Marchbank Handicap
Purse: $10,000 Added

Sixth Race   Tanforan - April 17, 1937

Purse $10,000 added. Three-year-olds and upward. 1 1-8 Miles. Main Track. Track: Fast.

Net value to winner $8,200; second, $2,000; third, $1,000; fourth, $500.

Horse	A	Wgt	Eqp	Odds	PP	St	1/4	1/2	3/4	Str	Fin	Jockey
Seabiscuit	4	124	wb	.40	7	2	1^4	1^5	1^2	1^4	1^3	J Pollard
Grand Manitou	4	110	w	29.30	4	4	6^{12}	6^{20}	5^h	2^h	2^h	D Summers
Sobriety	4	109	w	28.20	5	5	$4^{1/2}$	5^h	6^{30}	$3^{1/2}$	3^5	A Gray
Special Agent	5	113	wb	†2.50	3	1	3^4	$3^{11/2}$	$3^{1/2}$	4^8	4^6	N Richardson
Don Roberto	4	108	w	13.00	2	6	5^h	4^h	4^h	$5^{1/2}$	$5^{11/4}$	G Burns
Sir Oracle	3	103	wb	31.90	6	3	2^3	2^4	2^h	6	6	V Thompson
Indian Broom	4	116	wb	†	1	7	7	7	7	Pulled up.		R Neves

† Coupled as A. C. T. Stock Farm entry.

Off Time: 5:03   **Time Of Race:**   :22⅗ :45⅗ 1:10⅗ 1:36   1:48⅘
Start: Good and slow   **Track:** Fast
Equipment: w for whip; b for blinkers

Mutuel Payoffs

Seabiscuit	$2.80	$3.00	$2.80
Grand Manitou		11.00	8.20
Sobriety			7.40

Winner: Seabiscuit, b. c. by Hard Tack—Swing On, by Whisk Broom II (Trained by T. Smith).
Bred by Wheatley Stable in Ky.

Start good and slow. Won easily; second and third driving.
SEABISCUIT raced to the front soon after the start, was taken in hand after racing to a good lead rounding the first turn and, given a breathing spell around the far turn, was never fully extended and won well in hand. GRAND MANITOU moved up fast between horses after leaving the back stretch and, standing a hard stretch drive, gamely bested SOBRIETY. The latter made his move with GRAND MANITOU and finished with courage. SPECIAL AGENT lacked his usual early speed, but made a strong move after leaving the back stretch, only to tire in the final drive. DON ROBERTO was off rather slowly and made a good move approaching the far turn, but quit when put to a drive in the stretch. SIR ORACLE was closest to SEABISCUIT for the first half mile, but dropped back when the real racing began. INDIAN BROOM stumbled right after the start and, in close quarters while racing up on DON ROBERTO's flank going to the first turn, went to his knees and almost unseated his rider, losing all chance and just galloping far back in the field thereafter to be pulled up in the stretch.
Scratched—Watersplash, 100.
Overweight—Sir Oracle, 1 pound.

Owners: (7) Mrs C S Howard; (4) R Walsh; (5) Hunt, Beezley & Boeing; (3) A C T Stock Farm; (2) Why Worry Farm; (6) N W Church; (1) A C T Stock Farm

©DAILY RACING FORM/EQUIBASE

See page 25 for related story

Bay Meadows Handicap
Purse: $10,000 Added

Seventh Race   Bay Meadows - May 22, 1937

Purse $10,000 added. Three-year-olds and upward. 1 1-16 Miles. Main Track. Track: Fast.
Net value to winner $7,530; second, $2,000; third, $1,000; fourth, $500.

Horse	A	Wgt	Eqp	Odds	PP	St	1/4	1/2	3/4	Str	Fin	Jockey
Seabiscuit	4	127	wb	†.10	8	5	2^1	2^3	2^4	$1^{1/2}$	$1^{11/4}$	J Pollard
Exhibit	5	105	wb	†	4	4	6^2	$6^{1/2}$	6^1	4^1	2^n	L Josephson
Watersplash	5	103	w	45.80	7	8	8	8	7^h	5^1	3^1	R Neves
Boxthorn	5	111	wb	17.60	6	3	$1^{1/2}$	1^{nk}	1^1	2^3	4^1	R Tilden
Sallys Booter	5	110	wb	19.10	5	6	5^h	4^h	$3^{21/2}$	$3^{11/2}$	$5^{1/2}$	D Summers
Mickeys Man	5	101	wb	75.80	2	7	7^5	7^6	4^n	6^1	$6^{11/2}$	O Webster
Don Roberto	4	107	w	15.60	1	1	4^1	5^h	8	7^2	7^3	T Sena
Valiant Fox	4	103	wb	23.60	3	2	$3^{11/2}$	3^h	5^h	8	8	V Thompson

† Coupled as Mrs. C. S. Howard entry.

Off Time: 5:53   **Time Of Race:** :24   :47⅗   1:11   1:37⅗   1:44⅗
Start: Good and slow   **Track:** Fast
Equipment: w for whip; b for blinkers

Mutuel Payoffs

Mrs . C. S. Howard entry	$2.20	$3.00	$2.40
Watersplash			7.80

Winner: Seabiscuit, b. c. by Hard Tack—Swing On, by Whisk Broom II (Trained by T. Smith).
Bred by Wheatley Stable in Ky.

Start good and slow. Won easily; second and third driving.

SEABISCUIT acted badly at the post, but broke well and, after following BOXTHORN through the back stretch and around the far turn under steadying restraint, headed the latter in the stretch and was in hand near the finish. EXHIBIT was unable to keep up with the early leaders, but came very fast under hard urging near the finish to best WATERSPLASH. The latter made a strong move in the stretch and was going well at the end. BOXTHORN was rated while racing in front for three-quarters, then drew away slightly when called around the far turn, but tired badly after being headed by the winner. SALLYS BOOTER made a game move around the far turn, but tired in the stretch. DON ROBERTO dropped back after going a half mile. VALIANT FOX also tired. MICKEYS MAN seemed outclassed.
Scratched—Lloyd Pan, 100; Noble Count, 100.
Overweight—Exhibit, 1 pound; Mickeys Man, 1; Valiant Fox, 3.

Owners: (8) Mrs C S Howard; (4) Mrs C S Howard; (7) M C Walker; (6) E & W Janss (5) A Puccinelli; (2) W LeBaron; (1) Why Worry Farm; (3) N W Church

©DAILY RACING FORM/EQUIBASE

See page 26 for related story

Brooklyn Handicap
Purse: $20,000 Added

Fifth Race   Aqueduct - June 26, 1937
Purse $20,000 added. Three-year-olds and upward. 1 1-8 Miles. Main Track. Track: Fast.
Net value to winner $18,025; second, $4,000; third, $2,000; fourth, $1,000.

Horse	A	Wgt	Eqp	Odds	PP	St	1/4	1/2	3/4	Str	Fin	Jockey
Seabiscuit	4	122	wb	3.00	1	3	$1^{1/2}$	1^1	$1^{1/2}$	1^h	1^n	J Pollard
Aneroid	4	122	wb	2.50	9	1	3^2	3^h	2^3	$2^{11/2}$	2^5	C Rosengarten
Memory Book	4	114	wb	5.00	4	6	8^5	8^1	8^1	7^2	3^3	E Arcaro
Maeriel	4	105	wb	15.00	5	5	$5^{11/2}$	5^{nk}	7^2	$4^{1/2}$	$4^{1/2}$	M Sarno
Gold Seeker	4	107	wb	†3.00	3	9	9	9	9	8^1	5^h	J Stout
Bulwark	4	101	wb	40.00	2	2	2^2	$2^{11/2}$	3^1	3^1	$6^{11/2}$	N Wall
Rosemont	5	127	wb	†3.00	6	8	4^h	$4^{11/2}$	5^{nk}	6^{nk}	7^h	M Peters
Rust	5	106	w	20.00	7	7	7^h	7^1	4^h	5^h	8^5	J Longden
Scotch Bun	5	102	wb	20.00	8	4	6^1	$6^{11/2}$	$6^{11/2}$	9	9	S Renick

† Coupled as Foxcatcher Farms entry.

Off Time: 4:15   Time Of Race: :23⅗ :47 1:11⅗ 1:37 1:50½
Start: Good and slow   **Track:** Fast
Equipment: w for whip; b for blinkers

Winner: Seabiscuit, b. c. by Hard Tack—Swing On, by Whisk Broom II (Trained by T. Smith).
    Bred by Wheatley Stable in Ky.

Start good and slow. Won driving; second and third easily.
SEABISCUIT was rushed into command after the start, was rated along steadily, raced BULWARK into defeat, stood a long drive gamely and outlasted ANEROID in the final strides. The latter was taken back under restraint when outrun, improved his position steadily, came to the outside and closed with determination under pressure at the end. MEMORY BOOK began slowly and, outrun the first part, worked his way up steadily, came to the outside in the stretch and made up some ground. MAERIEL, from a slow start, responded to urging when called upon, came through on the inside and finished well. GOLD SEEKER dwelt at the start, was away slowly and closed gamely under urging through the stretch. BULWARK forced the pace from the start and then quit. ROSEMONT moved up with a rush on the inside nearing the far turn, but faltered steadily under pressure and pulled up slightly sore.
Overweight—Bulwark, 3 pounds; Rust, 1.

Owners: (1) Mrs C S Howard; (9) J A Manfuso; (4) Greentree Stable; (5) Maemere Farm; (3) Foxcatcher Farms; (2) H W Jackson; (6) Foxcatcher Farms; (7) L Strube; (8) A G Vanderbilt

©DAILY RACING FORM/EQUIBASE

See page 27 for related story

Butler Handicap
Purse: $20,000 Added

Fifth Race   Empire City - July 10, 1937
Purse $20,000 added. Three-year-olds and upward. 1 3-16 Miles. Main Track. Track: Fast.
Net value to winner $18,025; second, $4,000; third, $2,000; fourth, $1,000.

Horse	A	Wgt	Eqp	Odds	PP	St	1/2	3/4	1	Str	Fin	Jockey
Seabiscuit	4	126	wb	1.00	1	2	$1^{1/2}$	$1^{1/2}$	1^h	$1^{11/2}$	$1^{11/2}$	J Pollard
Thorson	5	107	w	4.00	2	1	6^h	5^4	4^4	2^1	2^3	J Longden
Corinto	5	109	wb	†2.60	3	6	$5^{11/2}$	3^1	2^h	3^1	3^1	H LeBlanc
Esposa	5	108	wb	5.00	5	5	3^1	$2^{1/2}$	3^h	5^{10}	4^1	N Wall
Caught	5	102	wb	20.00	6	4	2	$4^{1/2}$	5^5	4^h	5^{20}	S Renick
Finance	5	119	wb	†	4	3	4^h	6	6	6	6	C Kurtsinger

† Coupled as Mrs. E. Denemark entry.

Off Time: 4:27   **Time Of Race:** :23 :48 1:12 1:38⅗ 1:58⅗
Start: Good and slow   **Track:** Fast
Equipment: w for whip; b for blinkers

Winner: Seabiscuit, b. c. by Hard Tack—Swing On, by Whisk Broom II (Trained by T. Smith).
Bred by Wheatley Stable in Ky.

Start good and slow. Won driving; second and third easily.
SEABISCUIT handled his weight well, raced CAUGHT into defeat, then withstood determined opposition from CORINTO rounding the far turn, holding THORSON safe at the end. The latter was taken under restraint when outrun, worked his way up on the outside, made a determined bid in the stretch run but could not get to the winner. CORINTO was annoyed shortly after the break, moved up when clear, made a determined bid in the stretch, then faltered. ESPOSA was annoyed after the start, slipped through between leaders going to the turn, was again annoyed in the stretch and tired. CAUGHT, fractious at the gate, was guided towards the inside after the start and caused crowding, then tired. FINANCE was caught in close quarters after the start and knocked about. He pulled up lame.
Overweight—Caught, 2 pounds.

Owners: (1) C S Howard; (2) B M Byers; (3) Mrs E Denemark; (5) W Ziegler Jr; (6) J Butler; (4) Mrs E Denemark
©DAILY RACING FORM/EQUIBASE

See page 28 for related story

Yonkers Handicap
Purse: $7,500 Added

Fifth Race Empire City - July 24, 1937
Purse $7,500 added. Three-year-olds and upward. 1 1-16 Miles. Main Track. Track: Fast.
Net value to winner $8,225; second, $1,500; third, $750; fourth, $275.

Horse	A	Wgt	Eqp	Odds	PP	St	1/4	1/2	3/4	Str	Fin	Jockey
Seabiscuit	4	129	wb	.80	2	2	2^{5}	2^{4}	1^{h}	$1^{11/2}$	1^{4}	J Pollard
Jesting	7	108	wb	8.00	6	3	1^{h}	1^{2}	2^{4}	2^{3}	2^{3}	H LeBlanc
Corinto	5	109	wb	6.00	4	4	5^{6}	4^{nk}	3^{1}	3^{3}	3^{3}	J Westrope
Thorson	5	110	w	6.00	5	1	$4^{1/2}$	5^{5}	$5^{11/2}$	5^{1}	4^{1}	E Arcaro
Dark Hope	8	114	wb	6.00	3	5	3^{h}	3^{h}	4^{3}	$4^{11/2}$	5^{h}	E Steffen
Roustabout	6	109	wb	7.00	1	6	6	6	6	6	6	I Hanford

Off Time: 4:18 **Time Of Race:** :23⅗ :47⅖ 1:11⅗ 1:38 1:44⅕ (new track record)
Start: Good and slow **Track:** Fast
Equipment: w for whip; b for blinkers

Winner: Seabiscuit, b. c. by Hard Tack—Swing On, by Whisk Broom II (Trained by T. Smith).
Bred by Wheatley Stable in Ky.

Start good and slow. Won easily; second and third the same.
SEABISCUIT was taken back under restraint when outrun, improved his position when called upon, disposed of JESTING and finished in hand with speed in reserve. JESTING was rushed into command rounding the first turn, showed high speed under restraint and held on well under urging to the end. CORINTO was rated along forwardly from the start and finished well throughout the stretch run. THORSON was called upon going to the far turn and could not menace the leaders. He pulled up lame. DARK HOPE had no mishaps in the running. ROUSTABOUT, a trailer all the way, could not gain when placed under pressure.

Owners: (2) Mrs C S Howard; (6) Mrs E D Jacobs; (4) Mrs E Denemark; (5) B M Byers; (3) J W Y Martin; (1) C V Whitney

©DAILY RACING FORM/EQUIBASE

See page 29 for related story

Massachusetts Handicap
Purse: $50,000 Added

Fifth Race Suffolk Downs - August 7, 1937

Purse $50,000 added. Three-year-olds and upward. 1 1-8 Miles. Main Track. Track: Fast.
Net value to winner $51,780; second, $10,000; third, $5,000; fourth, $2,500; fifth, $1,250.

Horse	A	Wgt	Eqp	Odds	PP	St	1/4	1/2	3/4	Str	Fin	Jockey
Seabiscuit	4	130	wb	1.00	3	1	$3^{11/2}$	2^1	2^2	1^{nk}	1^1	J Pollard
Caballero II	5	108	wb	6.70	6	10	$6^{1/2}$	4^1	3^1	$3^{21/2}$	2^1	H LeBlanc
Fair Knightess	4	108	wb	37.40	7	4	$1^{11/2}$	$1^{21/2}$	1^1	$2^{1/2}$	$3^{21/2}$	R Howell
Grand Manitou	4	104	w	†26.30	13	7	12^3	10^{nk}	7^{nk}	4^h	4^h	J Deering
Calumet Dick	5	116	wb	12.10	5	12	13	13	13	7^{nk}	5^{nk}	J Wagner
Esposa	5	113	wb	15.70	1	2	9^1	$6^{1/2}$	6^{nk}	$6^{11/2}$	$6^{21/2}$	N Wall
Aneroid	4	128	wb	11.70	9	8	8^{nk}	7^{nk}	$4^{1/2}$	5^{nk}	7^{nk}	C Rosengarten
New Deal	6	107	wb	41.60	2	13	$10^{1/2}$	$11^{1/2}$	$10^{11/2}$	9^h	8^{nk}	E Smith
Trouper	4	100	wb	44.10	11	6	2^h	$3^{1/2}$	5^2	10^{nk}	$9^{11/2}$	D Morgan
Sahri II	6	110	w	6.10	10	5	7^1	9^1	9^{nk}	$11^{11/2}$	$10^{1/2}$	M Villena
War Glory	7	108	wb	90.20	8	9	5^1	8^h	$8^{1/2}$	$8^{1/2}$	11^3	W Ray
Black Gift	5	107	wb	†	12	11	$11^{11/2}$	12^2	$11^{11/2}$	12^3	$12^{21/2}$	K Knott
White Cockade	4	110	w	31.90	4	3	4^{nk}	5^{nk}	$12^{1/2}$	13	13	J Westrope

†Mutuel field.

Off Time: 5:19   **Time Of Race:** :23⅕ :47 1:11 1:36 1:49 (new track record)
Start: Good and slow   **Track:** Fast
Equipment: w for whip; b for blinkers

Mutuel Payoffs

Seabiscuit	$4.00	$3.20	$3.20
Caballero II		5.00	4.60
Fair Knightess			11.80

Winner: Seabiscuit, b. c. by Hard Tack—Swing On, by Whisk Broom II (Trained by T. Smith).
Bred by Wheatley Stable in Ky.

Start good and slow. Won ridden out; second and third driving.

SEABISCUIT went to the front at once, was steadied along in close attendance of the pace when FAIR KNIGHTESS raced into command, responded gamely when called upon and, moving to the lead near the eighth post, drew clear at the end. CABALLERO II was slightly restrained early, began improving his position midway down the back stretch and, closing in game fashion, wore down FAIR KNIGHTESS inside the last seventy yards. FAIR KNIGHTESS moved into the lead in the opening eighth, cut out a fast pace, and held on gamely to the end. GRAND MANITOU was unruly at the post, closed a lot of ground and finished with good energy. CALUMET DICK, a trailer until near the stretch, came with a belated rush in the last three-sixteenths. ESPOSA was on the inside, and dropped back going to the first turn. TROUPER had early speed. ANEROID never could reach contention. WAR GLORY swerved to the inside at the start and retired steadily after gaining a forward position. WHITE COCKADE quit.
Scratched—Mucho Gusto, 108.
Overweight—Black Gift, 4 pounds.

Owners: (3) C S Howard; (6) Mrs E D Jacobs; (7) H C McGehee; (13) R Walsh; (5) E K Bryson; (1) W Ziegler Jr; (9) J A Manfuso; (2) Araho Stable; (11) Mrs A R Smith; (10) C Shockley; (8) Mrs F A Carreaud; (12) L Carter; (4) T B Martin

©DAILY RACING FORM/EQUIBASE

See page 30 for related story

Continental Handicap
Purse: $10,000 Added

Fifth Race   Jamaica - October 12, 1937
Purse $10,000 added. Three-year-olds and upward. 1 1-16 Miles. Main Track. Track: Fast.
Net value to winner $9,250; second, $2,000; third, $1,000; fourth, $500.

Horse	A	Wgt	Eqp	Odds	PP	St	1/4	1/2	3/4	Str	Fin	Jockey
Seabiscuit	4	130	wb	1.00	2	2	1^h	1^h	1^{nk}	1^2	1^5	J Pollard
Caballero II	5	117	wb	6.00	3	1	2^h	$2^{1/2}$	$2^{11/2}$	$2^{11/2}$	2^2	A Robertson
Moon Side	5	112	wb	15.00	8	9	10^2	9^{nk}	6^h	4^3	3^1	L Haas
Thorson	5	112	w	10.00	7	3	6^2	4^h	3^h	$3^{1/2}$	4^4	J Longden
Chanceview	5	109	wsb	10.00	5	6	5^{nk}	6^1	9^2	$8^{11/2}$	5^h	S Renick
Preeminent	5	117	wb	20.00	10	5	$4^{11/2}$	$5^{11/2}$	$4^{1/2}$	6^{nk}	6^1	R Workman
Pasha	3	105	w	20.00	12	8	8^h	8^h	10^1	$7^{1/2}$	$7^{1/2}$	F Kopel
Danger Point	3	106	wb	20.00	6	7	9^5	$10^{11/2}$	7^h	$9^{1/2}$	8^2	J Stout
Rust	5	105	w	15.00	1	11	$7^{1/2}$	7^2	8^h	5^h	9^1	E DeCamillas
Two Bob	4	103	w	30.00	9	10	12	12	12	12	10^h	S Hebert
Strabo	3	108½	wsb	8.00	4	12	11^1	11^4	11^3	11^2	11^1	A Cooper
He Did	4	112	wb	6.00	11	4	$3^{1/2}$	$3^{11/2}$	5^1	10^1	12	L Balaski

Off Time: 4:39   **Time Of Race:**   :24   :48   1:12⅖   1:38⅗   1:44⅘
Start: Good and slow   **Track:** Fast
Equipment: w for whip; b for blinkers; s for spurs

Winner: Seabiscuit, b. c. by Hard Tack—Swing On, by Whisk Broom II (Trained by T. Smith).
    Bred by Wheatley Stable in Ky.

Start good and slow. Won easily; second and third the same.
SEABISCUIT slipped through on the inside going to the first turn, showed speed throughout while under steady restraint, shook off opposition when rounding the stretch turn and drew away to win with speed left. CABALLERO II, a forward factor from the start and on the outside of the leader, made a game bid rounding the far turn, but could not overhaul the winner. MOON SIDE was blocked and knocked around going to the first turn, improved his position and then finished well. THORSON moved up when called upon on the back stretch, but faltered at the end. CHANCEVIEW, well up in the early stages, dropped back while on the inside but came again at the end. PREEMINENT was in close quarters rounding the turn into the back stretch and was forced to ease back. PASHA ran in spots. DANGER POINT was bumped rounding the first turn. STRABO broke slowly. HE DID faltered after following the early pace.
Scratched—Fencing, 100.
Overweight—Danger Point, 4 pounds; Strabo, 1½.

Owners: (2) Mrs C S Howard; (3) Mrs E D Jacobs; (8) C Putnam; (7) B M Byers (5) A G Vanderbilt; (10) H P Headley; (12) M Selznick; (6) J D Norris; (1) L Strube; (9) Mrs E Denemark; (4) Mrs C O Iselin; (11) A Hanger

©DAILY RACING FORM/EQUIBASE

See page 31 for related story

Laurel Stakes
Purse: $7,500 Added

Fifth Race   Laurel - October 16, 1937
Purse $7,500 added. All ages. 1 Mile. Main Track. Track: Fast.
Net value to winner $4,275 each; third, $750; fourth, $350.

Horse	A	Wgt	Eqp	Odds	PP	St	1/4	1/2	3/4	Str	Fin	Jockey
†Seabiscuit	4	126	wb	.70	7	5	3^h	2^h	$2^{11/2}$	1^h	$1^{11/2}$	J Pollard
†Heelfly	3	114	w	6.20	6	2	7	7	7	$2^{1/2}$	$1^{11/2}$	G Woolf
Deliberator	4	116	w	24.20	2	3	1^h	$5^{11/2}$	3^h	4^3	3^1	J Wagner
Clingendaal	3	110	wb	4.35	3	4	$5^{11/2}$	$3^{1/2}$	1^{nk}	$3^{11/2}$	$4^{11/2}$	A Shelhamer
Fair Knightess	4	113	wb	9.30	1	6	4^1	4^h	4^{nk}	$5^{11/2}$	5^3	R Howell
Tabitha	5	108	w	§27.15	4	7	6^1	6^1	6^h	6^6	6^6	G Seabo
Floradora	4	108	wb	§	5	1	$2^{1/2}$	1^h	$5^{1/2}$	7	7	J Westrope

† Dead heat. § Mutuel field.

Off Time: 4:10   **Time Of Race:** :24 :47½ 1:12½ 1:37½
Start: Good and slow   **Track:** Fast
Equipment: w for whip; b for blinkers

Mutuel Payoffs

Seabiscuit	$2.40	$2.70	$2.50
Heelfly	3.90	4.00	3.50
Deliberator			8.20

Winner: Seabiscuit, b. c. by Hard Tack—Swing On, by Whisk Broom II (Trained by T. Smith).
Bred by Wheatley Stable in Ky.
Heelfly, b. c. by Royal Ford—Canfli, by Campfire (Trained by L. T. Whitehill).
Bred by Three D's Stock Farm.

Start good and slow. Won driving; third the same.
SEABISCUIT, holding a forward position early and racing on the outside of DELIBERATOR and FLORADORA, rallied strongly to take a slight lead in the last eighth, responded stoutly when unable to get clear and continued stubbornly until the close. HEELFLY, breaking blindfolded, dropped back after rounding the first turn, responded readily when shaken up and, finishing determinedly under a vigorous drive, was on even terms at the close while on the outside of SEABISCUIT. DELIBERATOR was taken back off the pace after reaching the back stretch, rallied nicely when put to a drive and finished with good courage. CLINGENDAAL, caught in tight quarters on the first turn, raced to the outside when taking the lead on the final turn, stayed close to the rail, but tired. FAIR KNIGHTESS was under strong pressure throughout. TABITHA was never able to improve her position. FLORADORA tired after going into the lead at the half-mile post while under light restraint.
Scratched—High Fleet, 108; Aneroid, 123; Infantry, 120; Rough Time, 114; Chanceview, 116.

Owners: (7) Mrs C S Howard; (6) T P Morgan; (2) Everglade Stable; (3) A C Compton; (1) H C McGehee; (4) A J Sackett; (5) E D Shaffer

©DAILY RACING FORM/EQUIBASE

See page 31 for related story

Riggs Handicap
Purse: $10,000 Added

Fifth Race   Pimlico - November 5, 1937
Purse $10,000 added. Three-year-olds and upward. 1 3-16 Miles. Main Track. Track; Fast.
Net value to winner $10,025; second, $1,500; third, $1,000; fourth, $350.

Horse	A	Wgt	Eqp	Odds	PP	St	1/2	3/4	1	Str	Fin	Jockey
Seabiscuit	4	130	wb	†.40	11	4	5^3	4^4	2^4	$1^{11/2}$	1^{nk}	J Pollard
Burning Star	3	114	wb	8.25	8	9	8^h	$6^{1/2}$	$6^{11/2}$	3^h	$2^{3/4}$	W D Wright
Caballero II	5	116	wb	†	10	8	$6^{1/2}$	$5^{1/2}$	5^1	4^h	$3^{1/2}$	E Arcaro
Aneroid	4	119	wb	11.35	1	2	4^1	3^h	1^h	$2^{11/2}$	4^1	C Kurtsinger
Unfailing	3	109	wb	15.50	7	7	9^4	8^1	$7^{11/2}$	5^4	5^2	J Westrope
Firethorn	5	120	wb	22.00	2	11	11	11	8^{nk}	6^3	6^5	H Richards
War Minstrel	3	110	w	45.20	3	1	1^1	$1^{1/2}$	3^{nk}	7^2	$7^{1/2}$	J Wagner
Thorson	5	115	w	57.30	9	3	$7^{1/2}$	9^3	9^3	9^h	8^h	J Longden
Chanceview	5	107	wsb	89.65	6	6	$3^{1/2}$	7^1	10^1	10^1	9^h	B James
Count Stone	4	105	wsb	48.95	4	10	10^2	$10^{1/2}$	11	11	$10^{1/2}$	F Kopel
Infantry	4	110	wb	38.70	5	5	2^3	2^h	4^h	$8^{1/2}$	11	C Corbett

† Mutuel field.

Off Time: 3:31   **Time Of Race:** :23⅗   :47   1:11⅗   1:37   1:57⅗ (new track record)
Start: Good and slow   **Track:** Fast
Equipment: w for whip; b for blinkers; s for spurs.

Mutuel Payoffs

Seabiscuit (Field)	$2.80	$2.30	$2.80
Burning Star		3.40	3.20
Caballero II (Field)			2.80

Winner: Seabiscuit, b. c. by Hard Tack—Swing On, by Whisk Broom II (Trained by T. Smith).
Bred by Wheatley Stable in Ky.

Start good and slow. Won driving; second and third the same.
SEABISCUIT, nicely ridden, was restrained within striking distance of the leaders while racing clear on the outside, entered into contention with the leaders at the turn out of the back stretch, wore ANEROID down slowly when reaching the stretch, then under strong urging outstayed BURNING STAR. The latter, starting slowly, began improving his position midway of the back stretch, circled his field and was wearing the winner down gradually near the end. CABALLERO II, saved a lot of ground at the first turn to reach a good position, responded readily in the last half mile when shaken up and finished gamely under severe punishment. ANEROID was hurried into contention, moved up with a rush to take a slight lead on the final turn, saved ground, but faltered under punishment in the last three-sixteenths. UNFAILING worked his way forward readily after being outrun early and was going strongly in the final drive. FIRETHORN made up a lot of ground in the last half mile after trailing his field. WAR MINSTREL set an extremely fast pace for three-quarters, then tired steadily. THORSON could not reach contention at any time. INFANTRY was used up forcing the fast early pace and quit badly from his efforts.
Scratched—Esposa, 113; Bow and Arrow, 105; Merry Maker, 102.
Overweight—Unfailing, 2 pounds.

Owners: (11) C S Howard; (8) Shandon Farm; (10) Mrs E D Jacobs; (1) J A Manfuso; (7) P Corning; (2) W M Jeffords; (3) Mrs E Denemark; (9) B M Byers; (6) A G Vanderbilt; (4) A H Waterman; (5) Millsdale Stable

©DAILY RACING FORM/EQUIBASE

See page 33 for related story

Bowie Handicap
Purse: $10,000 Added

Sixth Race   Pimlico - November 11, 1937

Purse $10,000 added. Three-year-olds and upward. 1 5-8 Miles. Main Track. Track: Fast.
Net value to winner $9,375; second, $1,500; third, $1,000; fourth, $350.

Horse	A	Wgt	Eqp	Odds	PP	St	1/2	1	1¾	Str	Fin	Jockey
Esposa	5	115	wb	14.85	5	6	$4^{11/2}$	3^h	3^h	3^h	1^n	N Wall
Seabiscuit	4	130	wb	1.25	8	3	5^h	$4^{11/2}$	4^1	1^h	$2^{11/4}$	J Pollard
Burning Star	3	114	wb	2.60	4	7	3^h	7^2	6^3	6^6	3^1	W D Wright
Firethorn	5	116	wb	†5.75	1	8	6^1	$5^{1/2}$	5^h	2^h	4^3	H Richards
Regal Lily	3	109	w	†	6	1	1^1	1^1	1^h	$4^{1/2}$	5^h	M Peters
Caballero II	5	113	wb	8.15	7	2	2^h	2^h	2^1	5^h	6^1	E Arcaro
Red Rain	4	106½	w	27.85	3	5	8	6^h	7^2	7^5	7^8	I Hanford
Challephen	4	107	w	67.80	2	4	7^{nk}	8	8	8	8	J Wagner

†Coupled as W. M. Jeffords entry.

Off Time: 3:24   **Time Of Race:** :25   :50½   1:15½   1:41   2:06⅖   2:32   2:45½ (new track record)
Start: Good and slow   **Track:** Fast
Equipment; w for whip; b for blinkers

Mutuel Payoffs

Esposa	$31.70	$9.80	$4.30
Seabiscuit		3.70	2.60
Burning Star			2.70

Winner: Esposa, ch. m. by Espino—Quick Banter, by Runantell (Trained by M. Brady).
Bred by Mr. W. Ziegler, Jr.

Start good and slow. Won driving; second and third the same.
ESPOSA, never far from the leaders after the start, rallied willingly to a hard drive in the last half mile, obtained racing room on the inside and, closing with determination, was up in the concluding strides. SEABISCUIT, nicely in hand while following the leaders, made a strong bid in the last half mile to reach the front in the last eighth and fought it out desperately to the end. BURNING STAR saved ground wherever possible after being hurried into contention in the first five-eighths and finished with a belated rush after dropping back midway of the back stretch. FIRETHORN loomed up dangerously rounding the final turn and lost ground in the late stages when forced to circle his field. REGAL LILY set a steady pace until caught, then tired when finishing between horses. CABALLERO II had much speed early, then tired when the real test came. RED RAIN lost ground in the last three-quarters and failed to rally. CHALLEPHEN was always outrun.
Scratched—Chanceview, 103; Merry Maker, 100; Thorson, 116.
Overweight—Regal Lily, 1 pound; Red Rain, 2½; Challephen, 1.

Owners: (5) W Ziegler Jr; (8) C S Howard; (4) Shandon Farm; (1) W M Jeffords; (6) W M Jeffords; (7) Mrs E D Jacobs; (3) Gwladys Whitney; (2) W L Brann

See page 35 for related story

San Antonio Handicap
Purse: $7,500 Added

Sixth Race   Santa Anita Park - February 26, 1938
Purse $7,500 added. Three-year-olds and upward. 1 1-8 Miles. Main Track. Track: Fast
Net value to winner $7,125; second, $1,200; third, $600; fourth $300.

Horse	A	Wgt	Eqp	Odds	PP	St	1/4	1/2	3/4	Str	Fin	Jockey
Aneroid	5	118	wb	7.90	4	1	1^1	1^1	1^1	$1^{1/2}$	1^n	C Rosengarten
Seabiscuit	5	130	wb	†.40	5	7	$5^{11/2}$	$4^{11/2}$	$4^{1/2}$	$3^{1/2}$	$2^{11/2}$	R Workman
Indian Broom	5	108	w	26.90	12	3	3^4	3^5	2^1	2^h	3^h	C Corbett
Time Supply	7	114	wb	25.90	13	11	7^1	$5^{11/2}$	5^4	$4^{11/2}$	4^h	E Steffen
Woodberry	4	108	wb	79.10	1	4	2^h	2^h	$3^{1/2}$	5^5	5^5	C Schultz
Frexo	4	110	w	100.20	3	10	11^1	13	10^2	9^6	$6^{11/2}$	C Stevenson
Gosum	4	109	wb	§14.00	9	12	12^h	11^h	8^1	7^h	7^4	A Gray
Calumet Dick	6	116	wb	20.60	6	5	$8^{1/2}$	$7^{1/2}$	6^h	6^h	$8^{1/2}$	A Shelhamer
Today	6	115	wb	27.00	7	9	10^1	$9^{1/2}$	7^3	8^h	$9^{11/2}$	G Woolf
Over the Top	4	112	wb	18.50	11	13	13	12^1	13	$10^{21/2}$	10^2	T Sena
Sahri II	7	109	w	§	8	2	6^h	8^h	9^1	$11^{11/2}$	11^h	F Maschek
Grey Count	4	109	wb	88.70	2	6	4^h	6^1	$11^{11/2}$	12^4	12^8	E Tucker
Limpio	5	110	w	†	10	8	$9^{11/2}$	10^h	12^h	13	13	R Howell

† Coupled as C. S. Howard entry; § N. A. Howard and L. Barker entry.

Off Time: 4:24   **Time Of Race:**   :23⅕   :47   1:11⅗   1:37½   1:50
Start: Good and slow   **Track:** Fast
Equipment: w for whip; b for blinkers

Mutuel Payoffs

Aneroid	$17.80	$3.60	$3.40
C. S. Howard entry		2.40	2.60
Indian Broom			6.00

Winner: Aneroid, b. h. by The Porter—Outburst, by Messenger (Trained by D. K. Kerr).
Bred by Llangollen Stable.

Start good and slow. won driving; second and third the same.
ANEROID broke quickly and, taking a short lead at once, was handled in excellent fashion and had enough left at the end to hold SEABISCUIT. The latter was in a trifle tight place after the start, but soon got his position and was taken under restraint in the back stretch, then made a game move when called upon and, finishing with courage, might have won had the distance been a trifle farther. INDIAN BROOM was always close to the pace and raced well to the finish TIME SUPPLY, turning in an excellent effort, followed the pace closely in the early stages and, making a strong move on the outside of the three horses rounding the stretch turn, was going well at the finish. WOODBERRY acted well at the gate and showed good speed, but was tiring a trifle near the finish. FREXO was outrun early, but closed steadily. GOSUM also finished fairly well. CALUMET DICK pulled up very lame, his rider dismounting and bringing him back to the judges' stand. TODAY was never a contender. OVER THE TOP lacked early speed and was badly outrun. SAHRI II was never dangerous and was hampered somewhat when a bandage came loose in the stretch. GREY COUNT and LIMPIO seemed outclassed.
Scratched—Whichcee, 108.
Overweight—Frexo, 4 pounds; Today, 5; Grey Count, 3.

Owners: (4) J A Manfuso; (5) C S Howard; (12) A C T Stock Farm; (13) Mrs F A Carreaud; (1) L B Combs; (3) R Walsh; (9) N A Howard; (6) E K Bryson; (7) McCarthy and Whitney; (11) A M Koewler; (8) L Barker; (2) E E Fogelson; (10) C S Howard

See page 40 for related story

Santa Anita Handicap
Purse: $100,000 Added

Sixth Race Santa Anita Park - March 5, 1938

Purse $100,000 added. Three-year-olds and upward. 1 1-4 Miles. Main Track (Out of chute). Track: Fast. Net value to winner $91,450; second, $20,000; third, $10,000; fourth, $5,000.

Horse	A	Wgt	Eqp	Odds	PP	St	1/2	3/4	1	Str	Fin	Jockey
Stagehand	3	100	w	††3.60	3	5	$9^{1\frac{1}{2}}$	7^{h}	$4^{\frac{1}{2}}$	3^{5}	1^{n}	N Wall
Seabiscuit	5	130	wb	1.90	12	14	12^{h}	$6^{\frac{1}{2}}$	1^{h}	1^{h}	2^{6}	G Woolf
Pompoon	4	120	w	4.00	11	10	7^{h}	$4^{\frac{1}{2}}$	5^{h}	$4^{2\frac{1}{2}}$	3^{2}	J Gilbert
Gosum	4	108	wb	108.10	10	17	$17^{\frac{1}{2}}$	17^{1}	14^{4}	8^{3}	4^{4}	A Gray
Aneroid	5	120	wb	8.30	7	2	2^{2}	$1^{1\frac{1}{2}}$	$2^{1\frac{1}{2}}$	2^{h}	5^{h}	C Rosengarten
Star Shadow	6	108	wb	§19.80	8	13	$14^{1\frac{1}{2}}$	$10^{\frac{1}{2}}$	8^{1}	6^{h}	6^{h}	C Corbett
Sceneshifter	4	112	w	††	17	12	10^{h}	$8^{1\frac{1}{2}}$	7^{h}	$7^{1\frac{1}{2}}$	$7^{1\frac{1}{2}}$	J Westrope
Warfellow	4	105	wb	†59.70	15	11	15^{1}	$11^{1\frac{1}{2}}$	11^{2}	10^{5}	8^{4}	L Knapp
Woodberry	4	110	wb	148.40	9	6	$4^{\frac{1}{2}}$	2^{h}	3^{1}	5^{2}	9^{2}	L Balaski
Frexo	4	111	w	†	2	4	16^{6}	15^{2}	16^{2}	11^{1}	10^{3}	C Stevenson
Whichcee	4	110	wb	11.20	1	3	1^{h}	3^{2}	$6^{1\frac{1}{2}}$	9^{h}	11^{h}	H Richards
Amor Brujo	6	120	wb	†††39.60	4	16	$11^{\frac{1}{2}}$	$9^{1\frac{1}{2}}$	15^{h}	12^{h}	$12^{\frac{1}{2}}$	F Maschek
Count Atlas	4	109	wb	†	13	8	$5^{1\frac{1}{2}}$	5^{h}	$12^{\frac{1}{2}}$	13^{2}	13^{6}	J Adams
Primulus	5	103	w	†††	6	1	3^{h}	13^{1}	$10^{\frac{1}{2}}$	14^{3}	14^{5}	F Miller
Top Row	7	123	w	§	14	7	6^{1}	$12^{\frac{1}{2}}$	$9^{\frac{1}{2}}$	15^{1}	15^{4}	D Brammer
Time Supply	7	118	wb	25.50	5	18	18	18	17^{2}	16^{3}	16^{5}	E Steffen
Townsman	4	102	wb	†	16	9	8^{h}	16^{h}	13^{1}	$17^{\frac{1}{2}}$	$17^{\frac{1}{2}}$	S Connell
Ligaroti	6	122	wb	42.80	18	15	$13^{1\frac{1}{2}}$	$14^{1\frac{1}{2}}$	18	18	18	A Shelhamer

† Mutuel field. ††Coupled as M. Howard entry; †††Kozinsky Bros and F. Smith entry; §Silver State Stable entry.

Off Time: 4:36 **Time Of Race:** $:22\frac{3}{5}$ $:46\frac{1}{5}$ $1:11\frac{1}{5}$ $1:36\frac{4}{5}$ $2:01\frac{3}{5}$ (new track record)
Start: Good and slow **Track:** Fast
Equipment: w for whip; b for blinkers

Mutuel Payoffs

M. Howard entry	**$9.20**	**$3.80**	**$3.00**
Seabiscuit		**3.40**	**2.80**
Pompoon			**3.40**

Winner: Stagehand, b. c. by Sickle—Stagecraft, by Fair Play (Trained by E. Sande). Bred by Mr. J. E. Widener.

Start good and slow. Won driving; second and third the same.
STAGEHAND soon gained a prominent place and, ridden in excellent fashion, moved up strongly and steadily to challenge SEABISCUIT in the stretch and won narrowly in a hard drive. SEABISCUIT met with serious interference when COUNT ATLAS bore over right after the start, then made a strong move in the back stretch to get to the front on the stretch turn and, hugging the rail in the run home under vigorous handling, barely missed. POMPOON swerved slightly at the start, but got his position early and clearly was not good enough. GOSUM made up much ground to finish fast and gamely. ANEROID had his early speed and got to the front in the back stretch only to tire in the stretch run. STAR SHADOW closed with courage. WHICHCEE raced to the front early and was taken in hand and, having no excuses tired in the stretch. SCENESHIFTER raced steadily, but was never a serious factor. AMOR BRUJO was done after making a brief move in the back stretch. TOWNSMAN and WOODBERRY had speed for seven-eighths then tired. TIME SUPPLY lacked speed at all times and was never a contender. TOP ROW showed a flash of early speed, then dropped back and pulled up very lame. PRIMULUS had some early speed. COUNT ATLAS bore over on SEABISCUIT at the start, then raced to contention, but dropped out of it when the real racing began.
Scratched—Indian Broom, 116.

Owners: (3) M Howard; (12) C S Howard; (11) J H Loucheim; (10) N A Howard; (7) J A Manfuso; (8) Silver State Stable; (17) M Howard; (15) Blue Moon Stable; (9) L B Combs; (2) R Walsh; (1) A C T Stock Farm; (4) Kozinsky Bros; (13) R C Stable; (6) F Smith; (14) Silver State Stable; (5) Mrs F A Carreaud; (16) Jean Chatburn; (18) Binglin Stock Farm Ltd

©DAILY RACING FORM/EQUIBASE

See page 42 for related story

Agua Caliente Handicap
Purse: $12,500 Added

Eighth Race   Agua Caliente - March 27, 1938
Purse $12,500 added. Three-year-olds and upward. 1 1-8 Miles. Main Track. Track: Fast.
Net value to winner $8,600; second, $2,500; third, $1,250; fourth, $750; fifth, $500.

Horse	A	Wgt	Eqp	Odds	PP	St	1/4	1/2	3/4	Str	Fin	Jockey
Seabiscuit	5	130	wb	.30	1	1	1^h	$1^{1/2}$	$1^{11/2}$	1^3	1^2	N Richardson
Gray Jack	5	103	wb	3.90	6	3	3^h	2^h	2^5	2^4	2^h	W Leischman
Little Nymph	5	98	wb	48.60	3	5	$5^{1/2}$	$6^{11/2}$	$5^{1/2}$	$3^{1/2}$	$3^{41/2}$	W L Johnson
Amor Brujo	6	108	wb	8.60	7	6	$6^{11/2}$	$4^{11/2}$	$3^{11/2}$	4^3	4^h	F Maschek
Warfellow	4	103	wb	16.80	5	8	8	7^h	$6^{11/2}$	5^1	5^3	M L Fallon
San Luis Rey	6	99	wb	†20.70	8	4	4^6	3^h	4^2	6^6	$6^{1/2}$	R Adair
Sir Ridgway	6	100	wb	†	4	7	$7^{21/2}$	8	7^5	7^{10}	7^8	R Varner
Top Radio	4	98	wb	28.50	2	2	$2^{1/2}$	5^h	8	8	8	C Bianco

† Coupled as Cox & Ketcham entry.

Off Time: 5:03   **Time Of Race:** :23⅖ :47 1:14⅘ 1:37 1:50⅗
Start: Good and slow   **Track:** Fast
Equipment: w for whip; b for blinkers

Mutuel Payoffs

Seabiscuit	$2.60	$2.20	$2.20
Gray Jack		2.20	2.20
Little Nymph			3.00

Winner: Seabiscuit, b. h. by Hard Tack—Swing On, by Whisk Broom II (Trained by T. Smith).
Bred by Wheatley Stable in Ky.

Start good and slow. won easily; second and third driving.
SEABISCUIT, away in front, took a short lead rounding the first turn, dropped back momentarily in the back stretch when SAN LUIS REY rushed up on the outside, went to the front again when his rider let out a wrap, then continued easily rounding the far turn and steadily drew away to a safe lead to win eased up at the finish. GRAY JACK, closest to the winner after going the first quarter, made a game bid for the lead going through the back stretch, but was no match for the winner, though closing strongly in the final eighth to save second from the fast-closing LITTLE NYMPH. The latter, outrun for the first half mile, closed very fast in the stretch and was catching GRAY JACK at the wire. AMOR BRUJO rushed up on the outside rounding the far turn and raced gamely to midway of the stretch, then tired. WARFELLOW came from far back in the final quarter and was going gamely at the end. SAN LUIS REY forced the pace the first half mile and showed in front for seventy yards in the back stretch, then tired. SIR RIDGWAY was always outrun. TOP RADIO showed good early speed and raced strongly for the first half mile, then quit badly.
Scratched—Marynell, 100.
Overweight—Warfellow, 1 pound; Sir Ridgway, 3; Top Radio, 3.

Owners: (1) C S Howard; (6) E E Fogelson; (3) Mrs R J Murphy; (7) Kozinsky Bros; (5) Blue Moon Stable; (8) Cox & Ketcham; (4) Cox & Ketcham; (2) J W Deel

©DAILY RACING FORM/EQUIBASE

See page 45 for related story

Bay Meadows Handicap
Purse: $15,000 Added

Seventh Race   Bay Meadows - April 16, 1938
Purse $15,000 added. Three-year-olds and upward. 1 1-8 Miles. Main Track. Track: Fast.
Net value to winner $11,270; second, $3,000; third, $1,500; fourth, $750.

Horse	A	Wgt	Eqp	Odds	PP	St	1/4	1/2	3/4	Str	Fin	Jockey
Seabiscuit	5	133	wb	†.20	7	5	2^h	$2^{1/2}$	2^2	1^1	1^3	G Woolf
Gosum	4	113	wb	10.90	3	2	6^3	6^4	5^4	2^3	$2^{13/4}$	A Gray
Today	6	112	wb	9.80	2	3	5^6	$4^{11/2}$	4^h	3^h	3^n	N Merritt
Advocator	4	109	wb	†	4	7	7	7	7	$5^{1/2}$	4^2	B James
Sweepalot	4	109	wb	12.80	1	1	$3^{11/4}$	$3^{1/2}$	$3^{1/2}$	6^1	5^1	J Adams
Primulus	5	105	w	8.60	6	4	1^1	1^h	1^h	4^2	$6^{41/2}$	F Maschek
Don Roberto	5	104	w	33.40	5	6	4^h	5^3	6^h	7	7	T Sena

† Coupled as C. S. Howard entry.

Off Time: 5:43   **Time Of Race:** :23⅗ :47⅖ 1:11⅖ 1:37 1:49 (new track record)
Start: Good and slow   **Track:** Fast
Equipment: w for whip; b for blinkers

Mutuel Payoffs

C. S. Howard entry	$2.40	$2.20	$2.20
Gosum		3.00	2.20
Today			2.20

Winner: Seabiscuit, b. h. by Hard Tack—Swing On, by Whisk Broom II (Trained by T. Smith).
Bred by Wheatley Stable in Ky.

Start good and slow. Won easily; second and third driving.
SEABISCUIT, off well, raced close to PRIMULUS under restraint for the first three-quarters, then gradually forged to the front when given free rein and, shaken up after entering the stretch, easily withstood a mild bid from GOSUM and was going away well in hand at the end. GOSUM was never far from the pace and came very fast rounding the stretch turn in a determined attempt to catch the winner, but was not good enough. TODAY ran his race and responded gamely to urging, continuing well to the finish. ADVOCATOR was going gamely at the end. SWEEPALOT was in rather close quarters rounding the first turn and dropped back when the real racing began. PRIMULUS set a good pace, but was used up and had nothing left for the stretch run, quitting badly. DON ROBERTO was a contender for three-quarters, then dropped back.
Scratched—Indian Broom, 111; Ligaroti, 119; King Saxon, 110; Patty Cake, 104; Count Atlas, 105; Rommy, 100.
Overweight—Primulus, 1 pound.

Owners: (7) C S Howard; (3) N A Howard; (2) N S McCarthy; (4) C S Howard; (1) Mrs H Curland; (6) F Smith; (5) Why Worry Farm

©DAILY RACING FORM/EQUIBASE

See page 47 for related story

Hollywood Gold Cup
Purse: $50,000 Added

Seventh Race Hollywood Park - July 16, 1938

Purse $50,000 added. Three-year-olds and upward. 1 1-4 Miles. Main Track. Track: Fast.

Net value to winner $37,150; second, $10,000; third, $5,000; fourth, $2,000; fifth $1,000.

Horse	A	Wgt	Eqp	Odds	PP	St	1/2	3/4	1	Str	Fin	Jockey
Seabiscuit	5	133	wb	.70	7	8	$9^{2\frac{1}{2}}$	5^{h}	4^{h}	2^{h}	$1^{1\frac{1}{2}}$	G Woolf
Specify	3	109	wb	§3.30	1	1	1^{6}	1^{8}	1^{6}	1^{4}	2^{n}	W D Wright
Whichcee	4	114	wb	†11.00	9	5	$2^{\frac{1}{2}}$	$3^{1\frac{1}{2}}$	$2^{1\frac{1}{2}}$	3^{5}	3^{5}	T Sena
Ligaroti	6	118	wb	3.70	4	7	$4^{1\frac{1}{2}}$	4^{4}	5^{h}	$4^{1\frac{1}{2}}$	$4^{\frac{1}{2}}$	N Richardson
Indian Broom	5	120	w	†	2	3	$3^{1\frac{1}{2}}$	2^{h}	$3^{\frac{1}{2}}$	5^{h}	5^{h}	S Coucci
Warfellow	4	105	wb	128.10	6	10	7^{1}	$6^{\frac{1}{2}}$	6^{4}	6^{6}	6^{h}	M L Fallon
Star Shadow	6	114	wb	§	10	9	10	10	9^{6}	7^{3}	7^{10}	A Gray
Sahri II	7	109	w	54.50	8	2	8^{h}	9^{2}	7^{h}	8^{h}	8^{2}	W Leischman
No Dice	4	105	wb	§	5	6	$6^{\frac{1}{2}}$	8^{h}	$8^{\frac{1}{2}}$	9^{10}	9^{7}	J Adams
Grey Count	4	105	wb	135.30	3	4	5^{1}	7^{h}	10	10	10	O Webster

† Coupled as A. C. T. Stock Farm entry; §Silver State Stable entry.

Off Time: 5:50 **Time Of Race:** :23$\frac{4}{5}$:47$\frac{1}{5}$ 1:11$\frac{2}{5}$ 1:37$\frac{3}{5}$ 2:03$\frac{4}{5}$ (new track record)
Start: Good and slow **Track:** Fast
Equipment: w for whip; b for blinkers

Mutuel Payoffs

Seabiscuit	**$3.40**	**$2.40**	**$2.20**
Silver State Stable entry		**2.60**	**2.20**
A. C. T. Stock Farm entry			**2.40**

Winner: Seabiscuit, b. h. by Hard Tack—Swing On, by Whisk Broom II (Trained by T. Smith).
Bred by Wheatley Stable in Ky.

Start good and slow. Won easily; second and third driving.
SEABISCUIT began racing slowly and between horses going to the first turn, was outrun for one-half mile, then moved fast to loom up dangerously entering the stretch and, cutting to the inside of SPECIFY when the latter bore out in the final eighth, staged a strong charge to get to the front in the last sixteenth and won going away. SPECIFY acted badly at the post, but beat the others away and, after opening up a good lead in the first quarter, increased his advantage on the back stretch, but was used up from his early efforts and, bearing out while tiring in the stretch, barely lasted to save second place. WHICHCEE was never far from the pace, saved ground in the stretch and, going strongly to the end, would have been second in a few more strides. LIGAROTI was bothered on the back stretch, but continued well and showed a creditable effort. WARFELLOW was in rather close quarters on the inside approaching the stretch turn but raced fairly well to the end. STAR SHADOW was badly outrun early and, although making up some ground in the stretch, was never dangerous. NO DICE was never a serious contender. SAHRI II and GREY COUNT seemed to be outclassed.
Overweight—No Dice, 1 pound.

Owners: (7) C S Howard; (1) Silver State Stable; (9) A C T Stock Farm; (4) Binglin Stable ; (2) A C T Stock Farm; (6) Blue Moon Stable; (10) Silver State Stable; (8) L Barker; (5) Silver State Stable; (3) E E Fogelson

©DAILY RACING FORM/EQUIBASE

See page 49 for related story

Special Stake Race
Purse: $25,000

Eighth Race Del Mar - August 12, 1938

Purse $25,000. Winner take all. Match race with Ligaroti. 1 1-8 Miles. Main Track. Track: Fast. Net value to winner $25,000.

Horse	A	Wgt	Eqp	Odds	PP	St	1/4	1/2	3/4	Str	Fin	Jockey
Seabiscuit	5	130	wb		1	1	2	2	1^h	1^h	1^n	G Woolf
Ligaroti	6	115	wb		2	2	1^h	1^h	2	2	2	N Richardson

Off Time: 4:26 **Time Of Race:** :23$\frac{3}{5}$:46$\frac{3}{5}$ 1:10$\frac{4}{5}$ 1:36$\frac{1}{5}$ 1:49 (new track record)
Start: Good and slow **Track:** Fast
Equipment: w for whip; b for blinkers

Winner: Seabiscuit, b. h. by Hard Tack—Swing On, by Whisk Broom II (Trained by T. Smith). Bred by Wheatley Stable in Ky.

Start good and slow. Won driving; second the same.
SEABISCUIT raced to the front at once to open up a short lead, continued gamely on the inside after being headed by LIGAROTI and again took a short lead nearing the stretch turn, but was forced to a hard drive near the finish and was all out to win. LIGAROTI, showing exceptional gameness, took the work of it by racing on the outside of SEABISCUIT all the way and, after being apparently beaten on the stretch turn, came again to be pressing the winner at the finish and seemed to meet with interference in the last few yards. LIGAROTI's rider claimed a foul, which was not allowed.
Overweight—Ligaroti, 1 pound.

Owners: (1) Mrs C S Howard; (2) Binglin Stable

©DAILY RACING FORM/EQUIBASE

See page 51 for related story

Manhattan Handicap
Purse: $5,000 Added

Fifth Race Belmont Park - September 20, 1938
Purse $5,000 added. Three-year-olds and upward. 1 1-2 Miles. Main Track. Track: Muddy.
Net value to winner $4,300; second, $1,000; third, $500; fourth, $250.

Horse	A	Wgt	Eqp	Odds	PP	St	1/2	3/4	1	Str	Fin	Jockey
Isolater	5	108	wb	6.00	3	2	1^{nk}	1^1	1^{nk}	1^{nk}	1^h	J Stout
Regal Lily	4	108	w	6.00	2	4	2^1	$2^{1/2}$	2^3	2^4	2^3	N Wall
Seabiscuit	5	128	wb	.90	4	1	5	5	5	3^5	3^{10}	G Woolf
Handcuff	3	109½	wb	3.50	1	3	$4^{1/2}$	4^{nk}	3^h	4^3	4^2	J Westrope
Piccolo	5	100	w	12.00	5	5	3^1	3^1	4^h	5	5	F A Smith

Off Time: 4:22   **Time Of Race:** :24⅖   :49   1:14   1:39⅓   2:05⅓   2:31
Start: Good and slow   **Track:** Muddy
Equipment: w for whip; b for blinkers

Winner: Isolater, br. h. by Blandford—Priscilla Carter, by *Omar Khayyam (Trained by J. Fitzsimmons).
     Bred by Belair Stud in England.

Start good and slow. Won driving; second and third the same.
ISOLATER set a fast pace from the start and, on the outside all the way, responded to urging in the stretch run and outlasted REGAL LILY in the final drive. The latter, in near pursuit of the pace from the start, saved ground entering the stretch and held on with good courage in the final drive. SEABISCUIT was carried wide rounding the first turn, was taken back under restraint, moved up with determination on the inside rounding the first turn and closed with a rush at the end. HANDCUFF saved ground rounding the first turn, was steered to the outside on the back stretch, lost ground on the stretch turn and then quit at the end. PICCOLO, close up on the outside rounding the first turn, faltered badly and was unable to keep up thereafter.
Overweight—Handcuff, 1½ pounds.

Owners: (3) Belair Stud; (2) W M Jeffords; (4) C S Howard; (1) Brookmeade Stable; (5) R A Moore

©DAILY RACING FORM/EQUIBASE

See page 53 for related story

Havre De Grace Handicap
Purse: $10,000 Added

Fifth Race Havre de Grace - September 28, 1938
Purse $10,000 added. Three-year-olds and upward. 1 1-8 Miles. Main Track. Track: Fast.
Net value to winner $8,175; second, $2,000; third, $1,000; fourth, $500.

Horse	A	Wgt	Eqp	Odds	PP	St	1/4	1/2	3/4	Str	Fin	Jockey
Seabiscuit	5	128	wb	.55	6	2	5^2	$3^{1/2}$	2^h	1^1	$1^{21/2}$	G Woolf
Savage Beauty	4	103	w	116.20	2	1	$2^{1/2}$	2^1	3^3	$2^{11/2}$	2^1	G Seabo
Menow	3	120	wb	5.25	8	3	1^1	$1^{11/2}$	$1^{1/2}$	3^3	$3^{11/2}$	L Haas
Rex Flag	4	111	wb	35.35	7	6	$6^{1/2}$	6^1	4^3	4^4	4^5	J Gilbert
Esposa	6	121	wb	7.75	3	7	$7^{11/2}$	$7^{11/2}$	6^1	$5^{11/2}$	5^1	N Wall
Two Bob	5	104	wb	102.20	1	5	8	8	7^h	6^h	$6^{11/2}$	L Dupps
Marica	5	124	wb	14.00	5	8	4^h	4^h	5^1	7^6	7^8	R Dotter
Masked General	4	114	wb	13.10	4	4	3^h	5^1	8	8	8	J Wagner

Off Time: 4;49 **Time Of Race:** :23⅗ :47⅗ 1:12⅗ 1:37⅘ 1:50
Start: Good and slow **Track:** Fast
Equipment: w for whip; b for blinkers

Mutuel Payoffs

Seabiscuit	$3.10	$3.00	$2.60
Savage Beauty		33.00	12.30
Menow			3.50

Winner: Seabiscuit, b. h. by Hard Tack—Swing On, by Whisk Broom II (Trained by T. Smith).
Bred by Wheatley Stable in Ky.

Start good and slow. won ridden out; second and third driving.
SEABISCUIT, bumped on the paddock turn, recovered quickly to hold a contending position, responded to intermittent punishment in the last half mile, reached the leaders readily, then moved to the front in the last eighth and drew out smartly. SAVAGE BEAUTY, forcing a swift pace while in close pursuit of MENOW, saved ground and held on tenaciously to the close. MENOW set a fast pace while being steadied, but tired in the last quarter mile when he went lame. REX FLAG bettered his position on the outside, but could not reach the leaders. ESPOSA lacked early speed and was never able to enter contention. TWO BOB trailed and was held safe when shaken up, then worked out an additional quarter mile. MARICA was sent up swiftly between horses going to the first turn and caused some crowding. MASKED GENERAL was rated nicely, but failed to stay.
Scratched—Nedayr, 117; Mr. Canron, 109.
Overweight—Savage Beauty, 2 pounds; Rex Flag, 1; Two Bob, 1.

Owners: (6) C S Howard; (2) W L Brann; (8) H P Headley; (7) Mrs L Viau; (3) W Ziegler Jr; (1) Mrs E Denemark; (5) T D Taggart; (4) Brandywine Stable

©DAILY RACING FORM/EQUIBASE

See page 54 for related story

Laurel Stakes
Purse: $7,500 Added

Fifth Race Laurel - October 15, 1938
Purse $7,500 added. All ages. 1 Mile. Main Track. Track: Fast.
Net value to winner $7,825; second, $1,500; third, $750; fourth, $350.

Horse	A	Wgt	Eqp	Odds	PP	St	1/4	1/2	3/4	Str	Fin	Jockey
Jacola	3	102	w	6.90	10	5	5^2	4^{nk}	1^1	$1^{1\frac{1}{2}}$	$1^{2\frac{1}{2}}$	N Wall
Seabiscuit	5	126	wsb	.60	11	6	8^h	6^h	$4^{\frac{1}{2}}$	2^2	2^3	G Woolf
The Chief	3	116	wb	13.45	9	4	7^h	$10^{1\frac{1}{2}}$	$7^{\frac{1}{2}}$	4^3	3^4	J Westrope
Aneroid	5	116	wb	6.50	4	1	2^h	3^1	2^h	3^2	$4^{1\frac{1}{2}}$	R Workman
Grey Gold	4	111	w	48.70	3	10	10^2	8^h	9^{nk}	8^1	5^h	R Howell
Accolade	8	114	wb	14.75	7	3	3^1	2^h	5^1	6^h	6^h	R Dotter
Mr. Canron	4	114	wb	†27.55	2	11	12	12	10^h	10^1	7^1	M Peters
Busy K.	4	118	wb	†	12	12	11^1	11^1	12	9^h	$8^{1\frac{1}{2}}$	R Eccard
Nedayr	3	116	wb	51.75	8	9	9^1	7^h	6^h	7^1	9^{nk}	C Kurtsinger
Mower	5	111	w	†	6	7	4^h	5^2	$8^{\frac{1}{4}}$	11^1	10^1	C Corbett
Finance	6	118	wb	112.45	1	2	1^h	1^h	3^h	5^h	$11^{1\frac{1}{4}}$	M Sarno
Masked General	4	114	wb	49.45	5	8	6^h	$9^{\frac{3}{4}}$	11^1	12	12	J Wagner

†Mutuel field.

Off Time: 4:08 **Time Of Race:** :23⅗ :47⅖ 1:12⅕ 1:37 (new track record)
Start: Good and slow **Track:** Fast
Equipment: w for whip; b for blinkers; s for spurs

Mutuel Payoffs

Jacola	$15.80	$5.20	$3.50
Seabiscuit		2.80	2.60
The Chief			5.00

Winner: Jacola, br. f. by Jacopo—La France, by Sir Gallahad III (Trained by S. L. Burch).
Bred by Mr. A. B. Hancock.

Start good and slow. Won easily; second and third driving.
JACOLA, rated in near pursuit of the leaders, raced to the front with a rush midway of the final turn, drew clear when reaching the stretch, rallied to pressure and came out smartly nearing the finish. SEABISCUIT, forced to race on the outside for racing room to better his position in the first seven-eighths, saved ground entering the stretch, responded to punishment, but could not reach the winner. THE CHIEF took back suddenly midway of the back stretch when caught in tight quarters, swung to the outside and finished with excellent courage. ANEROID was ridden hard to keep pace with FINANCE and he tired in the last five sixteenths. GREY GOLD, beginning slowly, worked his way forward steadily and was going gamely at the finish. ACCOLADE raced on the outside of the leader and was a strong contender for seven-eighths before tiring. MR. CANRON was away slowly and could not menace. BUSY K. was never a factor. NEDAYR raced in very tight quarters most of the trip. MOWER quit badly, as did FINANCE.
Scratched—Idle Miss, 115; Sun Egret, 108; White Cockade, 111; Gerald, 114; Kayak II, 105; Genie Palatine, 108.
Overweight—Aneroid, 2 pounds.

Owners: (10) E Friendly; (11) C S Howard; (9) M Howard; (4) J A Manfuso; (3) E W Duffy; (7) D Christmas; (2) W W Vaughan; (12) D A Wood; (8) W S Kilmer; (6) Millsdale Stable; (1) Mrs E Denemark; (5) Brandywine Stable

©DAILY RACING FORM/EQUIBASE

See page 55 for related story

Pimlico Special
Purse: $15,000

Sixth Race Pimlico - November 1, 1938
Purse $15,000. Seabiscuit and War Admiral. Winner take all. Walk-up start by George Cassidy.
1 3-16 Miles. Main Track. Track: Fast.
Net value to winner $15,000.

Horse	A	Wgt	Eqp	Odds	PP	St	1/2	3/4	1	Str	Fin	Jockey
Seabiscuit	5	120	wb	2.20	2	1	1^1	1^n	1^h	$1^{1/2}$	1^4	G Woolf
War Admiral	4	120	w	.25	1	2	2	2	2	2	2	C Kurtsinger

Off Time: 4:04 **Time Of Race:** :23⅗ :47⅗ 1:11⅘ 1:36⅘ 1:56⅗ (new track record)
Start: Good and slow **Track:** Fast
Equipment: w for whip; b for blinkers

Mutuel Payoffs
Seabiscuit **$6.40** **No place or show betting**

Winner: Seabiscuit, b. h. by Hard Tack—Swing On, by Whisk Broom II (Trained by T. Smith).
Bred by Wheatley Stable in Ky.

Start good and slow. Won driving.
SEABISCUIT and WAR ADMIRAL broke to a walking start with SEABISCUIT being sent into immediate command under pressure and drew clear going to the first turn. He hugged the rail rounding the turn and was placed to pressure after being straightened into the back stretch. Going to the half-mile post WAR ADMIRAL moved up strongly to drive abreast and he made repeated bids under punishment until the stretch was reached. In the last quarter mile SEABISCUIT was lightly punished after stalling off early efforts, then came out resolutely when Woolf urged his mount along at his best clip. WAR ADMIRAL, after joining SEABISCUIT at the half-mile post, failed to get to the front and fell back after reaching the stretch.

Owners: (2) C S Howard; (1) Glen Riddle Farms

©DAILY RACING FORM/EQUIBASE

See page 61 for related story

1940

Race Charts

San Antonio Handicap
Purse: $10,000 Added

Sixth Race Santa Anita Park - February 24, 1940
Purse $10,00 added. Three-year-olds and upward. 1 1-16 Miles. Main Track. Track: Fast.
Net value to winner $10,000; second, $2,000; third, $1,000; fourth $500.

Horse	A	Wgt	Eqp	Odds	PP	St	1/4	1/2	3/4	Str	Fin	Jockey
Seabiscuit	7	124	wb	†1.70	10	6	$5^{1/2}$	$2^{1/2}$	$2^{11/2}$	$1^{1/2}$	$1^{21/2}$	J Pollard
Kayak II	5	128	wb	†	5	7	10^{h}	9^{h}	5^{h}	$4^{11/2}$	$2^{1/2}$	A Shelhamer
Viscounty	4	110	wb	15.90	3	3	4^{1}	3^{h}	$3^{11/2}$	$3^{11/2}$	3^{4}	E Rodriguez
Preceptor II	7	112	w	§11.80	13	8	$9^{1/2}$	7^{h}	6^{2}	5^{3}	4^{2}	L Balaski
Heelfly	6	119	w	3.10	7	10	11^{h}	11^{2}	$8^{11/2}$	7^{3}	5^{h}	G Woolf
Wedding Call	4	110	wb	29.10	9	11	$8^{11/2}$	6^{2}	4^{1}	6^{2}	6^{2}	D Dodson
Anthology	5	110	wb	40.70	8	13	13	13	13	10^{h}	7^{2}	J Longden
No Competition	4	108	wb	16.10	6	4	2^{h}	$5^{11/2}$	7^{1}	8^{2}	$8^{1/2}$	C Bierman
Vino Puro	6	109	wb	6.40	12	5	3^{2}	$1^{1/2}$	$1^{1/2}$	2^{h}	$9^{11/2}$	B James
Arjac	4	104	wb	22.10	1	1	6^{1}	8^{h}	$10^{1/2}$	$9^{1/2}$	$10^{11/2}$	N Wall
Comet II	5	108	w	§	2	9	7^{h}	10^{h}	9^{3}	11^{3}	11^{6}	L Knapp
Sun Lover	4	117	wb	8.40	11	12	12^{6}	12^{6}	$11^{11/2}$	12^{8}	12^{12}	R Neves
Ra II	4	116	w	§	4	2	1^{1}	4^{h}	12^{2}	13	13	M Peters

† Coupled as C. S. Howard entry; § Binglin Stock Farm entry.

Off Time: 4:25 **Time Of Race:** :23⅕ :46⅘ 1:11⅕ 1:36⅖ 1:42⅖ (equals track record).
Start: Good and slow **Track:** Fast
Equipment: w for whip; b for blinkers

Mutuel Payoffs			
C. S. Howard entry	**$5.40**	**$7.80**	**$4.60**
Viscounty			**9.60**

Winner: Seabiscuit, b. h. by Hard Tack—Swing On, by Whisk Broom II (Trained by T. Smith). Bred by Wheatley Stable in Ky.

Start good and slow. Won easily; second and third driving.
SEABISCUIT, close to the pace from the start, moved up steadily after going half the distance and, easily heading VINO PURO when straightened out for home, drew into a safe lead in the last sixteenth. KAYAK II lacked early speed, but came very fast after going half the distance to the finish strongly, but failed to seriously threaten the winner. VISCOUNTY, well up from the start, made a game move after entering the stretch and went in courageous fashion to the finish. HEELFLY lacked early speed to keep up and, while closing some ground, was never a serious contender. VINO PURO showed fine early speed, but was not good enough and tired near the end. SUN LOVER began slowly and was never a serious contender. WEDDING CALL broke slowly and was used up reaching a contending position. ANTHOLOGY was off badly and had little chance. RA II showed fine speed for a half mile, then tired badly and probably needed the race. NO COMPETITION had early speed.
Scratched—Whichcee, 120; Step By, 105; Hysterical, 111; Can't Wait, 109.
Overweight—Preceptor II, 1 pound; No Competition, 1; Vino Puro, 1; Comet II, 2.

Owners: (10) C S Howard; (5) C S Howard; (3) Valdina Farm; (13) Binglin Stock Farm; (7) Circle S Stable; (9) Gaffers & Sattler; (8) G D Cameron; (6) Milky Way Farm; (12) Mrs J F Waters; (1) C M Willock; (2) Binglin Stock Farm; (11) Millsdale Stable; (4) Binglin Stock Farm

©DAILY RACING FORM/EQUIBASE

See page 73 for related story

Santa Anita Handicap
Purse: $100,000 Added

Sixth Race Santa Anita Park - March 2, 1940

Purse $100,000 added and Gold Cup to owner of winner. Three-year-olds and upward. 1 1-4 Miles.
Main Track (Out of chute). Track: Fast.
Net value to winner $86,650; second, $20,000; third, $10,000; fourth, $5,000.

Horse	A	Wgt	Eqp	Odds	PP	St	1/2	3/4	1	Str	Fin	Jockey
Seabiscuit	7	130	wb	†.70	12	5	$2^{1/2}$	2^n	2^h	1^h	$1^{1/2}$	J Pollard
Kayak II	5	129	wb	†	2	13	13	8^1	6^h	$3^{11/2}$	2^1	L Haas
Whichcee	6	114	wb	3.90	6	3	1^1	$1^{1/2}$	1^h	$2^{11/2}$	$3^{11/2}$	B James
Wedding Call	4	108	wb	96.60	1	2	5^h	3^h	3^2	4^1	$4^{1/2}$	D Dodson
War Plumage	4	107	w	26.80	9	7	11^1	10^2	$8^{1/2}$	$8^{1/2}$	$5^{1/2}$	R Neves
Heelfly	6	114	w	10.10	10	10	12^h	11^{112}	10^5	10^1	$6^{1/2}$	G Woolf
Viscounty	4	110	wb	28.20	3	4	$7^{21/2}$	6^1	5^h	$5^{1/2}$	$7^{21/2}$	E Rodriguez
Can't Wait	5	108	wb	34.00	7	9	8^2	$7^{1/2}$	4^h	7^h	8^h	J Longden
Specify	5	116	wb	16.10	5	1	3^h	$5^{11/2}$	9^2	$9^{11/2}$	9^h	H Richards
Royal Crusader	3	104	wb	50.10	13	8	$4^{11/2}$	4^3	$7^{1/2}$	6^4	10^3	L Knapp
Don Mike	6	112	w	§16.80	11	12	9^h	12^6	11^5	11^7	11^{15}	L Balaski
Ra II	5	118	w	§	4	6	6^2	9^h	12^5	12^6	12^7	M Peters
Kantan	3	100	wb	55.10	8	11	10^h	13	13	13	13	N Wall

†Coupled as C. S. Howard entry; § Binglin Stock Farm entry.

Off Time: 4:27 **Time Of Race:** :23 :47½ 1:11½ 1:36 2:01⅓ (new track record)
Start: Good and slow **Track:** Fast
Equipment: w for whip; b for blinkers

Mutuel Payoffs

C. S. Howard entry	$3.40	$2.80	$2.60
Whichcee			3.60

Winner: Seabiscuit, b. h. by Hard Tack—Swing On, by Whisk Broom II (Trained by T. Smith).
Bred by Wheatley Stable in Ky.

Start good and slow. Won driving; second and third the same.
SEABISCUIT, close to the pace from the start, was urged forward and out of trouble when it seemed as if he might be caught in close quarters nearing the first turn, then came on to catch WHICHCEE entering the final eighth and was going in his best form to the finish. KAYAK II, slow to get going, ran a sensational race to make a very strong move in the back stretch and might have been closer to the winner had he been vigorously ridden in the last sixteenth. WHICHCEE had his speed going to the front early and set a fast pace, but was clearly not good enough for the first two. WEDDING CALL, showing an excellent effort, was close to the pace in the early stages, made a determined bid rounding the stretch turn, but was forced to race a trifle wide and, although seeming to lack the class of the first three, went in superb fashion to the end. WAR PLUMAGE made a strong move nearing the stretch turn and was in close quarters rounding the turn, but turned in a creditable effort. HEELFLY lacked early speed and was never a serious contender, although closing fairly well. VISCOUNTY made a couple of bids to reach the leaders, but was not good enough. SPECIFY was never able to get to the front and failed to run his best race. ROYAL CRUSADER showed fine early speed and was a strong contender for seven-eighths, then faded. CAN'T WAIT, DON MIKE, and RA II were never serious contenders. KANTAN was clearly outclassed and did not belong in the race.
Scratched—Hysterical, 108.
Overweight—Royal Crusader, 4 pounds.

Owners: (12) C S Howard; (2) C S Howard; (6) A C T Stock Farm; (1) Gaffers & Sattler; (9) J C Brady; (10) Circle S Stable; (3) Valdina Farm; (7) M Selznick; (5) Silver State Stable; (13) R C Stable; (11) Binglin Stock Farm; (4) Binglin Stock Farm; (8) W L Ranch

©DAILY RACING FORM/EQUIBASE

See page 76 for related story

Photo Credits

Introduction
Seabiscuit with Red Pollard up (pg. 7), *Keeneland-Cook;* Mrs. H.C. Phipps (pg. 10), *Morgan Photo Service.*

1935-1936
Hard Tack (pg. 14), *Sutcliffe-Grayson;* Sunny Jim Fitzsimmons (pg. 15), *Bert Clark Thayer;* Mohawk Claiming Stakes (pg. 16), *Keeneland-Morgan;* Mr. and Mrs. Charles S. Howard (pg. 17), *Morgan Photo Service;* Scarsdale Handicap (pg. 18), *Keeneland-Morgan.*

1937
Brooklyn Handicap (pg. 26), *Keeneland-Cook;* Butler Handicap (pg. 28), *Keeneland-Morgan;* Seabiscuit after Yonkers Handicap (pg. 30), *Keeneland-Morgan;* Continental Handicap (pg. 32), *Keeneland-Cook;* Riggs Handicap trophy presentation (pg. 33), *Turf Pix;* Bowie Handicap (pg. 34), *Turf Pix.*

1938
Seabiscuit in the morning (pg. 39), *The Blood-Horse;* 1938 Santa Anita Handicap (pg. 43), *Carroll Photo Service;* War Admiral (pg. 46), *The Blood-Horse;* Special Stake with Ligaroti (pg. 52), *The Blood-Horse;* C.S. Howard and Samuel Riddle (pg. 55), *Joe Fleischer;* Seabiscuit working at Pimlico (pg. 59), *Joe Fleischer;* War Admiral working at Pimlico (pg. 60), *Joe Fleischer;* Pimlico Special finish (pp. 62-63), *Joe Fleischer;* Seabiscuit in winner's circle (inset pg. 62), *Joe Fleischer;* trophy presentation (pg. 64), *Joe Fleischer;* Seabiscuit (pg. 66), *The Blood-Horse.*

1939-1940
Seabiscuit working (pg. 71), *H.C. Ashby;* Swing On (pg. 74), *Sutcliffe-Grayson;* 1940 Santa Anita Handicap (pp. 76-77), *Keeneland-Morgan;* C.S. Howard and Tom Smith (pg. 79), *H.C. Ashby.*

1941-Beyond
Seabiscuit's statue (pg. 85), *Matt Goins;* George Woolf with Mr. and Mrs. Howard (pg. 86), *Carroll Photo Service;* Seabiscuit and sons (pg. 89), *The Blood-Horse;* Seabiscuit's sons in Santa Anita paddock (pg. 92), *Bert Clark Thayer;* Seabiscuit (pg. 94), *Vic Stein and Associates;* Man o' War (pg. 95), *Keeneland-McClure;* C.S. Howard (pg. 97), *News Bureau;* Mrs. Howard on Seabiscuit accompanied by Mr. Howard (pg. 98), *Vic Stein and Associates;* Mr. Howard and the statue of Seabiscuit (pg. 99), *Bert Clark Thayer;* Seabiscuit and Red Pollard (pg. 103), *Harold Williams;* Tom Smith (pg. 108), *H.C. Ashby;* Seabiscuit at Del Mar (pg. 114), *The Blood-Horse;* Pimlico Special post parade (pg. 115), *Joe Fleischer;* Santa Anita (pg. 119), *Bert Clark Thayer;* Red Pollard (pg. 125), *Morgan Photo Service.*

About the Editor

John McEvoy (1936–2019), a graduate of the University of Wisconsin, was a newspaper reporter and college English teacher who subsequently served as Midwest editor, then senior writer for *Daily Racing Form*.

He was the author of *Great Horse Racing Mysteries*, *Round Table*, and co-author with his daughter, Julia McEvoy, of *Women in Racing: In Their Own Words*. McEvoy also was the author of *Through the Pages of Daily Racing Form*, an historical overview of American Thoroughbred racing based on material that appeared in that newspaper's first one hundred years. In addition, McEvoy published a book of poetry.

He and his wife, Judy, lived in Evanston, Illinois; they have three children and three grandchildren.